One Consciousn...

An Analysis Of Bill Hicks' Comedy

By Paul Outhwaite

D.M. PRODUCTIONS

One Consciousness: An Analysis Of Bill Hicks' Comedy

by Paul Outhwaite

This edition first published in 2003 by
D M Productions
P.O. Box 83
Coulby Newham
Middlesbrough
TS8 0FX

Distributed by D M Productions

ISBN: 0-9537461-3-5 (3rd edition, revised and enlarged)

ISBN: 0-9537461-2-7 (2nd edition)

ISBN: 0-9537461-1-9 (1st edition)

"Great artists have no country"

Alfred Du Masset

For

Penny & Holden

Acknowledgements

One Consciousness has been around since December 2002, when about twenty copies were released, and in the blink of an eye withdrawn, for 'repairs'. A second, revised and limited edition was then released in February 2003. It served as a means of testing the water, and despite no funds to promote it, the feedback I received was encouraging enough to warrant another edition, for the first time in paperback. My intention was merely to use the text of the second edition, albeit with perhaps a few further corrections. However, the 'war' in the Gulf seemed an ideal opportunity to update the book with an additional chapter, especially as many commentators cited Hicks' routines when reporting the conflict.

In returning to the material Bill Hicks left behind, I found myself once again taken on that ride, once again being taken in by the sheer irresistibility of his narrative flights, to such an extent that new avenues of exploration opened up. A few additional notes became a notebook, resulting in a fuller re-draft than I had originally intended. Nonetheless, it proved a highly enjoyable experience, dealing once again with the subtle connections inherent in Hicks' comedy routines. This then is the version I have determined not to add to, case fuckin' closed!

I never met Bill Hicks, but I – like his fans – have connected to him through his work as a stand-up comedian. He has left a lasting impression, inspiring those who found in his material a philosophy and warmth that suggested everything good about humanity. Those closest to him, friends and family, speak of a person every bit as sincere and dedicated as that which his performances revealed.

In my communication with his fans, I have found them to be generous and passionate and certainly not precious about his legacy. There is none of that attitude often seen with fan worship where being the oldest fan somehow makes your love of Bill more heartfelt. With Hicks' fans there is a desire to spread the word, to share some of the inspiration they have felt.

In writing this book I am grateful to a number of people for their help, most notably Bill's mother, Mary Reese Hicks, for allowing me to use material from his published and unpublished work. That she also did some moonlighting as a proofreader is testament to her selflessness and desire to see that Bill's memory is kept alive.

I would also like to thank Larry Stern and Jack Boulware for helping me assimilate material for analysis as well as the writers noted in the reference section who were writing about Bill long before the current resurgence in interest. Good luck too to Kevin Booth with his own project about Bill. Fans eager for more Hicks' material appreciate his continued work with Sacred Cow Productions.

I have a debt of gratitude also for those souls who bought my last book, *Automatic Living*, whose kind words kept alive my enthusiasm and stopped D.M. Productions from going under. You know who you are and I will not forget you.

Finally, a special thanks to my unpaid proofreaders: to my wife Penny, and to Pete Firman. They had other things to do, but gave up valuable time to assist me.

1
__Introduction__

The first thing to say is that American comedian Bill Hicks was no ordinary stand-up. Not for him the archetypal motionless gag man under the spotlight reeling off a series of unconnected jokes. Hicks was a social commentator whose routines were part of a flowing narrative held together by a philosophy based on humanism and reason, and a desire to stimulate as well as amuse audiences. With him there was always an awareness of how our world, our society and its people are linked together. We are not separate entities going about our daily lives, we are all connected, physically by the planet on which we live and spiritually by what he referred to as "one consciousness." This is humanity connected through evolution, experience and a universal seeking of meaning through accumulation of knowledge. With this we therefore have a responsibility to each other. This responsibility encompassed individual and collective freedom and a belief that if we evolved intellectually then as a race we could progress.

He was idealistic in his vision of what the world could be, but equally he was angry with those who held the human race back, those not governed by reason and benevolent aspiration but by impulse and consumerist accumulation. Such diametrical oppositions fermented a comedic perspective raging with injustice, yet one that was lucid and controlled enough to convey the enticing possibilities of what life could be. Somewhere in between, Hicks' ironic take, his conveying of inconsistencies, exposing of lies, made a connection with searing, achingly funny accuracy.

He saw himself as a flame, Shiva The Destroyer, using comedy as a weapon to slay all the "fevered egos" polluting the planet, those individuals "tainting our collective unconsciousness" and obstructing humanity's evolution. He saw how governments and those in power lie to keep the masses dumb and malleable, exposing hypocrisy with a perceptiveness rarely matched before or since. That the comedy never suffered was testament to the sophistication of his wit.

At the age of 13 he did his first gig. Six weeks before his death, aged 32, he did his last. In the intervening years he frequently did over 250 gigs a year, trying to reach as many people as possible, to put them in touch with inner and outer space in a majestic flight of one consciousness thinking, inspiring friends and fans to join him on his imaginative ride.

People use and misuse the word tragedy all the time. It seems to accompany the death of anybody famous. But the real definition of tragedy evokes a sense of loss and poignancy, a sense of someone dying when they still had much to offer. Without hyperbole, Bill Hicks' death was a tragedy, for there was so much still to come from this creative, imaginative performer always brimming with new ideas. When he died in 1994 the world lost a rare talent, made all the more tragic by the fact that his voice had not reached as wide an audience as it should have, particularly in his home country. Yet, all mawkishness aside, his spirit and philosophy live on, not only through the growth of interest in him, but in the substantial body of material he left behind which, almost ten years after his death, is as relevant as ever.

Hicks once said, "As long as one person lives in darkness then it seems to be a responsibility to tell other people" (1). This encapsulated Hicks' philosophy, of shining light onto the world we live in as a means to better that world, be it by presenting truths and injustices often ignored or by succinctly using humour to bring clarity to issues obfuscated by government spin or media manipulation. For him, it is the role of every individual to do something to enhance the human condition. Unlike those we place our trust in - politicians and all manner of professionals - Hicks did it honestly and had a lot of fun along the way.

This book seeks to analyse his comedy and philosophy and place it in some kind of sociological and historical context. Though I have used a biographical structure, I am not intending to compete with either Cynthia True's biography of Hicks, *American Scream*, which covers Hicks' professional life thoroughly enough, or with Hicks' close friend, Kevin Booth, who is currently working on his own book.

The book has two strands. Firstly, it seeks to analyse the influences on and evolution of Hicks' stage act and career, achieving this through comparisons with other comedians and the world events that shaped his outlook and comedy, thereby placing Hicks in a historical and cultural context. Secondly, though not exclusively (in keeping with the overlapping strands of Hicks' comedy) there is an analysis of his philosophy and how its many threads are held together by major, unifying ideas such as freedom, truth and honesty.

His comedy was about the connections between people on our planet. In this sense his comedy and his life can be linked to world events. His routines merged ideas, his ironic perspective connecting themes and showing how we are all one consciousness. He referred to Carl Jung's theory "that all mankind shares a collective unconscious" which Hicks agreed with but thought, "it's not supposed to be unconscious" (2). It's a point that shows Hicks' belief that all the world's people and everything that happens are related; are parts of an evolutionary structure. This book adopts Hicks' theory, which is why even events from his early childhood have a connection to his later career and outlook, and by piecing them together we can see how his philosophy developed.

2
All You Need Is Love

The 1960s was a time of great cultural and social change in the world and the United States in particular, and as a child of this period many of these changes informed Bill Hicks' life and material. A decade that began with John F. Kennedy becoming the youngest man elected president of the United States in 1960, heralded, critically, the beginning of an era that saw television becoming the main source of information for the American public. Significantly, television debates between Kennedy and his opponent, Richard Nixon, presented the American public with a contrast between the easy going and open Kennedy and the tense and cold demeanour of Nixon. That the broadcast had such an impact on voters, helping as it did to sweep Kennedy into power, said everything about the emerging influence of a medium which so preoccupied Hicks.

Kennedy projected an idealistic image, his policies aiming to tackle poverty and advance the cause of civil rights. He was perfectly in tune with the America that had grown up in the post-war years with a liberalism founded in the 1950s of Elvis Presley, rock n' roll rebellion and young people becoming consumers with a voice. His inaugural address contained the oft quoted, "Ask not what your country can do for you - ask what you can do for your country." In it we see a desire for people to be selfless and unified in pursuit of a better world. This is the template from which Hicks worked, that of putting petty differences and hatreds aside in order to evolve collectively as a species.

Kennedy was not a politician separate from the people. This sense of connectedness and idealism was the Kennedy Hicks saw, one of the "good men" like John Lennon. Yet in late 1961 he ordered more help for the South Vietnamese in its war against the Northern Vietnam backed Vietcong, kicking off a chain of events that was to shape America's history profoundly and the sense of itself that was to follow.

Kennedy, like the sixties, had a darker side, though hindsight has viewed his bedding of Marilyn Monroe with little disdain. For Hicks' generation it demonstrated Kennedy's rock and roll credentials, a perspective that beyond his fight for good causes he also wanted to indulge in life's passions, thus giving him the imperfections that other whiter than white (and generally hypocrital) politicians denied.

Kennedy's anti-communist fervour has also been somewhat glossed over by history, all objective judgement clouded by his brinkmanship in the Cuban missile crises; a defining moment in Kennedy's presidency that saw him elevated to hero status. The contradictions of the president and the decade are apparent in Hicks himself. On one level, he is viewed as cynical, foul-mouthed and blasphemous, yet this opinion comes from only a surface reading of the man. Hicks had faith and was also very idealistic about the direction society could and should take. His apparent cynicism was always directed at the cynicism of others: those in power, those who claim to work and speak for the masses yet whose agenda is really tied to self-interest or the interests of faceless corporations.

William Melvin Hicks was born in Valdosta, Georgia on 16th December 1961 to James Melvin Hicks and Mary Reese Hicks. Less than a month later, in January 1962, the U.S. undertook its first combat missions against the Vietcong, whilst domestically a seeping sense of fear began to cloud the post-war optimism as all U.S. citizens were expected to know the location of bomb shelters in case of nuclear attack.

Hicks' voiceover at the beginning of the *Revelations* video describes the year of his birth as "the end of the American Dream, just before we lost our innocence irrevocably, and the TV eye brought the horror of our lives into our homes for all to see." The economic boom of the fifties and America's growth as a superpower, aligned with the sense of freedom created by a vibrant rock and roll revolution, had accorded Americans the feeling they were living the American Dream. In addition, Kennedy's presidency brought with it a belief that there would be social change for the better. Technological developments, allied with this new sense of liberalism, suggested positive progress would be made. A decade in which many ideas were trying to be heard saw many clashes, creating a chaos of possibilities. Then, on November 22nd 1963, Kennedy was assassinated, filmed footage of the moment beamed around a numbed nation and shocked world. Liberals, as Hicks could be loosely defined, saw hope lost, whilst right-wing "yahoos" celebrated. Indeed, there were reports that in some Southern universities students cheered on hearing the news. The sense of disbelief is apparent in Hicks' material where he would pluralize, noting that "we" as a collective were responsible. It was a disbelief in society, in the way people behaved and thought and were unable to recognise and seize the positive things about life.

13

Two days later, the apparent assassin, Lee Harvey Oswald, was himself assassinated on live television. The TV Eye was indeed bringing home the horrors of the world, more so with the escalation in the Vietnam War.

In August 1964, new president Lyndon Johnson and Secretary of Defence Robert McNamara told the American public the American destroyer *Maddox* had been attacked by North Vietnam, resulting in a congressional resolution allowing Johnson to begin military action. But there was no such military attack. As Hicks would often say, "All governments are lying cocksuckers" and Johnson had invented a pretext from which to involve America in a bloody conflict, one that would cause the country to lose its innocence irrevocably.

The Warren Commission delivered its report into the Kennedy assassination on September 24th 1964. It maintained there was no conspiracy and that Oswald acted alone, shooting Kennedy from the sixth floor window of the Texas School Book Depository Building. Many saw it as a whitewash of the facts, nothing short of a cover-up, the commission's single bullet theory mockingly referred to as "the magic bullet" by sceptics (a line later modified by Hicks for his routine on the Rodney King beatings, in which the L.A. police officers' interpretation of events was identified as "the magic baton theory"). The Warren report assumed Oswald's guilt, ignored his low rifle scores whilst in the military, and most damningly, it didn't investigate evidence of shots coming from the grassy knoll, which as Hicks said, "fifty-six witnesses testified was a gunshot."

Part of Hicks' fascination with the Kennedy assassination stems from his admiration of the president and the way subsequent events played out on television, leaving an imprint on the American public's consciousness forever. More significantly it was another example of the way governments can lie and be allowed to get away with it through the ignorance and indifference of the masses and the power of the political machine to manage information. Hicks saw it as a turning point in American history; the most transparent example of government lying to the public and an indication that democracy was just an illusion. In his act he would recall going to the Assassination Museum to see The Sniper's Nest, which the public weren't allowed near. The reason, Hicks thought, was because it would show Oswald couldn't have done it due to the impossible angle, pointing up the absurdity of a bullet hitting Kennedy's head from above yet the president's head going "back and to the left" as if he was shot from ground level.

Hicks, the truth-seeker who'd read many books on the Kennedy assassination, wanted to keep the debate going but believed the American public were more interested in the unstimulating pleasures of TV shows like *American Gladiators*. It echoes an internal memo sent on September 6th 1964 by Allen Dullen, a Warren Commission member who'd been sacked by Kennedy as C.I.A. director: "But nobody reads. Don't believe people read in this country. There will be a few professors that will read the record. The public will read very little." It perfectly captures Hicks' belief that government wants the public to remain dumb, docile and unthreatening: "Go back to bed America" indeed.

Whatever scepticism the Warren report stoked was buried by another distraction in the shape of the Vietnam War. By 1964 the conflict was escalating with Lyndon Johnson raising troops to over 60,000 in 1965. By 1966 this number was 385,000 and U.S. casualties were numbered at over 6,000 deaths. This figure pales in comparison to the 61,000 deaths for the Vietcong, statistics which connect to Hicks' later material on the 1991 Gulf War conflict and the disparity between "Iraq, one hundred and fifty thousand casualties; America, seventy-nine."

1964 also saw The Beatles first U.S. television appearance on *The Ed Sullivan Show*, the beginning of 'The British Invasion' of rock music. In 1965 The Rolling Stones released their worldwide hit *Satisfaction* with its satire on advertising "watching my TV and a man comes on and tells me how white my shirts could be, but he can't be a man 'cause he doesn't smoke the same cigarettes as me." Both groups would become synonymous with the decade and their members would, like Kennedy, be seen by Hicks as the good people, those with some soul, who played from their hearts, had artistic integrity and weren't afraid to speak their minds: John Lennon's pro-drugs stance resulting in a ban for the song *A Day In The Life* by the BBC in 1967. That same year, on June 25th an estimated 400,000,000 tuned into to the first worldwide live TV broadcast when The Beatles performed *All You Need Is Love*.

As a microcosm of the decade's mood and aspirations, The Beatles' broadcast was the apotheosis of Hicks' one consciousness thinking. The universal language of music could connect people, prompting a sharing of ideals and ideas with songs emphasizing collective hopes and the power of "coming together." The culture around Hicks was influencing him, and whilst others might say it was unconscious, for Hicks there was a meaning to the time he was born into. Therefore, we can see in Hicks' feeling of all the world's people sharing a consciousness an echo of the theory of "six degrees of separation." As a result of Harvard Social Psychologist Stanley Milgram's research in 1967, this theory proffered that each individual could be connected to someone else within six degrees. Thus, a person introduced to six strangers would find some connection with at least one of them. This "small world" theory is a central tenet of Hicks' philosophy as he looks at the wider world (and indeed, our place in the cosmos) and how we must acknowledge a shared responsibility if we are to evolve.

The psychedelic era ushered in by The Beatles' *Sergeant Pepper's Lonely Hearts Club Band* in 1967 saw a liberal attitude to drugs, a belief in loving your brothers and sisters and a sense of freedom. The Haight-Ashbury area of San Francisco – a city where Hicks could always be guaranteed a receptive audience - became a focal point for the counterculture movement. Allied to this feeling of love came a subversive spirit in the search for truth and justice, mirrored in the continuing struggles of the civil rights movement. Above all, there was a sense of hope amongst the younger generation. Yet this was a decade troubled by violence, not only in Vietnam, but also domestically.

1964 had seen the 'long, hot summer', a period characterised by civil unrest with hate crimes and revenge attacks and many demonstrations developing into riots. Despite Martin Luther King being awarded the Nobel Peace Prize that year, there existed a growing feeling in the black community that peaceful protest was getting their cause nowhere. In the black ghetto of Watts, Los Angeles, after police arrested a black man for drink driving, riots broke out. The National Guard had to be called in to restore order and, after 6 days, thirty-four people had been killed and $40 million of damage caused by the most violent outbreak since the Second World War.

The gun culture prevalent in America certainly brought a sense of democracy, allowing anybody to make the news in a series of high profile incidents that had begun with the Kennedy assassination. On 21st February 1965 Malcolm X was shot and killed. In 1966 a sniper, Charles Whitman, at the University of Texas in Austin, killed fourteen people from the university's bell tower before being shot by police (when incredulity consumed Hicks, there were occasions when he would sing "Oh, where's the tower, where's the gun?" to suggest that other people's ignorance and cynicism was driving him to immoderate measures to find relief). Then on April 4th 1968, a gunman murdered another of the "good men", Martin Luther King, a man whose speeches were both moving and compelling. We see in some of Hicks' material, particularly his closing conclusions, the eloquent and inspirational urgings of King and his attempts to influence through a potent marriage of passion and reason.

Two months after King's murder, Robert F. Kennedy – a politician many had placed their trust in and hopes for radical social change - was also assassinated. Hicks would align himself to these heroes, these voices of reason who were a threat to the corporate establishment, often ending his shows by making gunshot sounds and collapsing to the stage. He frequently referred to lone gunmen in his material, not only when pointing out the stupidity of news reports taking quotes from "a quiet loner who had a family of kids", but also with quips like "I've been having Lucas McCain fantasies at the mall." McCain was the wholesome character played by Chuck Connors in the TV series *The Rifleman* (1958-1963), the kind of character Hicks refers to in the *Revelations* introduction: "I always wanted to be the cowboy hero. That lone voice in the wilderness fighting corruption and evil wherever I found it, and standing for freedom, truth and justice." That Hicks would use McCain in the context of mass murder shows how far the American Dream has been distorted, that the new enemies are those who buy into a consumer culture that is indifferent to social depravation and is unwilling to take responsibility.

Sixties radicalism, the counterculture that didn't align itself to mainstream thought, had grown during the decade through music and protest, but up until 1968 public support for the Vietnam War had been fairly strong. In January 1968, the Tet Offensive resulted in 2,500 U.S. casualties and damaged that support. Now the TV Eye was beaming images of body bags into American homes on a daily basis, turning public opinion.

Republican president Richard Nixon took office in January 1969 after winning the election in late 1968. By April 1969 over 33,000 U.S. soldiers had been killed and there was little public support for the conflict. In the academic year 1969-1970, 313 student buildings were occupied in protests against the war. Such revolutionary spirit is a feature of Hicks' comedy and a reason why he often harked back to a decade when people didn't accept roles as mere passive onlookers. Anti-war feeling spurred Nixon on to beginning the slow process of withdrawal, coinciding with the American public's growing awareness of what had been happening in Asia. In November 1969 CBS television showed footage of the My Lai massacre, which had taken place on March 16th 1968. This had involved American troops from Charlie Company going on a four-hour rampage in the village of My Lai, raping women and girls, stabbing vaginas, disembowelling bodies and cutting off hands. At the end there were nearly 500 civilians dead. The level of brutality was unbelievable, as detached from American ideals and innocence as possible. Yet it was just one of many war crimes committed by Americans in Vietnam. The barbarism went up to the highest level with the C.I.A. under *Operation Phoenix* executing twenty thousand civilians without trial in South Vietnam under the pretext of them being suspected communists.

The sixties were coming to an end in a messy, barbaric way, it's last joyous gasp captured in the three day Woodstock concert, before darker events took over. In August 1969, followers of failed hippy musician Charles Manson murdered pregnant actress Sharon Tate and four of her guests, claiming some inspiration from The Beatles and their *White Album*. Hicks' other rock heroes, The Rolling Stones, were also involved in tragic events in December when giving a free concert at Altamont. The concert erupted into a riot with Hell's Angels stabbing to death eighteen year old Meredith Hunter. For many these incidents were seen as the consequences of allowing the sixties peace and love generation too much freedom. The counterculture had come to be perceived as a threat, the tide of public opinion more in tune with Nixon's conservative agenda, he having campaigned in television commercials with "we shall have order in the United States."

As the decade came to a close, 1969 saw the first moon landing and walk. Mankind's possibilities seemed endless. Hicks was certainly influenced by this historic moment. For him, the years ahead offered an opportunity to explore space, "both inner and outer," yet somehow in the subsequent decades petty hates, trivial concerns and an inability to evolve beyond self-interest and conflict meant mankind didn't take that chance. Hicks' material alluded many times to life beyond Earth, whether it be with his wish to be taken away from the hick towns he was playing or the drug trips in which he communicated with aliens. Beyond this, the "ride" that his shows took audiences on and the flowing poetry of his words gave him a perception of things as if looking down on Earth, seeing the bigger universal picture.

The new decade seemed set to offer little to the sixties generation, the decade closing with the prophetic film *Easy Rider* (1969) in which rednecks kill characters who embody the free spirit of that decade. In 1970, two symbols of the generation, Jimi Hendrix and Janis Joplin died whilst a third, The Beatles, split up amid acrimony a million miles from *All You Need Is Love*.

One death that year which the media rather neglected was that of John Kennedy Toole. A talented writer, he had committed suicide after the failure of his novel *A Confederacy Of Dunces* to find a publisher. The novel, finally published in 1980 and winner of the Pulitzer Prize the following year, was to become one of Hicks' favourites, its sparkling, witty dialogue and original, offbeat situations and characters appealing to Hicks - a voracious reader always on the look out for something unique. The novel's central protagonist, Ignatius J. Reilly, is one of the great literary creations, an hilariously over educated and opinionated cynic, ever willing to proffer his opinions, but too fat and lazy to do anything more than sponge off his mother and put minimal effort into a series of short-lived menial jobs. Though he has little in common with the hard working, purposeful Hicks, the two share a self-confidence and conviction in their own beliefs that refuses to bend to popular opinion.

On May 4th 1970, four Vietnam protestors were shot and killed at Kent State. It said everything about the conservative agenda now festering, snuffing out dissent like some South American dictatorship. Similar state power was also evident in September 1971 when Governor Nelson Rockefeller responded to riots at the Attica Correctional Facility by sending in armed guards whose brutal suppression resulted in 32 people being killed.

Amid this turmoil, Hicks' earliest cultural influence was Elvis Presley, a fellow Southerner born in Tupelo, Mississippi, who'd re-ignited his career with a comeback television special in 1968. It was not long after this that the seven-year-old Hicks began seeking out Presley's records, whilst in first grade, for his 'show and tell" he lip-synched to *All Shook Up* in front of the class. The appreciation in the reaction from his peers imbedded in Hicks a desire to perform.

Elvis Presley had kick-started the whole rock and roll era of the 1950s. He embodied its sex appeal and suggestion of danger, but by the 1970s his shows were more glitzy than dangerous, strictly show business as he cloyingly sought audience affection.

Hicks had seen Elvis perform twice, in 1970 and 1974, as impressed by the showmanship and theatrics as the music. This was a time when Presley, no longer making films, was playing Las Vegas frequently. On stage Presley would ad-lib, strike poses and go into long monologues, seeming to make it up as he went along and doing whatever his mood dictated. With his development into an American icon and evolution into caricature, there was a proliferation of Elvis impersonators in the mid seventies, a trend that continued and grew more widespread subsequent to his death in 1977.

After Presley's demise, the peculiarities of his personal life filtered through to the public, not only his drug taking and eating habits, but also his excessive spending on guns, his predilection for watching women in white panties and his giving away of free Cadillacs to strangers. Hicks would joke that it wasn't the drugs that killed Elvis but the bill he got for all the Cadillacs.

Hicks was always more interested in the second incarnation of Elvis, the bloated and paranoid 'Vegas Elvis'. He once joked "I'm the only guy in the country who does Elvis: the last hour" (3). Hicks' impersonation employs the Elvis' poses, exaggerating the curled lip, his hands raised shaking to the heavens. The routine featured in his earliest shows, from a simple impersonation of Elvis' mother chastising her son to the *Sane Man* show in which he imagines Elvis being a heavy smoker, still alive and doing hoarse versions of songs like *My Way*, or putting the microphone to his throat and Elvis singing through a voice box on his neck. At some shows, in full Vegas Elvis regalia, he would muster a damn good impersonation, performing songs like *Mystery Train, Are You Lonesome Tonight?* and *Suspicious Minds*.

Often Hicks' Elvis routines would become a prop in his shows, a kind of pause between material or a way to depart from subjects when he was doing two or three shows a night at the same venue. There were times when the routine took hold and took off as he improvised Elvis talking to Charlie Hodge. Like Elvis going into a long monologue, Hicks' Charlie Hodge routines would depart from the material the audience had come to see. Hodge was one of Elvis' entourage, one of the hangers-on, or as Hicks' Elvis says, "The man who brings me my scarves and water." As he mocked Hodge's feeding off Elvis, Hicks performed a dialogue between the two with Elvis asking Hodge to "put on some white panties and dance like a monkey," "scratch my balls" and "I want to film you mating with one of them dogs." Hicks is exaggerating the seemingly out of control Elvis that so fascinated him, picking up towels, beer bottles, table mats and anything else in the stage's area to wipe his brow and present to the audience.

Like JFK, Elvis had become an American icon, elevated to a mythic status that transcended their human selves. The fact that Hicks focused on both shows his fascination with American culture and whom it chooses as its heroes. He said of his fascination with Elvis, "I think he's an hilarious American story too. He had everything he could possibly want and he was still completely miserable" (1). Both Kennedy and Elvis seemed to convey something of the American Dream and also of an innocence lost. In Kennedy's case it was the dream of equality through social change, such idealism shattered by his assassination. With Presley it was the tale of a young, beautiful, virile, patriotic American whose music united a nation and transcended domestic and world borders. Yet by the 1970s he had become something of a caricature, a symbol of innocence despoiled by bloated excess, voracious pharmaceutical consumption and paranoia, even taking time to contact President Nixon with concerns about The Beatles' drug taking.

When Bill Hicks was seven, his family moved to Houston, Texas, to live in the Memorial area to the west of the city, a place called Nottingham Forest, which Hicks would later refer to as a "Southern Baptist ozone" such was the strictness of life there. It was a typical, comfortable middle class area with well cared for lawns, significant consumer spending power and a somewhat puritanical perspective. Too comfortable for Hicks, who was bored by the area and mystified by the appeal of living the so-called 'American Dream'.

In 1972 Nixon defeated the Democrat George McGovern who had campaigned against the Vietnam War and for social change to help the disenfranchised and poor of America. Nixon's landslide victory showed the country's fear of anything remotely liberal, Middle America's apprehension further intensified when the landmark Roe versus Wade case reached its conclusion in January 1973. Roe, a Texas woman, had sought an abortion, but the law only allowed abortions when they were necessary to save a pregnant woman's life. After many months, the U.S. Supreme Court ruled that women had a legal right to abortion, in effect legalising it. The laws of 46 states were affected by this ruling, and though it seemed a victory for liberals, it nonetheless mobilised the fundamentalists who were to become increasingly influential over the next two decades.

Abortion became one America's most contentious issues, provoking intense argument and leading to a situation where those anti-abortionists who called themselves "pro-life" decided that killing doctors who carried out abortions was the right way to present their argument. Though at the time of Roe versus Wade, the 11-year-old Hicks could not have appreciated the full implications of the case, the issue was so keenly felt in the Southern Bible belt that throughout his teenage years, with the case's ramifications still being felt strongly, Hicks grew increasingly aware of the debate. The subject featured, albeit simply, in some of Hicks' earliest comedy material, such as a throwaway line about babysitting for abortions. Nonetheless, before his teenage years were over, his rapidly developing comic instincts saw greater exploration of the subject. Naturally, for a person whose central philosophy concerned freedom of choice, Hicks opposed the anti-

21

abortionists and their imposition of values. Moreover, the pro-life brigade were a concoction of right-wingers, conservatives, fundamentalists and religious zealots, those whose ideology Hicks targeted throughout his career, mocking them for their venality and hypocrisy. Certainly, in the aftermath of Row versus Wade, those protesting against abortion including a considerable number who condemned anti-Vietnam War protestors as "un-American".

By March 1973 all U.S. combat soldiers had left Vietnam after 55,337 deaths, 150,000 seriously wounded and over 1,000 missing in action. Once again, there was a huge disparity in casualties with over two million Vietnamese military and civilian deaths. In total, seven million tons of bombs had been dropped on Vietnam, Laos and Cambodia.

America was looking to right wing politics for answers, the counterculture having disappeared underground, and its figureheads either happily growing into the mainstream or marginalized by government hounding. As societies do when they feel helpless, America turned to knee-jerk fundamentalism for answers. Nixon, in typical Republican fashion, began cutting back federal welfare and his New Economic Policy, after initial success, resulted in a steady rise in the cost of living. Hicks viewed all post-Kennedy politicians as corrupt and evil and Nixon's misdeeds were likely the start of this attitude. The president had covertly backed the overthrow of Chile's democratically elected President Salvador Allende, resulting in the pro-western fascist dictatorship of General Pinochet who set about killing and torturing Chileans opposed to his rule.

The "lying cocksuckers" were again evident when the Watergate scandal broke in 1973, evidence coming to light that Nixon's supporters had been behind a break-in at the Democratic Party headquarters in the Watergate building before the 1972 election. The President was accused of authorising the break-in as well as the subsequent cover-up. On the brink of his teens, though in truth his tastes, interests and outlook were beyond his years, Hicks couldn't help but notice the national and international scandal occupying news headlines for over a year. It transpired that not only had Nixon been secretly audio taping his meetings in the Oval Office, but also that they were a number of gaps and missing recordings from those that Watergate investigates would deem as significant. By 1974, further information was coming to light about Nixon's awareness of dirty tricks tactics during the last election, whilst several White House officials were being charged and convicted in connection with the break-in. Finally, tapes were released on which could be heard President Nixon saying "cover up or anything else if it'll save it – save the plan." Eventually, proven to be aware of the break-in and cover up and facing impeachment, Nixon resigned on August 9th 1974. The scandal had changed a nation's perception of politicians, now clouded by a distrust that infected Hicks, so that his comedy philosophy was essentially a mission to expose the "lying cocksuckers." In one final twist to the whole shoddy affair, Nixon was succeeded by Gerald Ford, the only surviving member of the Warren Commission that had put together the cover up surrounding Kennedy's assassination. Ford, naturally, granted Nixon a pardon.

The conservatism of Nixon and Ford was reflected in Hicks' home environment, where swearing and blasphemy were forbidden and going to church on Sundays was a must for all upstanding families. Hicks was watching preachers from an early age, subconsciously taking in performance, material, tone of delivery and audience reaction. Yet, as Hicks grew into a teenager he was already feeling alienated from the outlook religion offered. The sense of rules, routine and formality mirrored his home life and saw him retreating to his room to read and listen to rock music.

3
What's New, Pussycat?

Bill Hicks was a great fan of Mark Twain's writing, particularly *The Adventures Of Huckleberry Finn*, enthralled by the imaginative ride Twain took him on as Finn enjoys many adventures on his journey through the American South. Like Hicks' shows, Twain's story moves off at tangents but is held together by a developing narrative. The two are also similar in their focus on human nature and its peculiarities, their idealism never clouded by sentimentality as they use humour to expose hypocrisy. Thus, we have in *The Adventures Of Huckleberry Finn*, beneath the traditional adventure story, themes of corruption, the superficiality of religion and the unscrupulousness of those in power. As with Hicks, Twain saw the faults in humanity, calling man "The only animal that blushes - or needs to." Through sophisticated language and irony, Twain satirised society and its foibles, particularly those of the American South, creating the same grotesque, larger-than-life caricatures Hicks would employ in his shows.

Twain was as much a stand-up performer as a writer, appearing before hundreds of audiences in America, London and other parts of the British Empire. At ease with audiences, Twain said of them, "They quickly catch the point you are trying to make; oftentimes they anticipate it. Then you are put on your mettle to give a sudden turn to the story so as to bring out a new and unexpected point" (4). This compares to the way Hicks' narrative builds and takes the audience along before perceptive twists, which bring out the comedy but also help to make audiences look at things from a different angle. One example is his routine on smokers and non-smokers, asking who amongst the audience are non-smokers, leading the majority to cheer, expecting Hicks to rail against smokers. In the pause he pulls out his cigarette packet and announces, "bunch of whining little maggots." Similarly, he recalls being elated at seeing an old person smoking, giving him hope he will live long. "Nothing makes a smoker happier than to see an old man smoking," he tells the audience before approaching the smoker with "Dude, you're my hero! You're an inspiration, man" only to twist the gag when the man replies "What? I'm twenty-eight."

For Hicks, Twain was an American hero, the kind of artist America should be producing and celebrating. Later in his career he would lament the fact that beefcake actor Sylvester Stallone had millions whilst Twain died poor, the disparity a central part of Hicks' philosophy with its contrast between the intellectual aspirations he had for his homeland and the moronic reality of "bovine America" left contented by anti-intellectual entertainment.

The young Hicks was also interested in rock music, particularly the theatrical rock of the likes of Alice Cooper and KISS. As Twain gets into the skins of his characters, so KISS adopted stage personas and make-up with each member of the band as different characters: Gene Simmons as The Demon, Paul Stanley as Star Child, Peter Criss as Cat Man and Ace Frehley as Spaceman. Their stage shows were spectacular, Gene Simmons spitting fire at the audience or flying over them on a wire rig, and Criss' drum set rising off the stage.

This carnivalesque performance had a sense of power, as spectacular as another of Hicks' childhood heroes, Evel Knievel, who had grown to national fame in the 1970s through a series of stunts, predominantly involving jumping distances on his motorbike, attracting a record crowd at the Houston Astrodome in 1971 as he cleared 13 cars. Both Knievel and KISS impacted on Hicks because of their ability to draw in large crowds for events that created a shared experience, a uniting of people also apparent with Kennedy and Elvis.

Hicks was also a fan of the television series *Kung Fu* (1972-1975) starring David Carradine as Kwai Chang Caine, a renegade Shaolin priest who wanders late nineteenth century America searching for his brother. There is something of Hicks in the character, the lone wolf walking the Earth, confronting injustice, on the side of good and working outside the law. Caine's appeal wasn't just that he was heroic, but that he was searching for knowledge of the self and others, along the way offering mysticism in enigmatic utterances, certainly a feature of Hicks' comedy with his turns to "we are all one consciousness" and desire to explore "space, both inner and outer."

The major comedic influence of Hicks' youth was Woody Allen. Born on December 1st 1935, Allen's youth, like Hicks', was spent shying away into his bedroom, where he would practice magic tricks and play his clarinet. Going through the rituals practised by his Orthodox family made him as resentful of religion as Hicks, his comedy and magic a means to escape such constrictions. After writing for numerous TV comedians in the 1950s, Allen did his first comedy stand-up in 1960.

Allen's stand-up influences can be traced back to comedian Mort Sahl. Stand-up went hand in hand with the rise of the jazz clubs in the 1950s, where comedians were often employed as warm up acts. Sahl started out in these clubs, honing his act and finding an audience for his nonchalantly delivered routines. The emerging Beat Generation of writers in the late 1950s (and the movement's followers, known as 'Beatniks') had seen people such as Allen Ginsberg, Jack Kerouac and William Burroughs bring a more radical approach to writing, emerging as figures outside of the establishment with new and innovative ideas. With rock music and films also breaking down barriers, the 1960s saw stand-up comedians beginning to address the American experience, looking from the outside, pointing up its faults and employing more challenging material in contrast to the comedy of a generation reared on performers like Bob Hope. Golf playing, president schmoozing Hope was the antithesis of what the new generation stood for, the kind of comedian Hicks' father wanted his son to be like with his safe comedy and avoidance of swearing. To James Hicks' naively pointing out that Hope never needed to use foul language, Hicks would say, "Yeh, well Bob Hope doesn't play the shit-holes I play."

Sahl was something of an unconventional comedian for his time. His jokes weren't of the typical "take my wife" variety, but were instead political, rooted in the underground culture of jazz and the Beatniks, seeking to be as contemporary, original and thought provoking as the music and poetry of that scene. His comedy targeted the egos of Hollywood stars, satirising both left and right wing politics when addressing the Vietnam War, and causing something of a stir when he poked fun at McCarthy's communist witch-hunts. Whereas other comedians were content to boil the Warren report into Kennedy's assassination down to a selection of generalisations for their material, Sahl chose an analytical dissemination of the report's findings for his routines. Indeed, part of the reason Sahl was so marginalized was his refusal to cease doing material on the report's flaws. He was a true innovator with his sophisticated wit and perceptive take on issues and is still gigging today, railing at politicians and contemporary culture with a purpose to enlighten.

Sahl's style took influence from the free form structure of jazz music, employing stream of consciousness in his routines, going off at tangents in a smooth, non-contrived way, the result of Sahl's sophisticated and carefully crafted writing and shaping of material. When Woody Allen saw him in 1954 he was immediately impressed by the intellectualism and ease with an audience, though as Allen's career developed Sahl voiced his dislike of Allen's material.

Sahl was at the forefront of the satire boom of the 1960s, during which period shows like *The Steve Allen Show*, *The Ed Sullivan Show*, *Merv Griffin Show* and *The Tonight Show* were giving exposure to many stand-up comedians. It was *The Tonight Show* with Johnny Carson that Hicks was particularly enthralled with.

Carson had taken over *The Tonight Show* from Jack Paar in 1962 and was at his peak in the early seventies, on the way to becoming a national institution. Carson's style owed much to Mort Sahl, laid back in delivery, his nonchalance giving him a feel of sophistication as he kicked off shows with topical monologues. He included material on his personal life and connected with his audience, in tune with the national mood concerning current affairs. Carson gave exposure to new, young comedians, providing Hicks with a steady diet of different comedy styles. Many of the comedians were Jewish, the likes of Sahl, Carl Reiner and Mel Brooks. Their material concerned itself with themes seen in much of Hicks' work: religion, celebrity referencing and mockery, sexual disappointments, and the credulity of the public, material imbued with sarcasm and irony. Richard Lewis was another comedian who impressed Hicks when he appeared on *The Tonight Show*, again employing a stream of consciousness style as he based routines around his personal neuroses.

As well as this more homely material on the many TV shows Hicks was watching, there was also the socially conscious and political material of the likes of Dick Gregory with routines on the depravation in black communities, Robert Klein satirising Nixon and Watergate, George Carlin discussing drugs and Richard Pryor mocking Black Panther rhetoric.

These more controversial comedians owe much to Lenny Bruce, a comedian most often compared to Bill Hicks. Born on Oct. 13th 1925, Bruce emerged from Californian jazz clubs and strip joints in the 1950s before getting national television exposure on *The Steve Allen Show* in 1959. After a successful appearance at Carnegie Hall on February 3rd 1961, Bruce was at his peak in terms of material and acclaim amongst liberals and students. Thereafter, frequent drug busts and arrests for obscenity saw him tied up in legal battles and more concerned with defending his freedom of speech than being a comedian. By 1965, after spending all his money on lawyers, he was declared bankrupt. Constantly harassed by the moral brigade and police, he died on August 3rd 1966 from a drugs' overdose.

Bruce's short life saw him challenge the status quo like no comedian before him, targeting religion, race and sexuality as he attacked middle class America and its hypocritical attitudes. Liberal use of swear words and his raw perspectives on taboo subjects saw his material dubbed "sick comedy." Hicks didn't see Bruce as a major influence and didn't really like the connection. Just as Bruce said of himself, "I'm not a comedian, I'm Lenny Bruce," so Hicks thought of himself less in terms of being a comedian and more as a social satirist. For Hicks, Bruce was what he was and Hicks was what he was and the connection that critics made was certainly not by any design on his part. In an interview with Jack Boulware, Hicks said of the comparison: "I'm not really familiar with his material…he was a guy who talked extemporaneously from subject to subject, tied them all together somehow with a unified point of view, and talked about things that other people didn't talk about, and was very funny. If that's the comparison then I accept it" (5). Hicks, like the comedians of the 1970s, benefited from the battles Bruce had fought during his career, from being persecuted for using the word "schmuck" in a routine to going up against the powerful moralists who objected to his material on religion and persecuted him because of it. Bruce allowed people like Richard Pryor and Bill Hicks to walk through the barriers that he had helped break down so that analogies within the context of society and culture must be general and are therefore less relevant than comparisons of method and delivery.

In terms of style, Bruce is famed for his free association, the way ideas change and digress, yet are held together with themes often returning, a style taken from Sahl, and then later employed by Allen (though Bruce's manic delivery was certainly more fast paced than the laconic Sahl). Bruce's career blossomed at the same time as Sahl's, on the back of the growth of a café culture where jazz music and the Beatniks were at the fore, mingling, exchanging ideas and reciprocating inspiration. Bruce employs the hipster jazz lexicon in his routines, using words like a rhythm section. Hicks' free association owes less debt to jazz than Bruce's, though each uses the silences of jazz riffs to both enhance jokes and bring the audience in to the performance, leaving pauses as overwhelming questions. For Hicks, the meandering and digressions come from his confidence as a performer, his desire to open up new ideas on stage. Bruce's kinetic rampage through subjects is more a product of his love of jazz music and desire to integrate its mood and rhythms into his routines.

The comparisons between Hicks and jazz music are due to the way his routines – like Bruce's - are not the 1-2-3 beat of traditional stand-up, the 1) character/scene-setting 2) situation set-up 3) gag. This produces a stop start comedy and creates a distance between performer and audience, as if the audience are never allowed to get into the comedian's mind before another gag comes up. Hicks' jokes evolved and like Bruce he seeks to meet with the audience through the style of seeming to speak as himself, as a performer with anecdotal riffs taken from personal experiences and perspectives. This connection allows both comedians access to the audiences' minds so that attacking important issues allows more easily the re-shaping of pre-conceived ideas. Therefore, through initially shocking them, the audience are made to feel self-conscious and thereby question these issues.

Many critics have rightly identified how both comedians possess a fearless attitude, and how each uses this for comic insights that are controversial because they voice important truths, which many find uncomfortable. On his routine *Religions Inc*, Bruce criticises organised religion and sees figures like Billy Graham and Oral Roberts as little more than hustlers looking for a quick buck; a theme picked up by Hicks and Sam Kinison in their 1980s Outlaw Comics shows. Undoubtedly Bruce was taking more risks because at least the Outlaws could draw on the well-publicised scandals surrounding various televangelists for supporting evidence. Central to this fearlessness is a desire to expose hypocrisy in society, a theme seen in the way both comedians were interested in the power of language and the way it is used. Bruce sought to diffuse the potency of hateful language like "nigger," challenging the speciousness of being offended by words like "cocksucker" (having been arrested for using the word on stage in 1961). For him, moral indignation at such words only served to distract attention from important issues, Bruce more offended by words such as "segregation" and "late night television." He shares with Hicks a belief that outrage at dirty words is merely a means for moralists to suppress ideas and ignore the real problems in society.

One of Bruce's routines that stirred a lot of controversy was his joke about Jackie Kennedy and the way she reacted during her husband's assassination. He mocked how *Time* magazine had made out she was trying to help servicemen, when the reality, for Bruce, was that she was scared and looking for cover. The routine perfectly exemplifies Bruce's fearlessness in going against the national mood; such was his conviction that events shouldn't be viewed through rose-tinted spectacles. This uncovering of truth and exposing media manipulation are central themes in Hicks' routines (who also cared little for the restraints of popular opinion), and in this way both use the method of reversing a joke so that it becomes something different, attempting to open the audience's mind to see things from a different angle and not accept everything the media presents.

Of course, it is worth noting also that Bruce enjoyed drugs as much as Hicks. He would say, "Many people say 'why use narcotics?'" in a beat adding, "*Why* not?" But drugs destroyed Bruce. He became the addict that Hicks never did, the kind of addict mocked by Hicks' celebration of a drug user who never lost anything. And at the end of his career, Hicks' shows may have been bitter and angry but he never neglected the comedy. In contrast, Bruce – filled with the same sense of righteous injustice that often fuelled Hicks' most abrasive comedy – indulged in detailed analysis of his court cases and legal position for long periods during shows towards the end of his career.

Filmmaker John Magnusson's 1965 collaboration with Lenny Bruce, *The Lenny Bruce Performance Film*, intended as a document to be used as evidence that his material was not obscene, shows a comedian exhausted by the legal process, divergent from his comic instincts, instead engaging in tirades against the authorities who seemed to be involved in a witch hunt to silence him. Interestingly, John Magnusson also worked briefly with Bill Hicks and they made plans in 1993 to shoot a black and white concert film, based around the routines that later appeared on the *Rant In E Minor* album, but Hicks' ill-health prevented this.

In many ways, Bruce's material had already dated by the time Hicks was studying comedy and finding influences in the early 1970s. Hicks recognised the importance of Bruce and George Carlin as pioneers, calling both a "breed of individuals who believe in their art and love it and want to evolve it" (2). These were comedians on the peripherals of the mainstream, unlike the big comedy star of the decade, Bob Newhart. Newhart had started doing stand-up in 1959, his 1960 album *The Button-Down Mind Of Bob Newhart* going to number one in the charts. He, too, regularly appeared on *The Tonight Show*, finding an appreciative audience for his deadpan style and one-sided conversations. Though sophisticated, Newhart was a safe comedian, his material concerned with clever observations that had a broad appeal. His TV series, *The Bob Newhart Show* (1972-1978) had him playing a Chicago psychologist surrounded by oddball characters, cleverly tapping into America's growing interest in therapy and self-help which was to dominate 1980s culture and was again mirrored in Newhart's next TV show, *Newhart* (1982-1990) about a Vermont inn owner and writer of self-help books. An accomplished performer, Newhart nonetheless offered none of the challenge to audiences offered by Bruce and Carlin.

It was George Carlin who took up the baton of the controversial comedian after Bruce's death. Carlin had formed a comedy duo with Jack Burns in 1960, moving from radio to the stage with an appearance on Jack Paar's *The Tonight Show* the same year. In 1962 Carlin began his solo career and got another appearance on *The Tonight Show*, hosted by Mort Sahl. There followed a period of sustained gigging and frequent television appearances before the release of his first album, *Take Offs and Put Ons* in 1967. At the time, Carlin's act was pretty tame, matched by stage attire of suit and tie, but by the early 1970s, using acid to expand his awareness, dressing more casually and growing a beard, he was moving towards social and political comedy. His 1972 album, *FM & AM* (which won a Grammy and went Gold) marked the change, the title symbolic of the transformation in his material. Despite his success, Carlin found that like Lenny Bruce, his material offended moralists, and he was arrested in July 1972, a liberal use of sexual swear words provoking the authorities to charge Carlin with obscenity. As his cocaine habit developed and he railed at Nixon he found more television work and hosted the first *Saturday Night Live* in 1975. Frequent television specials and comedy albums cemented his reputation as a cutting edge comic, although in Reagan's America he found his voice somewhat marginalized. Moreover, a second heart attack and his determination to get over his cocaine addiction saw Carlin produce some subdued material, more observational than political, until a return to form and resurgence of interest in the 1990s, culminating in a Lifetime Achievement Award at the American Comedy Awards of 2001.

Hicks was a fan of Carlin's and as well as the socio-political material, there is also some similarity in the way they (like Twain and Bruce) play with language. For Carlin's lines like "Whose cruel idea was it for the word 'lisp' to have an 's' in it?" and "Isn't it a bit unnerving that doctors call what they do 'practice'?" there is Hicks' early ponderings of electric bills saying "thank you for the opportunity to serve you," when there is no other choice. Most tellingly, Hicks' famous routine about a desire to perform fellatio on himself is a reworking of Carlin's routine about seeing a dog lick its own balls and noting "If I could reach I'd never leave the house" (5a).

Though the ideas and style of Carlin and Bruce and their valorous confronting of important issues and strongly individualistic points of view can be seen in Hicks' work, it was Woody Allen he cited as his main influence.

Initially, Woody Allen was a somewhat nervous performer, yet this became something of a trademark, fitting in perfectly with the self-mockery and neuroses that were central to his act, slowly building a following with several appearances on *The Ed Sullivan Show* and Jack Paar's *The Tonight Show* in 1962. He also capitalised on the early sixties boom in the popularity of comedy albums, Allen releasing his first on Colpix in 1964. That same year he did a week as host on *The Tonight Show*, standing in for Johnny Carson. Never at ease in the medium, pretty soon Allen was moving away from stand-up, doing his last gig in 1972, concentrating instead on films.

Hicks initially came into contact with Allen through his stand-up routines for television appearances. With friend Dwight Slade, Hicks formed a double act, The Losers, and began writing material, most of it taken from comedians they had seen on television, most notably Woody Allen. As twelve year olds, their act involved Allen impersonations and the copying of his routines and style.

When Hicks got a portable television in his bedroom in his early teens he began watching more diverse comedians, but his admiration for Woody Allen was cemented when he first saw Woody Allen acting in *What's New, Pussycat* (released theatrically in 1965). The film, a loosely plotted sex farce written by Allen, concerned a womaniser (Peter O'Toole) seeking help from psychiatrist Peter Sellers. Though Allen takes only a supporting role as Sellers' friend, the film is characterised by the kind of witty one-liners Hicks so enjoyed; snappy pay-off dialogue that was a central component of Allen's stand-up.

Hicks would make audio recordings of Allen's TV appearances, then listen back and learn the routines, attempting to find a comic voice through re-writing Allen's material superimposed on his own limited experiences. His bedroom was his self-contained universe, a place where he and Dwight would develop characters based on his school life, like Dumb Jock, or taken from his father (Goober Dad) and his mother (Mumsy). There was always affection in the routines he developed around his family, yet these innocuous and gentle stereotypes were the early seedlings of characters that would be developed to savagely expose the stupidity of Americans.

When he was thirteen, Bill went away to a church camp where he did his first solo stand-up. He had about fourteen minutes of material written, half of it stolen, including a Woody Allen gag about being breast-fed by "falsies". Of the experience Hicks recalled "People laughed, then looked at me like I was the antichrist". It was an early indication that Hicks had no time for a didactic morality, a hint of the stand against narrow-mindedness that was to be a key theme in all areas of Hicks' philosophy and routines. It also showed his willingness to say whatever he liked regardless of whether it was accepted or not.

As mentioned, Hicks and Slade copied Allen's style in their early routines as a double act. Here was a performer on television whose nervous mannerisms and eager to please vocals were akin to the tentative steps the double act were taking into stand-up. His personal neuroses and failures gave him a connection to the audience, much as Hicks would include self-mockery in his act. Allen, the nerd, the loser, transcended his persona with quick and clever quips that seemed to suggest he was better than other more athletic types. Perhaps for Hicks it mirrored his feeling of separation from the Dumb Jocks at high school. Added to this was material about a 'rough' childhood, which obviously appealed to Hicks' feelings of being stifled by his home life. His upbringing – though in truth not that rough - formed a central part of Hicks' earliest material before he had experience of the world beyond its confines.

In his routines, Allen would string together anecdotes using short sentences, emphasizing syllables and sounds within those sentences. Excessive use of "and" connected ideas in the story, each one painting a picture for laughs. In this sense there was a somewhat staccato build-up, allowing Allen to pause and to digress. Though more free flowing, Hicks builds his routines in a similar way, taking an initial idea before moving it to other levels.

Allen does this in his routine *The Moose*, beginning with the recounting of hitting a moose whilst driving, then strapping it to his car. He takes it to a party where it mingles with guests before losing out to two humans each dressed as a moose in a fancy dress competition. Allen mistakenly takes the humans to release back into the woods where hunters then shoot them. Hicks has this style of taking an idea to an absurd level in his earliest routines. Concerning the mid-eighties debate on prayers being made illegal in schools, he would imagine some kind of vice squad bursting into school to arrest people for praying, and then imagine children, huddled like smokers, in toilet cubicles, secretly praying, vice squad like figures kicking down the door to arrest those in the cubicles. Similarly, when Hicks talks of going into an adult bookstore in the U.K., the routine moves between several places and becomes as equally absurd as Allen's tale. Hicks buys a pornographic magazine, goes back to his hotel and notices blue dots on all the graphic pictures. This leads him to muse on what live sex shows must be like as he physically acts out the role of the man whose job it is to hold a blue dot over the more graphic scenes.

The surreal elements of Allen's stand-up (and early films) certainly influenced Hicks, where like Allen he could play with proportion, as in Allen's routine about being hypnotised into thinking he was a fire engine, then being pulled up by the cops and wondering how they could get a fire engine into a police car (*The Great Renaldo*). This is much the same as Hicks on drugs encountering cops whom he thinks are miniature, leading him to contemplate putting them into a jar.

Allen's digressions took the young Hicks on an imaginative ride, much as Hicks' even more diverse going off at tangents would with his audiences. One example of Allen's routines digressing is seen in *Second Marriage*, which does not follow a straight path, but more a circuitous route covering the draft, drugs, stoned police horses and car rental. Allen's words create a storyline in the audience's mind, his attention to seemingly insignificant details seeking to colour in the picture and help the audience visualise. For Allen these digressions were solely for the laughs, for Hicks they were used to connect ideas, opening out routines to view the bigger picture. As he said to John Lahr, "The best thing I do is make connections. I connect *everything*" (6).

Hicks and Allen are both first person comedians, in the sense that they are not telling jokes about situations from which they are disassociated, but instead both build material from themselves, from their voices, carefully drawing in other people's lives yet keeping these vignettes connected to their own outlook and feelings, which are often coloured by disappointment and frustration.

Comedy is often about the individual being unhappy in his or her environment, and with Allen and Hicks we have two comedians as outsiders, looking on the wider world with some disbelief and scepticism. For Allen, this was more due to his shyness and insecurities, whereas for Hicks it was by choice, a way to avoid being assimilated and diluted by the mainstream: "I get a certain kick out of being an outsider constantly. It allows me to be creative. I don't like anything in the mainstream and they don't like me" (7). This is similar to Allen's feelings about the cool reception given to his film *Stardust Memories* (1980), of which he said in 1992, "One critic said my audience left me, but the truth is, I left my audience. The backlash really started when I did *Stardust Memories*. People were outraged...I was just trying to make what I wanted, not what people wanted me to make" (8).

Allen is the outsider, alienated from the modern world and its trends, his routine *Mechanical Objects* capturing this disassociation from contemporary things: "I have a sun lamp, and as I sit under it, it rains on me." Hicks was not a beach person, separate from those who populate such places with their tanned skin and white teeth whilst he has "White skin, tanned teeth"; a similar disassociation as Allen saying, "When I go to the beach I don't tan, I stroke" (*Private Life*). The two are detached from popular trends, from those activities that seem to have mass appeal. Hicks would feel distance from nightclubs and dancing, would see himself as an outsider not in tune with popular American culture, unlike the test audiences turned off by the sex scenes in the film *Basic Instinct*: "Boy, is my thumb not on the pulse of America." Hicks is the outsider in all the meetings he missed, like those on "the miracle of childbirth" or "When did we start listening to pre-pubescent white girls? I must have missed that meeting." Indeed, there were many missed meetings that concerned his not being into the music that was selling millions in America: "Hammer. There was another boat that left me on the island." Both Allen and Hicks use their outsider status on one level for self-mockery to allow the audience to empathise, but also as a way to convey their frustration with the world: a world that seems superficial and is permanently distracted by ephemeral pleasures and anti-intellectualism.

Perhaps the greatest appeal for the continually reading Hicks was the sophistication of Allen's material, his cleverness with language giving him an air of nonchalance, his choice of material eschewing the ordinary and everyday for references that exhibit his intellect. For example, Allen does a gag about where "I cheated in a metaphysics exam. I looked into the soul of the boy in front of me" (later repeated in *Annie Hall* (1977). Hicks makes a nod to this in his early eighties shows with the dumb jocks taking philosophy exams and referring to it as a "quiz."

Beyond sophisticated references, Allen, like Mark Twain, has anecdotes filled with detail, elevating the material to a literary level, often ending narrative threads with an unexpected twist. However, in terms of composing the material Allen and Hicks were very different. Allen, his early career based around writing sketches for other stand-ups, crafted his material more consciously, building a long plotted story onto which he could add funny remarks. His stand-up material would go through several drafts before he was ready to perform it. Often he would "condense a twenty minute thing to six minutes" (9). When taking the material to an audience, Allen stuck to his set, in contrast to Hicks, placing "no premium on improvisation as an end in itself" (9). Though in delivery he gave the sense of digressing with ease, Allen was too nervous a performer and had spent too much time writing material to veer from his set.

Through almost endless touring Hicks had a body of work to take on a stage, but with each show he could give material previously covered a new twist. Because his targets were large, for example government deception, he could open up new pockets as they came to him during his act, crafting material on stage, improvising, evolving ideas through several shows. He would often play two or three gigs a night at the same venue and part of the reason for improvisation was not wanting to cheat an audience as well as not wanting to bore himself. On the composition of his material, Hicks said, "I write everything on stage...I don't sit around and write all day. I write ideas down" (10). These ideas would be illuminated on stage, and though he would repeat routines, the sense that he was composing on stage can be seen with Hicks' witty remarks often being added to different subjects in his routines. He could even change for different audiences, so that the Sharper Image reference became Tandy in the U.K. and to trailer parks were added council flats.

Allen's material is rooted in a New York perspective and like his films he never really leaves that environment. Whilst a Southern background heavily influenced Hicks' material, he went beyond this to create a more expansive outlook. It is the taking of material from one's own background and embellishing it that appeals to Hicks. Allen's love for New York is evident in his material, but he is not averse to mocking the pretensions of New York intellectuals. Hicks' love of the South is more implicit, more seen through his absorbing of Southern peculiarities and archetypes for use in routines. His ridiculing of his background has far greater savagery than Allen's, not poking fun at those at the top of the intellectual ladder, but those at the bottom whose intent it seems to be to drag the rest of society down to.

After seeing *What's New Pussycat*, Hicks also became a fan of Allen's films. His earliest features were still connected to his stand-up, little more than a series of sketches and clever one-liners hung on simple, if surreal plots. Films such as *Take The Money And Run* (1969), *Bananas* (1971) and *Sleeper* (1973) indulged in slapstick humour reminiscent of old *Keystone Cops* and Charlie Chaplin silent features. This can be seen in Hicks' film collaboration with Kevin Booth and David Johndrow, *Ninja Bachelor Party*. Set in the suburbs, the film concerns Clarence Mumford (Booth), a Robitussin cough syrup addict and would-be Ninja. Mumford is the Woody Allen nerd character, the central role Allen often cast himself in, and like these characters Mumford comes out on top in the end. In its major fight scene Mumford faces off with Dr Death, the Ninja Grandmaster (Hicks), in a set piece that owes much to Allen with its exaggerated sound effects of crashing and hitting, falling over and anti-macho, poorly coordinated fighting. Ridiculous and surreal, Mumford and Death run through streets, into a building, fighting in a lift and then on top of the building. It employs speeded-up scenes like the chase scenes Allen used in *Sleeper*, as when Dr Death ends up in a washing machine and it spins around. Likewise, Allen has characters surreally moving out of context to engage with things incongruous to the situation. In *Bananas* there is an army of rebels stopping off at a diner to order sandwiches and coke, whilst in *Ninja Bachelor Party* the serene Master Ninja (again, Hicks) in a Korean wilderness, takes out a phone and accepts credit cards for his teaching of Mumford, before driving off in a car.

Despite the wild anarchy of these films, they did have aspirations to be more sophisticated than his stand-up, particularly as he became more at ease with the medium in the mid 1970s. As with his stand-up routines, Allen fills his films with literary, philosophical and artistic references such as Hemmingway and Freud. The knowing parody of the science-fiction genre (*Sleeper*) and crime film (*Take The Money And Run*) show Allen revealing his sophistication, albeit none too subtly. Nonetheless, in parodying the Russian literature of Dostoyevsky and Tolstoy in *Love And Death* (1975) and adeptly skewering pretentious philosophising of the human condition, Allen is conveying his literary influences and intellect more cleverly. Such referencing takes him above the nerd persona, just as Hicks' unashamed referencing of Freud, Van Gogh, Beethoven and Carl Jung elevates him to something higher than the image of merely a sex/shock comedian.

Although not apparent after the early 1980s when his political views were moving to the right, there is some political satire in Allen's work. Material from his stand-up career suggested left-wing leanings, one of Allen's quips being that he was "Working on a non-fiction version of the Warren report." The film *Bananas*, boasting a performance by the next decade's dunderhead hunk, Sylvester Stallone, deals with political and television manipulation and even has a satire of left and right wing politics. At one point a U.S. soldier asks a general whose side they are fighting on and receives the reply, "The American government is not taking any chances. Some of us are fighting for, some are fighting against."

The film *Sleeper* has Allen's character waking up in the year 2173, the sleeping idea symbolic of political apathy, the kind Hicks would rail against as he denounced America's disinterest with politics and its pliability through television. The society Allen depicts in 2173 is self-satisfied and unquestioning, its revolutionary spirit seen in the need to overthrow a fascist government, again a satire of left and right wing politics. *Sleeper* also deals with a theme of the loss of individuality, much like *Love And Death* where the individual is lost amidst the mindless nationalistic following of a path to war. The basis of Hicks' philosophy was that the individual should have the right to choose his or her own destiny as long as it didn't infringe upon the rights and freedoms of others. He would swim against the tide of superficial mass opinion, "the ain't life keen" outlook that doesn't seek the truth behind the superficiality, standing as an individual unwilling to be absorbed.

Allen identifies the centre of superficiality as Hollywood, and its world of celebrities ass-kissing their way to fame and fortune. His love of New York directly correlated to his hatred of L.A. "They don't throw their garbage away, they use it to make TV shows" (*Annie Hall*). *Annie Hall* in particular seeks to contrast the falseness of the West Coast with the intellect of New York, much as Hicks would do in his routine about phoning the West Coast and hearing boasts about it being perpetually sunny, with people laying by the pool and talking to TV producers, contrasting this image with people back East "reading a book. Yeah, we're thinking back East. Yeah, we're evolving".

Both *Stardust Memories* and *Celebrity* (1998) focus on the vacuity of stardom, the way it isn't the be all and end all of human existence, mocking the way the public seems to place famous people on a pedestal like they are the role models for what ordinary people should aspire to, an idea at the centre of Hicks' tirades against the TV and music industry. Meanwhile, *Zelig* (1983) again focuses on the loss of individuality with its main character a man who can transform himself to fit in with his surroundings and therefore make those around him feel more comfortable. In this it also deals with the way people embrace and follow anyone who seems to be a celebrity. Hicks frequently worked in Los Angeles but hated the place, hoping one day that an earthquake would wash it into the ocean, leaving just the "cool, beautiful serenity called Arizona Bay." For Hicks, it was a place where non-entities proliferated, where the obsession with fame meant no one engaged with real issues. Fame seemed to be the pinnacle of achievement and it could be guaranteed with the most simple-minded and obnoxious television shows and films.

On a more base level, Allen's obsession with sex can be seen in much of Hicks' material. For example, Allen's line "Sex is a beautiful thing between two people" (pause) "between five it's fantastic" (*Vegas*) can be linked to Hicks' "It's gonna take a very special woman" (pause) "or a bunch of average ones." Their sexual material evolves from sexual and relationship failures and the exaggeration of them, but for both there is the desire to be seen as more than just sexual comedians with Hicks' desire to escape dick jokes and Allen's nerdish sex mad characters balanced by intellectual asides. It is the dilemma best seen in Allen's *Stardust Memories* with its main character, director Sandy Bates, desiring to escape a past of funny but inconsequential earlier films. Bates (closer to the real Woody Allen than many of his films) wants to be taken seriously as an artist but is constantly told by fans that they liked him more with his earlier funny films. Hicks grew frustrated too at being perceived as a dirty comedian who only did dick jokes, often sarcastically making reference to dick jokes to criticise the mentality of the audience. Ironically, Hicks too would become less interested in Allen's movies in the early 1980s when Allen was trying to make more serious films.

Allen frequently referred to the pleasures of masturbation with the likes of "don't knock masturbation. It's sex with someone I love" (*Annie Hall*) and "Don't go knocking my hobbies" (*Hannah And Her Sisters*). Hicks took the idea to much darker levels, not just masturbation over magazines and films, but men giving themselves blow jobs. Both talk about it naturally, uninhibited by a false morality, which doesn't want to acknowledge that it even happens. With this willingness to cut loose from constrictions of rectitude comes a more surreal perspective on sex. *Bananas* has TV sports reporter Howard Cosell commentating as Allen's character has sex. Hicks' update had Dan Rather commentating on a riot of sex in the streets as a cure for the A.I.D.S. virus is found.

The surrealism apparent in Allen's *Everything You Always Wanted To Know About Sex But Were Afraid To Ask* (1972) with its segment based around Gene Wilder fucking a goat, can perhaps be seen as some inspiration for Goatboy, the randy Satan-goat with which Hicks took the sex angle much much further, having sex with priests and young virgins. Another segment of the film, *What Happens During Ejaculation* is even closer to one of Hicks' routines. In the film sperm are personified, taking messages from the brain and talking to each. Allen, as a sperm, contemplates smashing his head against rubber or ending up on the ceiling if the body is masturbating. Hicks not only uses his physical body on stage to become a sperm swimming, but has a routine in which he sees the sperm as people, wiping vast continents from his chest. Both performers attach the surreal to a subject many would find distasteful, but in this they are pointing up a more profound truth about where life begins, seeking to confront audience tastes with an exaggerated vision of what is natural.

Allen's material on sex is a lighter attack on sexual hypocrisy than Hicks', though both are using the material as a kind of escape from their religious upbringing. Allen, more agnostic than atheist, was fascinated by the idea of a God. It permeated his film work, but is also evident in his stand-up material. In his routine *Private Life* Allen recounts practising for a role as God, doing the method acting thing and staying in character for a day before he "got into a fight with a guy and forgave him." Hicks had a similar line when confronted by Christians who didn't like what he said in his show, countering their post-gig grievances with the quip, "Then forgive me." Both comedians see the hypocrisy of fundamentalism, the disparity between beliefs and reality. Hicks' references to a second coming have Jesus shocked that people are still wearing crosses, their insensitivity likened to the wearing of rifle pendants in memory of John F. Kennedy. Incredulity becomes anger with Hicks' routine about Jesus shooting those in society who have misinterpreted his ideas. It's a point seen in *Hannah And Her Sisters* (1986) when Allen quips, "If Jesus came back today and saw what was being done in his name, he'd never stop throwing up." And though both perspectives seek to criticise organised religion, there is an implicit acknowledgement of the value of Jesus' original ideas.

Part of their religious outlook includes a fascination with death, giving a philosophical streak to their work, Allen's developing more throughout his longer career and maturing in his late 1970s film work. Cynthia True's *American Scream* biography of Hicks recounts his and Dwight Slade's audition for a school talent show, the duo employing a scene called *Death* which had been inspired by Woody Allen's play *Death Knocks*. Both efforts use the same surreal technique of personifying Death and surrounding the character with contemporary accoutrements for comic effect. In Allen's play, first published in *The New Yorker* in 1968, Death is challenged to a card game. With Hicks and Slade, Death visits an apartment and is seen by its occupant (Hicks) as a charity collector. It is appropriate that Hicks and Slade should tap into a theme central to much of Allen's work, with many of his film personas plagued by the possibility that life may just be meaningless and that death is an inevitability that leaves mankind helpless. He is aware his trivial neuroses may not be important in the open scheme of things, but the agnostic in him means he can neither escape his guilt if there is a God nor his fears of death if there isn't. Though Hicks attacked organised religion, he did have faith that there was a higher being, a God of some sort and that beyond death there was some higher experience. For him, life's trivialities held the human race back. When Hicks mused on death, heaven was a comical world rooted in human culture. Unlike Allen musings on death suggesting life is meaningless, Hicks was more concerned that his mother might discover his "porno wing" after his death, whilst his heaven had Yul Brynner and Jimi Hendrix partying in the afterlife. For Hicks, the rock and roll comedian with the rock and roll perspective, God was a rock and roll deity.

Woody Allen was never a rock n' roll comedian though and Hicks would move quickly in his evolution to other comedians who embodied some of that rock n' roll spirit. He did an audiotape of Steve Martin's first appearance on Johnny Carson's *The Tonight Show*, listening to it regularly, a continuation of the studying of comedy that had begun with Woody Allen. When he played the tape for Slade, Hicks would perform the visual gags, using his physical features to help his one-man audience visualise, and at the same time learning how visuals could enhance a routine, something that was to become an essential part of the act Hicks was developing.

4
Wild And Crazy Guys

In early 1975, NBC was looking for a new television show for Saturday nights; something to replace the slot lazily being filled with Johnny Carson re-runs. TV writer Lorne Michaels (who had written for many comedians, including Woody Allen) had an idea for an innovative live show with a satirical edge mixing sketches, movie parodies, mock news reports and music. *Saturday Night* debuted on October 11th 1975, hosted by George Carlin. Its appeal lay with a young audience who had grown up during the TV boom of the fifties and sixties and were now playing an active part in the medium's development as well as becoming a key audience demographic. As an audience, they were bored with the old order, turned off by television and a predominance of shows that belonged to another era. *Saturday Night* appeared at exactly the right time, building on the successful excursions into television of performers such as Richard Pryor and George Carlin, ushering in a new and vibrant generation of comics whose attitude and material were relevant to a vast audience that had previously been ignored.

It was something of a natural successor to *The Carol Burnett Show* (1967-1978), a variety show mixing character comedy and skits and some tame topical satire with a broad appeal. The comedians on *Saturday Night* brought fresh ideas; the new production having an anything goes vibe, its seeming unpredictability giving it a sense of danger. Although the show indulged in Nixon bashing and had satirical elements it was hardly subversive, its anarchic spirit never really threatening to the establishment. Nonetheless, it was new and fresh enough to blow away the cobwebs of the old guard of comedians.

By 1976 the show had become a big hit, gaining 4 Emmy awards and producing a new generation of comedy stars like John Belushi, Dan Aykroyd, Chevy Chase, Lily Tomlin, Steve Martin, Bill Murray and Andy Kaufman, kicking off the late seventies comedy boom in America. This was the generation of comedians first linked to rock music. Indeed, stars such as Belushi, Chase and Aykroyd were playing their rock star parts by indulging in cocaine and partying with Keith Richards and Paul McCartney.

These comedians were overturning the conventions of comedy, quite willing to have ideas fall flat in the pursuit of originality. By the time the programme became *Saturday Night Live* in 1977, John Belushi was the show's star. His comedy was filled with raw energy, his manic performances perhaps more about his physicality than his material. Steve Martin's stage show was also about how he used his body and face, but his skills were subtler than Belushi's. From noting how Woody Allen's mannerisms could be an integral part of his performance, Hicks saw how Steve Martin took physicality a step further, making it central to his act.

Born in Waco, Texas, in 1945, Martin moved to Southern California when he was five years old. Like Allen, his early act involved magic before moving into writing for TV shows when he was 21, then beginning as a stand-up in the early seventies. By 1975 he had established a large cult following, hosting *Saturday Night Live* for the first time in 1976.

The political humour satirising Nixon and attacking the Vietnam War was not Martin's thing and anyway, audiences had grown bored with hearing the same old gags about Nixon's dishonesty. Moreover, those maimed and injured in Vietnam were now visible reminders of the war's terrible consequences, having returned to towns and cities all across America. Martin's offbeat humour found an audience, the same demographic who watched *Saturday Night Live* for its unconventional zaniness. Self-dubbed "the wild and crazy guy," his manic energy and physical presence on stage gradually drew large, adoring crowds with people attending his gigs wearing Martin's trademark bunny ears or sporting a plastic arrow through the head. His first comedy album *Let's Get Small* won a Grammy in 1977 and cemented his reputation as a lively and original performer. An efficacious counterbalance to the resolutely political and purposeful comedy that had characterised stand-up since the late 1960s, unlike most comedy albums it managed to capture the essence of the performer, conveying not just Martin's zestfulness and eccentricity, but also his subtle use of pauses, his confidence with comic timing and the underlying sophistication of his playing with language. Martin's two subsequent albums, *A Wild And Crazy Guy* (1978) and *Comedy Is Not Pretty* (1979), re-worked the same formula effectively, showing an assured performer able to work a live audience with aplomb.

It is easy to see the appeal of Martin's stage show to the adolescent Hicks, with frenzied routines mixing the surreal and absurd in much the same way as Woody Allen's films did. Take for example Martin pondering the human body and what life might be like if the mouth had ended up situated under the arm. His surreal idea is played out as he flaps his arm and mimes shoving food beneath it, like the physical grotesque of Hicks pondering the idea of women priests and imagining a priest "with gills and a trunk", extending his arm as the trunk curls up.

Hicks' fascination with rock music and rock performers such as KISS found no connection with Woody Allen's stand-up. In contrast, Martin's stage shows had a much more rock and roll feel, the comedian persona of Martin some distance from his real self, echoing the front employed by rock performers (usually a rebellious one). Martin's ability to play with and sustain this artifice allows him to seem (to an audience) as inscrutable as those cool, enigmatic rock stars. He is unlike the majority of stand-ups who generally seek audience connection through appearing to be ordinary. Even if they are not being themselves, most are at least offering a realistic, everyman persona in order for the gags to hit home because they are easy for an audience to relate to. Martin's skill was to adopt this anarchic artifice so that his nonchalant detachment exuded confidence, the kind of disinterest in conformity that is a feature of rock star posturing. In addition, as an adept banjo player, he would use musical routines during his act, which saw crowds not only laughing but also whooping and cheering like those at rock concerts. The way he worked the audience established a similar connection as that created by rock performers, Martin employing his famous routines such as *The Wild and Crazy Guy*, *King Tut* and *Happy Feet* like musicians use their most well known songs. Indeed, the audiences demanded such routines, having become familiar with them through their inclusion on his albums, whilst catchphrases such as "Well, excuuuuse me!" would have the crowd delirious like a band returning for an encore of their biggest hit.

This sense of performance was further seen through Martin's use of physical comedy. Hicks was never influenced by comedians eager to get snappy gags out, preferring instead to play out physical comedy with attention to detail so that it is not merely slapstick. Martin too has this sense, going beyond snapshot mugging in a routine where he drops water onto the stage floor, then sends a shiver through his whole body to denote an electric current going through him as he touches the microphone. There is laughter, but Martin has the timing perfected enough to go back to the microphone and take several shocks, the exaggeration paradoxically reinforcing the realness of the electric current. The same attention to detail is a part of Hicks' physical comedy, undoubtedly a result of his audio recordings of Martin requiring him to perform the visuals (to Dwight Slade) with technical accuracy.

Hicks was known to copy Martin's physical and facial gestures as a youngster, and when his career developed, Hicks' using of the stage's space was similar to Martin's. Martin is constantly fidgeting in performances, skipping around the stage, flailing his arms, moving his feet, and exaggerating mundane gestures. His *Happy Feet* routine has his feet dancing around the stage, taking over his whole body, pulling it unwillingly in all directions. His carefully choreographed movements are aligned with a use of props, not just those at hand as Hicks would use – a microphone, its stand and a stool – but bringing in other objects like apples to juggle or balloons to blow into shapes, using them to seemingly improvise. It gives the performance an extra dimension, a busyness and aura of anarchy that has all the colour of a rock performance. Yet such is his skill that it gives his show a sense of ease, his style seeming like improvisation and allowing him to at times appear almost amateurish, like he's making it up as he goes along. This allows his connection with the audience through creating a sense of thinking on his feet, as if he is responding to their encouragement. They are thus fundamental to the performance, with Martin feeding off the resulting atmosphere of participation and delightedly helping form a bond with the audience.

The ease of connection obviously appealed to Hicks, with the nonchalance of Martin apparent in his languid slipping into song being similar to Hicks' improvised reciting of lyrics from songs by The Rolling Stones, Bob Dylan and most notably Elvis Presley. Martin manoeuvres into a variety of accents and voices, using them to maintain the mask of his stage persona (The Wild And Crazy Guy) rather than to create fully rounded characters, in contrast to Hicks' employment of voices to create more clearly defined characters, albeit archetypes. The simple tool of a deep voice for serious figures is seen in much of Hicks' comedy, but the closest comparison in terms of voice is Martin's *I'm A Ramblin Guy*, in which we get the sense of a man lost in his own explanations that will go nowhere. Martin has the same rise and fall of intonation and syllable emphasis as the unsure ramblings of Hicks' characters who sold weapons to Iraq thinking it was for farming and the fundamentalist who is trying to explain why the Earth is only 12,000 years old, their voices trailing off as their arguments falter.

There is also something about Martin's comic timing that appealed to Hicks, the way that like Twain and Woody Allen, anecdotes built up a picture only for an amusing twist at the end. For example, a routine in which Martin eulogises dreamily about the beauty of a 400-year-old cathedral in France, at length conveying his awe before easing in the line "as I was writing my name on it with a can of spray paint." It's intellectualism bludgeoned by ignorance, an accentuated contrast skilfully displaying the comedian's confidence by showing them toying with intellect to suggest they have nothing to prove. We get a similar undercutting of intellect when Hicks talks of finding his perfect woman in England, his beautiful and sensitive description climaxing with, "We can sit quietly together and watch a leaf turn colour in the fall, and both turn to each other and smile," before a pause leads to "and then fuck like a rabbit" (3). Similarly there is Martin going to a girlfriend's house and liking her "pussy," then feigning indignation at the audience's assumptions, telling them he was referring to a cat before muttering under his breath, "That cat was the best fuck I ever had."

These twists gave his comedy the surreal quality that Allen's films had. Hicks, always one to seek a new way of looking at things, appreciated the comic potential of the surreal emerging from the mundane. Martin gripes about the price per square feet of carpet before going beyond mundane with the punch line that he "bought two square feet and strapped them to my feet." Part of the exhilaration of Hicks' comedy was the way an idea evolved from mundane beginnings, the way that his well structured routines took off and didn't allow the audience a pause to think 'hey, that's just silly.' Martin does it with a routine that begins with his general musings on cats and develops into a tale of his cat embezzling him and buying $3,000 worth of cat toys. It follows a similar path to Allen's *Moose* story and Hicks' many surreal digressions.

Pockets of sophistication are evident in Martin's stand-up with asides that refer to metaphysics and the meaning of the universe. Again, for Hicks this set him apart from other comedians, giving him an intellectual superiority and therefore power. Martin's film career was to develop his sophistication, though it started with the broad slapstick of *The Jerk* (1979). Nonetheless, the progress of Martin's film career offers testament to his performing skills as he gradually became more successful, broadening his range with writing and directing and ultimately leaving stand-up behind.

Similar in style to Martin was Andy Kaufman. Something of an enigma in the comedy world, Kaufman's originality and constant endeavouring to test the boundaries of what is perceived as comedy made him more a performance artist than straightforward stand-up. Significantly, Kaufman's emergence coincided with the growth of interest in performance artists, a 1970s movement spearheaded by figures such as Laurie Anderson, whom

46

Kaufman met in 1978. Like Hicks, Kaufman was switched on to Transcendental Meditation, using its opening up of the body and soul in his somewhat avant-garde approach to performances. His career began in the early 1970s, appearing on stage as the naïve fish-out-of-water, Foreign Man, and doing poor "emetations" of Richard Nixon and Ed Sullivan, as well as a sparkling Elvis Presley. He appeared on the first *Saturday Night Live* in 1975, lip-synching to the theme from *Mighty Mouse* cartoon, the kind of unorthodox routine on which the show was being built, so that throughout the decade he continued to appear on *Saturday Night Live* as well as other TV shows, including several appearances on *The Tonight Show*. In the successful TV series *Taxi* (1978-1983) he was part of an ensemble cast, which included one of Hicks' bete noirs, Tony Danza. Kaufman appeared as the loveable fool Latka Gravas, though the show's success was something of an aberration in Kaufman's career and he quickly came to loathe the show and its restrictions.

After a supporting role in the film *God Told Me To* (1976), he featured more prominently in two other movies: *In God We Tru$t* (1980) alongside Richard Pryor, and *Heartbeeps* (1981), but both bombed. In 1982, his appearances increasingly belligerent and challenging, he was voted off *Saturday Night Live* by an audience phone-in. Though he had more exposure on television than Hicks (after *Saturday Night Live*, the 1980s saw frequent appearances on David Letterman's show) Kaufman too found television generally unresponsive to his talents, generally unable to accommodate his unique comic contrivances. His special for ABC, filmed in 1977, was not shown until two years later. When he died in 1984 many thought it a set-up, but in the intervening years his reputation – like Hicks' – has blossomed, culminating in a biopic with Milos Forman's *Man On The Moon* (1999) starring Jim Carrey.

Kaufman was more at home with his stage act. His shows were oddball affairs, often including wrestling where he billed himself as Inter-Gender Wrestling Champion, using the persona to delightedly taunt women in the audience. He even did shows centred on a comprehensive reading of the novel *The Great Gatsby*. Like Hicks, he had an Elvis obsession and included an impersonation in his act; the young virile Elvis as opposed to Hicks' Vegas Elvis. Hicks' comedy was about personas being used as conduits for the message he was seeking to convey; whereas Kaufman's stage shows featured characters that were a comic end in themselves. As well as Foreign Man he had lounge singer Tony Clifton, complete with dress, prosthetics and make-up. Foreign Man was initially the amiable and warm fish out of water character, but as Kaufman's career progressed and audiences began to expect Foreign Man (or perhaps, Latka Gravas from which Foreign Man evolved), he used Foreign Man as an anti-warmth statement. When crowds chanted for the character it frustrated Kaufman, so that he delighted in giving only snippets, exaggerating the character's warmth to reveal its insincere underbelly. This can be compared to Hicks and his "dick jokes" as they become a means to mock the audience's stupidity and base needs. Moreover, the obnoxious Tony Clifton character allowed Kaufman to unleash his darker side, Clifton indulging in alcohol and cigarettes unlike the teetotal, non-smoking Kaufman. This is closest to Hicks' Goatboy with its unleashing of sexual desires. In essence, Hicks' personas and Kaufman's characters are both about revealing deeper aspects of their own feelings, and beyond this they allow the performers to throw the focus back onto the audience, to examine their reactions and what it says about them.

Beyond both being physical performers, the most striking similarity between Kaufman and Hicks is their relationship to audiences. In his shows Kaufman would often change material, like Hicks bored with any set routine and not really caring about audience reaction, playing both to and against them. Kaufman wanted to challenge audience expectations of the stand-up comedian, often testing their limits with performances like his singing of *A Hundred Bottles Of Beer On The Wall* all the way through. For Peter Firman, "He craved their emotional involvement in whatever form, they hate him, they're bored, they love him, they laugh or they cry" (11). This is similar to Hicks hoping the audience are "at least emotionally involved…even if it's anger." Hicks often tested an audience's limits with his long monologues from Goatboy (even acknowledging the audience's discomfort with asides such as "enough already…"). Likewise, when Hicks slips into Elvis and Charlie Hodge dialogue he is often unwilling to let it go. Just as Kaufman employed silence to resist expectations, so Hicks continues with the Charlie Hodge routine as if to reclaim himself, to go against audience expectations. Women often jeered Kaufman because of his wrestling escapades, but this was merely a ruse with female plants in the audience often leading the jeering. Like Hicks, he wanted to keep the audience's mind open, and like Hicks he enjoyed the twisting of expectations and changing perceptions, Kaufman delighting in making the audience realise they were being had (though he was equally happy to keep them in the dark).

Kaufman too was interested in exposing the falseness of the show business world. Part of the reason he came to loathe *Taxi* was because it exemplified that superficial and deceitful world with the careful management of the studio audience, through prompts and, if necessary, the addition of canned laughter. This contrasts starkly with what Kaufman sought from his comedy: "I just want real reactions. I want people to laugh from the gut, be sad from the gut, or get angry from the gut." It's a demand paralleling Hicks' desire to have rock stars who "play from their fuckin' heart!" Kaufman used his arrogant persona, consumed by superiority and false sincerity, to mock Hollywood types, presenting an exaggerated version to expose the self-interest and vacuity of those types. Through this unsympathetic character, Kaufman was also accusing the public of being blind to the shallowness of stars, *The Andy Kaufman Show* (1983) seeing him refer to the audience with "What a bunch of sheep!" For him, there was a dichotomy between his 'art' as he saw it and the audience's response, the same dichotomy for Hicks between sex jokes and the often unpalatable truths he wanted to convey. Taking this to a logical end, Kaufman wanted to expose the entertainment industry's manipulation of audiences by using elaborate set-ups, like his appearance with wrestler Jerry Lawler on David Letterman's show when he threw coffee at Lawler. In shocking both Letterman and the audience he was pointing up the way they accept the stage-managed set-ups television engineers. Hicks' methods of irony and the dissemination of language and image were for the same ends, making visible the chasm between reality and unreality.

Hicks' early education in comedy had taken in the tail end of the satire boom and the new wave of more absurdist, surreal comics like Martin and Kaufman. Both strands are prevalent in his comedy. For Andre Breton, surrealism "was dedicated to revising our definition of reality…to change our perception of the world and hence to change the world itself" (12). This is similar to Hicks' idea that "in order to change the world, we have to change the way we perceive it" (3). The surrealism Hicks was seeing, initially with Woody Allen's films, and more so with Steve Martin's stand-up, gave him a means to tap into the caricatures of Americans and point up their flaws.

As this new direction in comedy took off, Bill Hicks began Stratford High, a typically bland school with pupils from families much the same as Bill's. He found he and Dwight had little in common with other students, more fuel to his Dumb Jock character than anything. Dwight and Bill began researching mysticism, transcendental meditation and yoga; such interests evidently the beginnings of Hicks' exploration of "inner" space, of the possibilities of the mind. He had a sense of his position within the universe and the insignificance of mankind, a perspective that evolved and became a central cohesive idea in his comedy. It aided the growth of his sense of irony, the fact that people didn't look at the big picture, didn't realise how foolish and trivial their actions and concerns were.

At this stage, Hicks was still undecided on whether he wanted to be a rock star or a comedian. His routines appealed to the school crowd in the canteen and at the local Wendys diner where he and Dwight performed with jokes like, "I'm not too popular in high school. Last night the cheerleaders wrapped my house. With toilet paper." At the same time, Hicks was developing quick gags, which worked in the clever pay off that was to be a defining feature of routines throughout his career, as in being given a 3-by-6 board in high school, and told to make something out of it, so Hicks makes a 2-by-4 board. At Stratford, in the ninth grade, he and Dwight befriended Kevin Booth, a year older and heavily into rock music and being a musician. They formed a band, Stress, and Hicks focused on that for some time, but the three-minute crash boom bang of punk rock wasn't going to give him that connection of ideas with an audience.

When Jimmy Carter became president in 1976, only fifty-three per cent of those eligible to vote had done so. Public dissatisfaction with politicians was at an all time high, still not recovered from Nixon's misdeeds. Carter paid lip service to social causes yet still ploughed millions of dollars into the military and continued the protection of corporate wealth. Under pressure, he soon backed away from his desire to decriminalise marijuana. Meanwhile, the U.S. continued its support for governments that tortured and murdered dissenters in countries like Iran and Indonesia. Indonesia had invaded East Timor in 1975, beginning a process of genocide that led to over 200,000 massacred by 1978, the year that Carter increased arms sales to Indonesia. Though Carter has the noteworthy distinction of being the only U.S. president since 1945 not to send Americans into battle (indeed, he was awarded the Nobel Peace Prize in 2002), his tenure in office was rather bland and ineffectual. Increasingly, society looked to the entertainment industry for answers, at the radical films being made in the 1970s and the inventiveness of television comedy. Those on the margins of society looked to crime.

In February 1978 the Comedy Workshop in Houston was looking for stand-ups for comedy nights. Hicks and Slade did three gigs there, Hicks sneaking out of his room at night and being driven to the club by Kevin

Booth. Their routines were still shaped and somewhat limited by their experiences, he and Dwight joking about the parental punishment of having their legs taken away for a week or poking fun at the characters in *Hardy Boys* mysteries.

Hicks was using material based around his family and the attitudes of the society he was growing up in. His father, the Goober Dad persona, had Hicks adopting the upright moral tone in his voicing of out of touch views and adhering to an irrelevant conservative perspective, wearing his Bermuda shorts and worrying about his lawn. Within this there is the beginnings of criticism of concern with trivial things in life, but also apparent is an increasing cleverness with language. One routine has the typical kid's boast of, "My dad can beat up your dad", returned by Hicks with "When?" He joked about his father buying him a dictionary when all the other children were getting go-carts. When his father said, "Look Bill, it's got go-cart in," Hicks would add "so is jerk, dad. Look, here's cheapskate." His mother, Mumsy, is played with right hand on hip, stomach pushed forward and mouth stretched. The voice is a drawl, mixing the same conservative outlook as Goober Dad with frantic concerns for her son's well being. He has his mother telling him about all the friends and relatives who have deadly diseases, or seeing things from a well meaning if naïve perspective.

Nonetheless, Hicks was doing material beyond his age, including adult stuff about nobody on the *Gilligan's Island* TV show wanting to fuck Ginger or Mary Anne, or a routine which has Hicks talking about his father getting fired from a mortuary because of having relations with corpses, and Bill shocked because "We all knew it was purely platonic."

Hicks got a taste for it but did his last show with Dwight in June 1978 as not soon after Dwight left the area, leaving Bill at a loose end. He had a good rapport with Slade and didn't yet feel confident with going solo in a proper stand-up venue. At the same time his alienation was increasing, prompting him to see a psychiatrist, partly a spiritual thing, partly down to his feeling of lacking direction. He certainly wasn't interested in all the false soul searching, as he would later mock the Californian types who tried to get in touch with their inner child by demanding they "get in touch with your outer adult!" Torn between rock music and comedy and seeking an outlet for his accumulating ideas, he continued to write material and practice with Stress, not quite drifting (Hicks was always working on something) but certainly at a crossroads, awaiting a fresh impetus in his life.

5
Breaking The Rules

August 1979 was another turning point in Hicks' career when The Workshop in Houston opened the Comix Annex next door and called Bill with an offer of some stand-up work. Fortuitously (or perhaps, in Hicks' one consciousness universe, events could be put down to fate) James Hicks' job meant Bill's parents moving to Little Rock. Not wanting to disrupt their son's education, Hicks stayed behind, ostensibly to finish at Stratford, though in reality it gave him the freedom to work at the Annex, make money and continue honing his routine.

In 1979 comedy was peaking as the new cool. Comedians like Andy Kaufman and Richard Pryor were overturning conventions and being written about in highbrow publications, elevated to the status of artists. Comedy was original, dangerous, relevant and groundbreaking with *Saturday Night Live* having led the way, making such an impact that its anarchic, semi-improvised style intoxicated not only popular television, but also film. As the decade drew to a close, the original *Saturday Night Live* alumni - stars like Dan Aykroyd, John Belushi, Steve Martin and Chevy Chase - were moving into films, leaving behind a show that no longer stood out so distinctly from the competition. Moreover, in 1979 the show's original creator Lorne Michaels left, along with its best writers. Mediocre replacements didn't take the programme any further, its appeal never reaching beyond the U.S., a slump in creativity following until Eddie Murphy became the show's star in the early 1980s.

Hicks' routines in 1979 were still fairly innocent, focused on things like his family and his middle class life, joking about working as a bouncer in a salad bar and recollections of a childhood trying to be Evil Knievel, jumping friends on his bike and landing on their nuts. However, there was a more risqué element than before, Hicks newly inspired by Richard Pryor's *Live In Concert* album. In addition, through his material, Hicks was beginning to go a little deeper, criticising America and recognising complacency. Some audiences were offended by his attacks on family values: a heckler at one gig - frustrated by an inability to counter Hicks' arguments - pulled a gun on him.

On November 4th 1979, the U.S. embassy in Tehran was taken over by protestors, holding fifty-two hostages, demanding that the Shah of Iran be returned from America to face punishment for the crimes of murder and torture he had committed against its people. As the siege dragged on through 1980, America was a place unsure of its stature. Blind patriotic fervour manifested itself, the media demonising Iran's Islamic leader Ayatollah Khomeini, playing perfectly to Ronald Reagan's right-wing agenda as he positioned himself to replace President Jimmy Carter. The country was undergoing a sea change, ready to return to a conservative ideology, dragging the entertainment industry with it.

Just as the seventies had been an exciting time for television comedy, so American cinema had been pioneering with films like Francis Ford Coppola's *The Godfather* (1972), Bob Fosse's Lenny Bruce biopic *Lenny* (1974), Martin Scorsese's *Taxi Driver* (1976) and Sidney Lumet's TV satire *Network* (1977) with its cry of "I'm as mad as hell and I'm not going to take this anymore." The morally ambiguous films of the decade weren't afraid to ask questions of American society and come up with unpleasant truths about greed, violence and alienation. But after *Jaws* (1975) cinema began offering less challenging films, more for escapism and mass-market appeal. In addition, those exciting television comedians like John Belushi, who worked so well within the medium, were now more interested in making films. His appearance in John Landis' *National Lampoon's Animal House* (1978) expanded his audience, the film becoming a massive commercial success and heralding a slew of inferior and increasingly juvenile imitators like *Porkys* (1982) where dumb tits and ass gags and pratfalls were the order of the day. Belushi went on to make films such as *1941* (1979) and *The Blues Brothers* (1980), expensive and self-indulgent exercises which said everything about the decade ahead.

Scorsese's masterpiece, *Raging Bull* (1980), was a commercial flop and heralded in a new era of blockbusters and mindless action movies throughout the eighties from the likes of Don Simpson and Jerry Bruckheimer, films which were perfectly in tune with the Reagan years of greed and self-interest. Screenwriter Robert Towne summed it up with "So much of the 70s was about revealing the disparity between what the country said it was, and what filmmakers perceived it to be...When the 80s came along, we entered a world of steroided-out superheroes...Sly, Arnold, even Bruce Willis would re-fight the Vietnam War, and win. A country that in LBJ's words had truly become a helpless giant, needed a fantasy where it was not impotent" (13).

A new breed of comedy going against the mood of the Reagan era was emerging at The Workshop, where Hicks was not only performing but also hanging out with other comedians, learning from their acts and honing his skills. Despite the early influences of Woody Allen and Steve Martin and the way they had helped him see comedy as a performance, he still hadn't found in it the controversy and subversive spirit that appealed to him in rock music.

The scene at The Workshop offered him that connection to rock music, particularly with comedian Sam Kinison who was also beginning his career there. Born December 8th 1953, Kinison's routine was pure fire and brimstone, much as would be expected from a former preacher. His spell in this occupation saw Kinison frequently at odds with other preachers, unconcerned as he was with the business of raising money whilst also refusing to employ sermons based on fear and indoctrination. Typically rebellious, he had to leave the ministry in 1978 after getting divorced, turning to stand-up instead.

Kinison and Hicks were part of a comedy group variously dubbed 'The Outlaw Comics' and 'The Comic Outlaws'. The group performed together like some rock band, their reputation formed by their hedonism and uncompromising style and material. This evolving group – not all necessarily full time members of the performing combo – included the physical comedy of Carl LaBove, the storytelling style of Ron Shock and the likes of Jimmy Pineapple, John Farneti, Steve Epstein, Andy Huggins and Riley Barber, all playing off and influencing each other and developing material from their associations. It was Jimmy Pineapple who first used the phrase "case fuckin' closed," which Hicks would often use to bookend routines. This was a sharing of material rather than copying, the group sessions involving philosophical discussions that opened up new avenues for each to explore.

The Outlaw Comics had something of a love/hate relationship with the South, mocking its characteristics and ways, but also implicitly celebrating its larger than life quality. Hicks would draw from Southern types characters that epitomised ignorance. They would be the people in trailers with wonky teeth who had a dog, Skeeter, and who watched "*The Dukes Of Hazzard* every night" yet "has to have it explained to him." Though caricaturing this dumbness, they were as much trying to show that the stereotypes of TV shows like *The Dukes Of Hazzard* (1979-1985) were an unfit representation of Southerners, particularly unlike the politically and socially aware Outlaws.

Like Hicks, Kinison and Carl LaBove and many of the other Outlaw Comics moved to Los Angeles to play at the city's Comedy Store (Kinison arrived in early 1981 with LaBove, both initially working as doormen). When they reformed in Houston in the mid eighties, they went on the road with themed shows focusing on politics, drugs and *Outlaw Comics Get Religion*. After running up a $3500 bar bill, they did a show called *The Texas Outlaws Pay Their Bar Tab*. Though angry and more than willing to employ swearing, they were philosophical too, using comedy to detail the faults they saw inherent in humanity by using American society as a microcosm of the world. For Hicks, the perspective evolved from a belief that Texas wanted its own government and didn't trust the national government. The state, through the oil boom, had become emblematic of America, vast skyscrapers and wealth conveying the kind of patriotic invulnerability in tune with Reagan's view of the country. Implicit in this image was the buying into Reaganomics that the Outlaw Comics did not share.

Hicks was captivated by Kinison's anger, his own philosophy and routine influenced by Kinison's no holds barred attacks on religious hypocrisy. Hicks' upbringing had been permeated with religion and he had long felt it phoney and intolerant, unable to accept the idea of an avenging God who'd created hell: "that's an insane God and therefore not mine" (3). Kinison questioned accepted truths and delved into taboo subjects fearlessly, employing experiences from his own time as a preacher. After an upbringing spent being forced to go to church and listen to sermons he didn't agree with, Hicks was seeing the kind of preacher he'd always wished to see, Kinison's material not only concerned with preaching an alternative gospel but also the rise and fall of his delivery being like that of a preacher.

The ascendance to prominence of religious zealots in the South was of concern to its comedians who saw in them grotesque caricatures of intolerance, spreading fear instead of love and demanding money in God's name. Pat Robertson (founder of the Christian Broadcast Network) had become a powerful figure by 1975 when he was broadcasting to over 100 million homes. The Reverend Jim Bakker and his wife Tammy soon followed with their own TV show, the *Praise The Lord Club*, a kind of religious version of *The Tonight Show*. These preachers were leading the masses with an illiberal ideology and the masses seemed to be lapping it up without questioning, none more evident than when the Reverend Jim Jones persuaded over 900 people to commit suicide (amongst them, parents forcing cyanide into their children) at his Jonestown compound in 1977.

In 1979 Jerry Falwell founded the Moral Majority, a movement venomously against pornography, homosexuality, abortion and unmarried couples having sex. They even employed Hitler's tactic of burning books, yet Ronald Reagan praised their crusade, and their archaic views found an audience of millions prepared to follow and give money blindly.

The material Kinison and Hicks were doing in the mid and late 1980s betrays the closeness of their relationship, their reciprocation of ideas evident in the similarities between both comedians' routines attacking organised religion. Each saw through the veneer of family values being espoused by hypocritical figureheads such as Jim Bakker, someone as corrupt and phoney as they come, who in 1986 was paying himself a $1.9 million salary and owned 47 bank accounts. He'd resigned on March 19th 1987 after being caught with secretary Jessica Hahn (with whom Kinison later had a short relationship). In addition, he was convicted on 24 counts of fraud. Kinison's comedy pinpointed the corruption of such televangelists, mocking their desire for money with the idea that a collection is necessary not for aiding a community's sick and needy, but because, "Jesus wants us to build a Ferris wheel." Another scandal followed in 1988 when Jimmy Swaggart confessed his sins on live TV, which included an encounter with a prostitute. To Kinison, these were the kind of dishonest characters he'd encountered whilst a preacher, calling Bakker a "hypocritical self righteous bastard," and musing on the possibility that "Judas is up in heaven thinking 'maybe I'll get a reprieve'" whilst Jesus looks down from the skies, filled with disbelief at what Bakker has been doing in his name.

Celestial beings and deities having a voice featured in much of Hicks' material. He has God as a joker, running around burying dinosaur fossils to test people's faith: "We'll see who believes in me now. Ho-ho, I'm a prankster God. I am killing me." Then there is Hicks' Jesus looking down upon Earth's population, baffled that they are still wearing crosses: "Man, they're still wearing crosses. Fuck it, I'm not going dad," just as Kinison's Jesus looks down, unwilling to return as he contemplates the holes in his hands. These messiahs were observing such figures as Bakker and Swaggart, angered at what they were doing in the name of God. By giving them voices, Hicks and Kinison were showing that the Jesus or God they loved was not distant from ordinary people, not the strict and unforgiving figures the zealots presented them as. These deities were in tune with humanity, were in fact amongst us and easily reachable through state of mind rather than cash donations.

Hicks, like Kinison, believed in Jesus and God, but both were incensed by the way phoney preachers and televangelists appropriated religion for their own agendas. When Hicks said, "I believe in Jesus and God, I just don't believe in suffering" (1), he was making a specific point about religions extorting money by enforcing a rigid morality and threatening eternal damnation. In his act in 1988 he would talk about how Pat Robertson had been told by God to run for president, to which Hicks, who thought Robertson a "Nazi hillbilly fuck", responded "God didn't tell me to vote for him " mocking the likes of Robertson, George Bush and Jerry Falwell who were "Christians for stronger nuclear armament," angrily lambasting them with "amen, amen, amen" as his arm gestures Nazi salutes, their rhetoric more fascistic than humanitarian.

That these religious figureheads are distant from the people is evident in Sam Kinison's inspired routine about the Pope getting shot, prompting him to travel in a protective mobile that made him look "like Robo-Pope." It cleverly points out the contradictions of religious ideology and its desire to adhere to traditional ethics being compromised by the violence of contemporary society, with Kinison's Robo-Pope one who "loves God and hates crime." With Hicks, the premise is opened out to become a question of faith, the armour-plated mobile suggesting the Pope's lack of it. Just as Kinison has Jesus coming back to face his wife after being away for his death and resurrection, so Hicks' has an Uzi toting Jesus coming back to gun down the hypocrites. Both routines seem to suggest the need for religion to evolve, to become more in tune with contemporary values if they are to remain relevant.

In the late seventies and early eighties, Hicks and Kinison were influencing each other and sharing ideas, their material often overlapping. Yet though they shared a rage against the world, Hicks' material had greater warmth. He took some of Kinison's anger and ideology, shaping it into something more metaphysical, tying religious beliefs to a wider perspective on humanity. There was an element of spirituality and looking at the big picture in Kinison's act as he mused on "Anybody who tried to bring peace and love in the world, his name is target," as he referred to the killings of Jesus, Ghandi, the Kennedys and John Lennon, before adding, "that's why they only wounded Reagan." With this Kinison points out his disbelief at humanity and seeks to align himself to the good people who preach peace on a world stage. It is a line Hicks uses too, only with a subtle difference as, after each name, he emphasizes the word "murdered" before reeling off Reagan's name with a silent beat preceding the word "wounded." In this Hicks is more accurately skewering the complicity of humanity by repetition of the human act of murder, each rhythmic repetition accentuating and accusing before the contrast of "wounded" hangs in the air to suggest his incredulity at finding no explanation for such injustice.

There is no question of either comedian stealing material from the other, for central themes like religious hypocrisy and Reagan only being wounded were shared starting points, from which the Outlaws would develop their own angles. Kinison's perspective saw him generally staying within the parameters of American society, whilst Hicks saw the connection between American society and how it led world trends and opinion.

Kinison wanted to puncture the lies told in the name of religion. He intended his comedy to shock, but more than that it was about breaking down barriers, be they religious or sexual. Kinison loved to talk graphically about sex in his routines, and although Hicks' early career included routines about sex, Kinison's influence was to take it up a level. Sex had been a taboo topic for Lenny Bruce to puncture during his career, whilst Woody Allen would develop a more innocuous and surreal approach. Richard Pryor and Sam Kinison both had this surrealism laced with graphic descriptions. Kinison mused on researchers "trying to invent the artificial pussy" before extending the idea with an image of people queuing for such a product. Further developed, Kinison changes tone, using an archetypal TV commercial voiceover: "Yes, you've got to make it to Kansas City, you don't have time to stop, you reach in for Bronco's pocket pal, and you put that partner on and you ride that ride with a smile...K-Tel's new elastic bush."

This kind of sexual surrealism is seen in much of Hicks' material, from both his Outlaw period and beyond, as with his mid-eighties routine about a diabetic going down on a woman wearing candy panties, moving beyond reality as he pushes his head then body inside the woman's vagina, his hand subsequently only "coming out for cigarettes once in a while." In a society inhibited and offended by sexuality (to the point of being embarrassed to talk about it), such provocative imagery is necessary. In reaching out to the extremes, it is hoped that the banality of sexuality will be acknowledged and therefore allow society to turn its attention to more serious issues.

From a series of disappointments in love, Kinison purged his frustration and anger through dark routines about relationships. Hicks, no stranger to such disappointments, also went off on some candid and unflinching, yet darkly poetic, fantasies. In one mid-eighties routine he remembers a woman, one "I gave my heart to…" before hoping that, "One day this girl is going to be living in a trailer park…with clouds of A.I.D.S. mosquitoes swarming around…nine naked little babies with rickets…rats laying babies in their ears. And they bring home dead animals…to eat…She lives with this ex-welder, doesn't have a job. He's got fur all over his back…six hundred pounds and he makes love to her with a broom handle…One night he's gonna be romancing her with that stick, his heart is gonna explode and she's trapped under six hundred pounds of flaccid, sweaty, fish-bellied cellulite that's moving like the tides of the ocean…Blood and phlegm and bile pours out his mouth and nose and into her face…And just before she drowns in that vomit, she turns to the TV, and I'm gonna be on it." Undoubtedly graphic, the routine is nonetheless coloured with such detail and narrative verve that it becomes a compelling construction of images, Hicks' tone perfectly pitched as it leads us to an ingenious climax.

By linking the routine to his ex-girlfriend, Hicks makes his bitterness more personal, not seemingly addressed to all women. Kinison's bitterness manifested itself in routines that were about women in general, laying him open to accusations of sexism. Like the Hicks rant, Kinison's bitterness in *Sexual Diaries* sees him looking to the future of the woman he has dated, telling men presently in relationships to "Do every nasty thing you can think. Be the nastiest, darkest chapter in her sexual diary…Fuck her every single place and way you can think of…Then if she leaves you for another fuckin' guy you just made this guy's life real fuckin' interesting…women love to talk about the last fuckin' guy…" as Kinison looks ahead to a woman scarred by the way he has treated her, fucking her with a bottle and making her next relationship a misery. We don't have Hicks' vivid picture, the attention to detail that suggests his own personal hurt. Kinison, with the impersonal "women," is almost inciting all men to mistreat their partners; his comic ends somewhat subservient in such a general context.

Both comedians played guitar and were passionate in their love of rock music "with balls," music a million miles away from the anaemic candyfloss that would clog up the music charts in the 1980s. The fact that The Outlaw Comics toured together like a rock band only made their affinity with the medium stronger, their style influenced by it, their shows appealing to the same young crowd who were interested in rock music for its rebellion and elements of danger.

Kinison had ideas on rock music that Hicks could identify with and gain inspiration from. Kinison railed against rock stars in anti-drug commercials, calling them "rock n' roll pussies" and commenting, "It's like Christians against Christ...Rock created drugs. What are they talking about?" It is similar to Hicks' tirades against the likes of 1980s boy band New Kids On The Block as he mocks their proclamations that "we're rock stars against drugs." Kinison is perceptive in seeing rock without drugs as nonsensical, cheekily linking it to religion, but the routine doesn't develop or take off like Hicks', where he links rock stars against drugs to selling out and the dumbing down of popular culture. Indeed, Kinison's musical tastes were for artists with little credibility and artistic endeavour themselves: Bon Jovi, Billy Idol, Motley Crue, all denizens of the bleached blonde, permed hair L.A. rock brigade.

Amongst the Outlaws, Kinison was the most imposing physical presence on stage. Hicks watched as he prowled and ranted, a ball of energy letting personal demons loose. Early wild routines involved him jumping off stage and pretending to homosexually rape a man from the audience. More than this, Kinison would use his physical presence to denote other characters on stage. Like Hicks, Kinison would roll his eyes back into his head as he got into dumb characters, and also denote both official or establishment figures by putting the microphone close to their lips and booming out a deep, slow voice which addresses the comedian with a "sir" at the end of the sentence. There is also the similarity of each comedian turning his profile to the audience as he imitates a phone call and each placing a hand over the microphone before using his mouth for a whispered comment from a persona.

Kinison's use of facial expressions, allied to his use of voices, allowed a multi-character dialogue on stage, helping the audience to visualise a scene beyond a mere stand-up performance. The high-pitched, pious female voice in a routine about eating pussy (another of Bill's favourite topics) can be seen in many of Hicks' characters, as in the voice sanctimoniously pondering, "what about *American Gladiators*, is it too violent?" This multi-character dialogue is also employed by Kinison when he gets into the character of an audience member, voicing usually shocked comments on his performance like "what kind of jokes are these?" or "Jesus God, this is the sickest most disgusting joke I've heard on stage." It can be seen with Hicks doing the same: "I feel like we're being lectured by some kind of pale demon," and in Hicks' long Goatboy routine from *Revelations* where at intervals he is a voice in the audience saying "Okay Bill, stop with the Goatboy thing."

When Kinison resumes the voice of his own persona, the tone of throwaway lines like "If he was any kind of man, he'd take his life" (Jim Bakker) and "What a dick" are found in Hicks' work. The delivery of such throwaway lines indicates the influence the two had upon each other, an influence beyond just material.

Kinison was renowned for his penetrating scream and there are times when Hicks' rants reach such a fever pitch of indignation and incredulity that language becomes redundant and he too is compelled to scream, albeit less manically (as can be seen in the "heyheyheeeey" squeal as hotel room service walks in on Hicks whilst he's masturbating). Kinison's routines would build like a fuse hissing towards explosion, his anger and bewilderment rising as he railed against society, unleashing the scream not only as a release, but also as an indication that he can do no more, that he is impotent against the tide of conservatism and blind acceptance. The scream is against a society that needs to hear the truth but is too self-satisfied to want to listen. This build up is evident in many of Hicks' riffs as he uncovers endless injustices and widespread banality and can't understand why his voice of reason isn't being heard. Though generally he doesn't seek to employ Kinison's scream as a form of catharsis, there is something of a purgation going on with his attack on clean teen pop group, New Kids On The Block in his *Relentless* show. Having mocked their wholesomeness and adherence to conservative values, Hicks becomes a seething ball of energy as he ridicules an opinion that rock musicians should be good role models. His raging contempt is apparent as he contrasts an anodyne contemporary music scene with rock and roll mythology, demanding to have more rock stars who kill themselves on stage, pouring scorn on the New Kids' conformity with his militaristic marching on the spot and furious seig heils.

Hicks saw in Kinison a comedian at ease with performing, able to employ a variety of techniques, not trying to do gag after gag, but instead letting routines build, using pauses to create a sense of thinking on his feet, giving a feeling that he was close to the audience, almost a raconteur. He could change tone and pace easily, pulling the audience in before beginning the escalation towards his mad primal scream.

Kinison would also make use of stage accessories, such as the microphone. In a routine about being married, he uses the microphone as a dick, unscrewing it from the lead (a trick later used by Eddie Murphy) to suggest that, post-nuptials, it is now owned by the wife, who pockets it as a method of control. In a similar vein, Kinison has the microphone as a dildo, a female plaything to taunt her partner with, but though it may satisfy a woman, ultimately it "can't pick up the cheque." Like Hicks, Kinison could use the microphone as a prop and employ the sounds it created, like crashing it to his hand on the stage floor as he acts out nailing Jesus to the cross, or banging it against his heart rapidly to boom out the sound of its increased beating after a big cocaine hit. Hicks too uses the microphone in this way: for a beating heart, for housekeeping knocking at his hotel room door, and when he head-buts it to elicit the sound of moths hitting light bulbs. Like Steve Martin's use of physicality, tone and props, this creates a busyness to the performance, again with all the exhilaration of a rock show.

As the eighties progressed, Hicks and Kinison partied together, their new experiences reflected in routines about alcohol and drugs. Both did routines about the joys of drunk driving and the benefits of pot, Hicks' routine about giving people stuck in traffic marijuana to calm them down very close to Kinison's "Pot makes you a more considerate driver. You wave people passed. You let them cut in front of you." And for mystical visions of Hicks seeing the pyramids in psychedelic trips, there's Kinison seeing Aztec temples.

The Outlaws were still touring together in 1987, but somewhere along the way there was a falling out with Kinison and though they encountered each other and partied together in the mid-eighties, it was a different kind of friendship. In truth, their comedy was always going to go its separate ways. Though they both toured relentlessly, doing several hundred gigs a year, Kinison played to crowds as if desperate for validation, seeking to force involvement by whooping them up like some hackneyed rock n' roller so that it became a more visceral experience than Hicks' cerebral connection with audiences. Although the experiences and partying were a valuable part of Hicks' learning curve, he would move on from the haphazard, unchecked humour of Kinison and The Outlaws.

Kinison's career progressed in the mid eighties after Rodney Dangerfield gave him a television break in 1984 on a young comedian's special. He released his first album *Louder Than Hell* in 1986 and made five appearances on *Saturday Night Live* the same year, including one as host. His next album, *Have You Seen Me Lately?* was released in 1988 with the major backing of Warner Brothers. Eventually he was filling arenas, on the cover of *Rolling Stone* magazine, making it big, appearing in Dangerfield's movie, *Back To School* (1986). As his fame grew his material seemed to become diluted, all intimacy lost in huge arenas, where shows were even more focused on sex and shock tactics. Though both comedians were proud of their non-PC credentials, Hicks wanted to move away from being perceived as a "dick joke" comedian. Hicks did continue to use visceral and graphic sex routines as part of his act, but increasingly they were being used as a kind of pause, a break before the truth bearing.

Despite his admirable fearlessness, Kinison's appeal was rooted in an American macho image and with that came routines about A.I.D.S. that were deeply homophobic and offensive. When he screams to the audience "Do we like to wear rubbers guys?" as if to distance himself from homosexuality, he gets a big virile "No!" hollered back, an apparent celebration of ignorance. In spite of this, it would be unfair to compare him with Andrew Dice Clay's repugnant brand of homophobia. At least Sam's aim was to tackle subjects with a satirical edge. Indeed, his routine about homosexual necrophiliacs, with its use of physical comedy as Kinison acts out a dead body being buggered, is, against the best liberal's efforts, hilariously funny. Moreover, towards the end of his career he even offered apologies to the gay community. He disliked Andrew Dice Clay, whom he called "That retard in Fonzie's jacket" (14), hated the way Clay stole his material and added more shock value. At least with Kinison there was something authentic, a deep frustration with his own disappointments in love, unlike Clay who just set out to crudely mock women. Those who did lump them together, like Randy Lewis, still accepted that Kinison had more to offer than Clay: "Kinison, unlike Clay, knows how to structure a joke that is created out of a unique (albeit generally base) perspective...Clay substitutes unbridled repugnance for viewpoint, odious epithets for insight" (15).

Gay activists protested at Kinison's gigs and Warner Brothers even inserted an A.I.D.S. awareness leaflet into his *Have You See Me Lately* album. There is an argument that Kinison was breaking down barriers in order to confront taboo subjects without the phoney hysteria, but whilst he undoubtedly went some way towards exposing ignorance and opening up a debate, his aim was a little skewed at times and what the audience was laughing at was too often unsubtle and occasionally right wing, such as the inexcusable assertion that A.I.D.S. began "because a few fags fucked some monkeys." It seemed he was targeting the disenfranchised whereas Hicks was targeting those in power.

Hicks' mid-eighties material on homosexuality and A.I.D.S. was no less ill informed, pondering what counselling A.I.D.S. victims could possibly want and concluding that it could only be a suicidal gunshot. Yet caveats that he had nothing against gays prefaced such stuff as "I could never participate in an activity which disrupts my bowel movement" before he turned the joke on himself being a drinker and not being able to have a solid shit anyway. It would be fair to take his material to task on this, but in mitigation there was still a great deal of ignorance about the disease at this time. Not until film star Rock Hudson died of A.I.D.S. in 1985 did American society begin to seek more knowledge about the disease. Hicks did mature in this way and subsequent material, like gays in the military, opened out to a bigger picture and showed that his concern was not with sexual preference but with the media hysteria that went with it. Moreover, the routine offered a criticism of the military itself and its nonsensical, homophobic reasoning: "I don't want a bunch of gays around me when I'm killing children." Similarly, a routine that begins with a focus on women priests and at first seems sexist, develops to a mockery of religion in general: "I don't care, that's priests of both sexes I don't listen to."

Kinison seemed to have created something bigger than himself, his initial purpose of exposing hypocrisy through raw language and uncompromising images being subsumed by the sheer outrageousness of those images. Audiences were there to delight in the intolerance and seemingly glory in the hateful values suggested by Kinison's political incorrectness.

Kinison also seemed to want to acquiesce to the mainstream. That's not to say he sold out, but such things as a guest appearance on the inane TV show *Married...With Children* in 1990 were beneath him. He was better than that and the short-lived sit-com, *Charlie Hoover*, in which he appeared in 1991 as the 12-inch high alter ego to actor Tim Matheson's character, urging him to indulge in pleasures.

He said he'd stopped doing cocaine in 1990, but unlike Hicks who wouldn't denounce drugs, Kinison's stance was somewhat reactionary, urging audiences to stop doing drugs because "you're gonna get sick and die." In fact, he hadn't actually stopped, but his binges had become less regular.

The distance between Hicks and Kinison is most obvious in their takes on the Gulf War of 1991. Both saw the disparity between the might of the U.S. and Iraq with Hicks saying, "A war is when two armies are fighting," contrasting the advanced technology of U.S. missiles with Iraq having "muskets" and mocking the inaccuracy of their outdated Scud missiles. Kinison's routine on the *Live From Hell* album employs a similar starting point, calling the conflict "an impression of a fuckin' war", and as Hicks talked about U.S. weapons from a Sears catalogue, Kinison's routine on the inaccuracy of the Scud had "If K-Mart was a weapons dealer, they would make the scud missile."

Kinison alludes to the media's manipulation of Iraq's might with "The fourth largest army in the world? How scary are you if you're number four?" It's an observation similar to Hicks' "Iraq had the fourth largest army in the world...After the first three armies, there's a real big drop off," a segment concluded with a neat quip about Hare Krishnas being "the fifth largest army in the world." The divergence between the two comics is apparent with Kinison employing the line in a somewhat throwaway manner whilst Hicks builds a whole routine around satirising the media coverage, thus uncovering its deception. His material is anything but patriotic, whereas Kinison appeared to be proclaiming American power by mocking Iraq's vulnerability and stupidity for starting the war. The jingoistic mood of Kinison's Gulf War routine and its implicit celebration of America's victory is most obviously exemplified in his unforgiving deriding of Iraq's need for aid after the conflict: "Fuck you. Eat your poisoned fish, breath your black air, and kiss my American ass."

There is none of Hicks' subtlety or elucidation, Kinison's crass revelling in America's triumph playing to established prejudices. When Hicks talked about soldiers "in hog heaven out there" he was criticising the bloodlust and the media (particularly television's) presentation of the war as some kind of dumb jock adventure. As with the predominantly sanitised reporting, these soldiers either ignored or were unaware that in war there are casualties, Hicks' routine having them flicking through weapons catalogues, choosing the most eye-catching weapons and revelling in their destructive power. He voices these soldiers as disengaged Southern yokels, representative of an army and a country that is blissfully unaware of the realities of war, particularly when they are shown video footage of so-called "smart bombs" hitting their targets with unerring accuracy (in fact, significant numbers missed their targets too). Hicks wondered if such advanced technology could be used to feed hungry people, his own thoughtful ruminations on technological possibilities contrasting with the "hog heaven" attitude that represents a race with its priorities all wrong. Kinison's sledgehammer approach does not seek to edify and though he paints a picture of generals getting drunk and rewinding tapes of smart bomb video footage, he seeks to emphasize their delight in watching the tapes, whilst his tone, his roar and the audience's whooping suggest he too is revelling in the destruction.

Kinison died in a car crash on April 10th 1992.The tragic irony of a man who'd celebrated drunk driving in his routines being killed by such a driver is similar to Hicks' dying of cancer after years of celebrating the joys of cigarettes. Bill movingly spoke of Sam in the *Halloween Special*, Sacred

Cow's first ever live broadcast on 31st October 1993, laying some ghosts to rest: "Sam was a great, great comic, and he was a friend for a while. Like most people we had a falling out..." before an inspired joke "Sam, oddly enough, went straight to Heaven…Apparently his life was so hellish, God gave him a big reprieve" (16).

6
<u>Richard Pryor & Physical Comedy</u>

For Hicks, moving to Los Angeles in 1980 was a chance to further his career. At the time his attitude to the place was more ambivalent than in his later career when he derided its artificiality so ruthlessly. Yet he was still in tune with its weirdness and eccentricity, saying that his dream whilst there was to date actress Linda Blair. As James Pineapple recalled in the *Austin Tribute Show*, Bill said "when you date the girl from *The Exorcist* you can kiss her on the mouth when you fuck her up the ass."

L.A. was the place where all comedians drifted to in the early eighties, where stand-ups like Richard Pryor and Robin Williams were making it big, playing places like The Comedy Store. In the autumn of 1980, the eighteen year old Hicks was also performing at the venue, doing short sets lasting between fifteen and twenty minutes. The Comedy Store had opened in 1972, gradually cementing a reputation as an important place for new and established comedians, giving exposure to performers like Jay Leno and David Letterman, whilst Hicks often shared the stage with other young comedians like Jerry Seinfeld, who were just starting out in stand-up.

His routines were evolving a little slowly, much of the material still based around his family and the idiosyncrasies of Southern life. He was using more of the religious material and delving into his darkest recesses for riffs on sex whilst also developing some funny, if pretty uncontroversial material about bums. At this stage Hicks, influenced by Richard Pryor, was more concerned with cultivating his use of sound effects and body movements.

He also appeared in a pilot for a planned TV series called *Bulba*. It was to star Lyle Waggoner, who'd been the first playgirl centrefold in 1973 and had played Major Steve Trevor in the 1970s TV show *Wonder Woman*. Hicks played a marine guard at a madcap American embassy where each week, it was proposed, wacky escapades would ensue. Fortuitously, the pilot didn't do anything.

As ever, Bill was restless, still not where he wanted to be with comedy, still not quite finding his voice. He did get lumped in with the gratuitous comedy of Andrew Dice Clay, of whom he later said, "Dice Clay's a moron" (17) or "the Republican Red Foxx" (3). He disliked the link intensely, saying "consider me the antidote" to Clay's brand of empty-headed nastiness directed at women and minorities. As ever, he was on a mission, a continued creative drive, reflected in a letter he wrote to Dwight Slade in October 1980 concerning his ambition to be "ever more funny, original, hilarious, refreshing, creative, loveable, wonderful, perfect" (18).

On December 8th 1980 John Lennon was shot and killed outside his apartment by crazed fan Mark Chapman, a man obsessed with J.D. Salinger's novel *The Catcher In The Rye* (first published in 1951). Interestingly, Hicks once said, "I'd like to be more like the J.D. Salinger of comedy" (5). On a simple level he was seeing himself as an outsider, like the reclusive Salinger, and like the novel's main character, Holden Caulfield. Like Caulfield, Hicks saw the phoniness of people and felt alienated from the world. He probably identified too with the subversive spirit of the novel, which some American schools banned, believing it would influence pupils adversely. Perhaps the influence was to show young people the truth about the world in which they lived, the kind of objective Hicks' routines had. More broadly, Salinger's short stories would often weave in characters from other stories, much like Hicks' material would have returning riffs, re-employing characters from different situations. Chapman's obsession with the novel was more about himself than a wider society, though he justified his actions by claiming that Lennon had become a phoney. In imitating Holden Caulfield's steps in the novel, prior to killing Lennon, Chapman's actions offered a telling example of a society unable to think for itself. Another of the "good men" had been killed and Chapman's reasoning said everything about the 1980s obsession with celebrity.

By the following summer, Dwight Slade had moved to L.A. to work with Hicks on a script called *The Suburbs*, which they eventually finished in January 1982. Of the idea, Hicks said, "Our characters will appeal to people like us, hating hypocrisy, mixed up, confused by stupid people" (18). Still rooted in his Southern upbringing, it was intended to lift the lid on that world, something akin to David Lynch's film *Blue Velvet* (1986), but with jokes. Despite some praise from those who read it, *The Suburbs* could find no backing for it to be filmed.

In 1981, after 444 days, the American hostages were released in Iran on the day President Reagan was inaugurated. The 1980 election had seen only a fifty four per cent turn out of those eligible to vote, meaning only twenty-seven per cent of the country had voted for Reagan. Yet from this platform, which Reagan referred to as "Morning in America", he began a series of sweeping right-wing reforms which were to instil in Hicks an anger that turned him from a comedian to a social commentator and satirist.

In Los Angeles Hicks caught a Richard Pryor performance at the Comedy Store. Pryor was doing material in preparation for his *Live On The Sunset Strip* stand-up movie, which when released in 1982 had a major impact on Hicks' career, such was Pryor's brilliance in it.

Hicks had, from his early teens, long been a fan of Pryor through watching his television appearances and listening to his stand-up albums. The two have often been linked together in the context of raw comedy with a socio-political edge, though in terms of personalities and experiences they were a long way apart.

Born December 1st 1940 (five years to the day after Woody Allen), like Hicks he started out performing in front of his class at school. However, Pryor's childhood was certainly closer to the 'rough childhood' comics have always traded on, including Woody Allen and Hicks himself. Raised in brothels in a violent, alcohol fuelled and abusive family environment, Pryor's youth also saw him committing crimes, smoking marijuana and having his first child at age 16 (to a woman his father had also slept with). Nonetheless, he worked hard at stand-up and got his television debut in 1964 on Rudy Vallee's *On Broadway Tonight*. By the time Hicks had discovered him in the mid-1970s, through his appearances on television shows, Pryor had already released several comedy albums and developed a dangerous cocaine habit.

In terms of material, Hicks and Pryor share some similarities of theme, both avoiding the shtick of the artificial comedian lying about his life, but rather taking experiences, exaggerating them and giving them a universal feel. They were also gritty and undaunted by taboos, their comedy about real things that matter; Pryor's naked honesty reflected in Hicks' material.

They contemplate sex and sexual hypocrisy and are prepared to mock male ego and machismo, Hicks admitting to being "hung like a seahorse" whilst Pryor – on the look out for some new pussy – receives his wife's retort of "Another coupla inches of dick and you'd find some new pussy right here" (18a). Both comedians speculate on masturbation and eating pussy in a way that presents their gender as either pathetically one-dimensional or subservient. Like Kinison, Pryor conjured up surreal images with his sex material; in one routine talking about being caught up in "The great pussy drive of the fifties" much like Hicks would confess to being "a pussyholic". This personification by the comedians gives their material a less sexist twist, subverting macho stereotypes by seeing males as creatures unable to control their desires, presented instead as dumb slaves to the pussy's power.

Though less extensively in Pryor's case, both also see the hypocrisy of religion. One routine has Pryor as a mid-west radio preacher, the kind Hicks and Kinison mocked, saying "'Hark there friends and neighbours, has God touched you today? Well if he hasn't touched you, you send us a dollar eighty-nine cents and we'll send you, absolutely free, a touch from God." However, growing up in a whorehouse, in an environment were hookers, pimps and drug fiends gave little countenance to conventional morality, Pryor is less concerned with religion's contradictions.

Despite their upbringings being in sharp contrast, both Hicks and Pryor craft material that is strongly informed by their backgrounds, each employing character facets and personas drawn from their own formative experiences. Moreover, Pryor exposes the racism all around him whilst Hicks attacks the implicitly racist agenda of right wing Southern conservatism. They are both raging against the ignorance of their environments, Pryor's viewpoint being shaped into a wider social and political perspective due to the prevalence of racism in society. This makes him much more of a political comedian than Kinison as he is dealing with universal themes, centring on humanity and its dark underbelly. In Pryor's world there are guns, not referenced flippantly, but as entities used in a society where depravation sees its inhabitants resort to crime. His humour points up the reality of the black experience with its social exclusion, endemic poverty and festering drug culture, his material populated by desperate malcontents seeking to eek out a living. Although Pryor does not directly attack government like Hicks, he points up injustices and thereby makes a political statement, not just about white society's ignorance of the issues, but also about how black society reacts in this environment.

There can be seen another small link between the two comedians with their experiences of television. Hicks never got the exposure he deserved, certainly not like Kinison did, and for some time the mainstream shied away from Pryor. Though he wrote Mel Brooks' spoof western *Blazing Saddles* (1973), he was rejected for the lead role, considered by studio executives to be too much of a loose cannon. Whilst his early television appearances concerned a more innocent, less confrontational Pryor, someone middle class America could accept, by the time he appeared on *Saturday Night Live* for the first time on December 13th 1975 (then in its incarnation as *Saturday Night*) NBC put in a five second delay. In addition, his NBC series *The Richard Pryor Show* ran for only four episodes in 1977 before Pryor quit, frustrated at the station's censors cutting material. Although television's manipulation was not a major concern in Pryor's material, he told *Ebony* magazine in January 1978: "One Hundred and twenty-seven million people watch television every night, that's why they use it to sell stuff...They're not going to write shows about how to revolutionise America. The top-rated shows are for retarded people."

What links Hicks and Pryor most strongly is the physicality of their comedy. Hicks acknowledged this with, "He shows me the body movement to back up the material and the honesty of feelings. It showed me what could be done" (19). Hicks had become a huge fan of Charlie Chaplin in the early 1980s and had seen the way physicality could not only emphasize a gag but be humorous in itself. Pryor's uses of visuals, his facial and bodily movements, were akin to performance art. Indeed, they were the focal point of his early act. For example, his appearance on television in *The Kraft Summer Music Hall* had Pryor first miming the difficulty of starting a car, complete with cacophonous sounds, indulging in a little patter before closing with a mime, using the microphone stand as a set of heavy dumbbells which he lifts with difficulty before losing his grip. Such was the innocence and simplicity of Pryor's early material. Not until the late sixties/early seventies did the socio-political, cursing Richard Pryor begin to take shape with the release of his second album *Craps (After Hours)* in February 1971. What hadn't changed was the use of his face and body for physical comedy, Pryor having honed it to become subtler, a facet of his performance rather than that from which the routines were built. His first concert film released in January 1979, the hugely successful *Richard Pryor-Live In Concert* showcased his physicality perfectly.

From Woody Allen, Steve Martin and Sam Kinison, Hicks was influenced by their use of voices, mannerisms and employment of physical comedy. Though Kinison had been a profound influence on Hicks, Pryor embodied everything Hicks wanted from a stand-up: the energy, the physicality, the controversy, the hedonistic lifestyle and, critically, the hard-hitting socio-political content.

In his performances, Pryor constantly strolls the stage back and forth, as if wanting to address the audience and draw them in. There is a nonchalance and ease about it whereas Hicks – rarely still on stage – paces rather than strolls, his body frenzied in a series of limb, head and facial gestures, as if to convey his anger and eagerness to get across the message. For Eric Bogosian, "there's this sort of tornado moving around the stage and cycling around and throwing all this energy out at you" (20), effectively compelling the audience to connect with him.

What both comedians do is use their physicality to make use of stage space as a character (s). Through mime and gestures they give the stage a sense of presence and distance, meaning that the performances open up the stage beyond just the comedian standing under a spotlight. Their shows have a theatrical quality with audiences made aware of things going on around the comedian, that there are many characters acting out a story, thus giving the stage depth. As Hicks said, "I don't believe comedy and drama are too far off" (3), and in this way he sought to take from Pryor the physicality which made his shows more than just stand-up. This theatricality is achieved through their skills as physical comedians and their close attention to detail. A simple example is when Pryor performs standing in a queue, his head miming looking over a shoulder in front of him, then looking behind him in the line. The act is played out precisely, Pryor even waiting before taking a short step forward as the queue moves on. It's as simple and closely observed as Hicks imagining smokers passing out in cold weather because they "don't know when they're done exhaling." It is not just a collapsing to the ground that Hicks acts out, but there is the detail of the smoker drawing on a cigarette, looking into the skies unknowingly as Hicks lets his body fall in deliberate stages. Such subtle nuances can be seen in Hicks' routine about the inaccuracy of Iraq's scud missiles during the Gulf War. The missile is compared to a station wagon, "the Buick scud," with Hicks in the driving seat as the missile is launched, his immediate space representing the confines of the vehicle, his facial expressions conveying the flight of the missile/Buick before it misses its target and sinks into water. Hicks has one hand on the wheel, creating air bubble noises and, well aware of the physics of such a situation and the density of water, lowering his body slowly as the vehicle sinks. The final nuances perfect the routine as Hicks gestures wipers swishing and a horn honking, the accompanying noises becoming more distant as the vehicle sinks further.

Pryor uses his body more often from almost stationary positions to create presence and distance on the stage. He has a clear sense of the dimensions of the stage and the audience's perception of it, allowing him to create that theatrical display through his physicality. When Pryor recalls pulling a gun on a Mafia boss during his time as a young comedian in Las Vegas, his young self is in profile assuming the gun holding position. However, whilst in character he looks over his shoulder, becoming a different character as he addresses the audience as Richard Pryor now, looking back, his quick remarks giving the anecdote an extra layer. Presence is felt as the over the shoulder Pryor forms an affinity with the audience, as if stepping out of the comedy situation, the older Pryor like a conduit to an easy connection with the young Pryor in profile. It brings the audience in because he seems to step into the gallery and watch with them the young Pryor's foolishness. Similarly, in disconnecting with his young self the audience get the sense of a scene being played out somewhere else on the stage, sharing with Pryor his bemusement at his young self.

Hicks believed that during a great show it was as if he were sitting in the audience, calling the experience "a great feeling of power, a great feeling of control, and a feeling of accomplishment when you actually create on stage, and it's a real rush cos you're in the audience too at that point" (10). Hicks performs what he would want to see if he were an audience member and the ease of his and Pryor's performances create a closeness to the audience. Indeed, as has been noted, Hicks employs asides like Kinison in which he is an audience member commenting on the show. Pryor's characters, be they animals or inanimate objects personified, are often talking to, advising or admonishing Pryor, informally addressing him as "Rich," therefore showing, like Hicks, an awareness of being watched.

As the routine continues, the Mafia boss (Pryor now more upright to denote the change of character) is played with him bending his right elbow and wrapping it round the microphone stand in a hug. The perspective has seamlessly shifted and the young Pryor is the microphone stand, three characters now cohabiting the stage's space. Pryor's attention to detail can be seen when he gestures a rubbing above the microphone holder to denote the mafia boss rubbing the young Pryor's head. Further developed, the mafia boss talks to characters stage left and stage ahead, to incidental mafia heavies, so that there is the presence of five characters on stage, each one carefully positioned by Pryor's use of physicality.

Hicks can accomplish the same thing, a multi-character set-up created in his routine about putting terminally ill people in movies. Hicks first becomes a grandson, his face forward, body bent, lip curled, frowning in an expression of disbelief: "How come you dressed my grandmother up as a mugger?" He then clicks his body upright to denote the film director ordering, "Shut up and get off the set," his finger jutting forward for "Action!" Quickly Hicks becomes a helper on the film set, miming the pushing of the grandmother in front of the cameras, weighting both his hands behind the space where the grandmother is. Like Pryor, he is using a small space but through the creation of characters is giving the impression of a larger one. Hicks then inhabits the grandmother's frame, eyes tight, hands limp at his chest, head looking up and around to suggest her disorientation. Hicks has her shuffling long enough to convey her frailty and accentuate the contrast and impact of him straightening his body to become Chuck Norris delivering a karate kick to the old woman's head. Back to the grandmother, Hicks slaps his right hand to his forehead, making a loud "ksssh!" sound into the microphone as the kick comes through the air, before falling backwards onto the ground. The perfect structuring of the routine is apparent when Hicks effortlessly switches back to the amazed grandson with, "Wow, he kicked her head right off her body!"

Hicks' physical comedy saw him exploding around the stage, mimicking Iraq's Elite Republican Guard as he stomps around the floor space, and weighting his movements to suggest the size of the "ten feet tall desert warriors" as his vocals boom in time to the steps. We have him running around haphazardly; disorientated, representing a member of the American public who has just realised that the government was lying about the Kennedy assassination. In his routine concerning Neanderthal man finding mushrooms, Hicks carefully uses a large area on the stage to create a sense of the open spaces of Stone Age Earth. He is hunched over, moving ape-like around the stage as he tries to catch a cow, his eyes squinting into the distance as the cow escapes. Hicks will not rush the picture he is articulating, for that would not create the space and theatrical sense and illusion he requires. It would not convince the audience, so he takes his time in bending down to pick a mushroom from the cow turd, at first unsure and tentative. Then when he takes the mushroom there is sniffing and curiosity before he eats it. His eyes widen, his body movements become more animated, gradually taken over by laughter, pointing at things to suggest Neanderthal man's gradual awareness, colouring in the stage with imagined objects scattered amidst the sparseness of Stone Age Earth. Then he leans back on his stool and says, "I think we can go to the moon." The stage now moves beyond theatre, opens up into the vast universe, Hicks balancing on one leg and gesturing up to outer space.

Beyond physicality, Hicks' material is also creating presence and distance. The way his ideas connect, develop and take off helps the audience imagine a fully sketched world. From an ape-like shuffle, Hicks is twirling the microphone stand in a nod to the monolith from *2001:A Space Odyssey*, humming the music – *Thus Spake Zarathustra* - from that film, and taking the audience to the moon (the *Revelations* stage set complete with a moon shining brightly, top left).

Pryor, more the skilled actor, could remain stationary to open up the stage. Pryor tells of two cheetahs casually chatting about hunting down a gazelle and from an almost stationary position he opens up the space of the stage. The first cheetah is Pryor in profile, looking to his left, slightly toward the audience, his body loose. When he talks to this first area of space he is addressing the second cheetah, but he also creates another area of space by pointing across the stage at the supposed gazelle in the distance. The second cheetah is then given a voice with Pryor in complete profile, its eyes staring across the stage to accentuate the space where the gazelle is. The routine bounces off these three positions in perfect synchronicity, the audience so involved with Pryor's character conception and evoking of distance through his eyes that they are almost forced to accept it is a jungle environment to keep up with Pryor. He understands their preconceptions of the jungle and is therefore aware that he only need add well-sketched characters and the subtle creation of space through eye movements for the audience to easily form a picture.

Hicks too has this sense of dimensions and distance, exemplified in his routine about America's selling of weapons to poor countries then blowing them up, comparing this to Jack Palance's actions in the movie *Shane*. Like Pryor, Hicks looks into the distance to open up the stage, licking his lips as he portrays Palance, tall and mighty, staring ahead, his eyes fixed on some point. Hicks then switches to the simple farmer looking back. By contrasting their body language, Hicks conveys their apartness and opens up the space of the stage. For the farmer, Hicks has his head slightly down as he meekly looks back at Palance, moving uneasily on the spot, trepidation and anxiety conveyed as he subtly moves his right arm and hand with nervous indecision. Then Hicks' body tenses, his eyes looking down to the stage where a gun is supposed to be. Several times Hicks plays out this nervous looking down then looking at Palance. The stagecraft is excellent, beautifully poised to create a sense of distance, and like Pryor, Hicks plays on the audience's preconceived notions, this time from stand-offs they have seen in western movies. It is played out long enough for the audience to visualise before the farmer goes for the gun and is shot, Hicks dropping his body to the stage.

Pryor's stationary body is used to build characters whereas Hicks' was often for a visual gag, like when he imagines parachuting down to "Dick Joke Island", his body on the spot swaying from side to side, gently lowering as he descends down, again precisely aware of the physics of a parachute moving through air. It's a simple comedic moment, amongst many that come during his shows, as in swimming gestures when he imagines himself as a sperm or when he is on one leg, straining as he leans his body to the left to show his political affiliations. Such regular and brief physical comedy moments not only keeps the energy of his shows alive but the constant variety also allows the audience to be switched on to its theatrical sense.

Both comedians keep their free hand in almost perpetual motion, gesturing, improvising, and almost lecturing. Pryor also uses it effectively as part of his routines like when he imagines facing kidnappers who are pointing a shotgun at him. His left hand is scared, giving in to the kidnappers easily: "Fuck you!" it says into his ear before Pryor quickly pulls it behind his back. There is a pause before the hand zooms into view, darts to Pryor's ear a second time and, as if to justify its cowardice, says "It's a shotgun asshole" then returns behind his back. From here the hand calls to Pryor, "Give me that rope" with Pryor subtly looking over his shoulder. Again Pryor's attention to detail helps create a sense of presence with the fingers on the left hand flapping as it speaks. Pryor's body moves into profile, "I'll tie myself. Is this a good knot?" says the hand, Pryor looking one way whilst the handed is extended in the opposite direction. The hand seems to be separate from Pryor himself and in profile we get the sense of two characters back to back, tied together.

In this the hand is no longer just a part of the comedian's body but is another character on stage, adding to the performance's theatrical sense. When Hicks watches the terrible news stories and imagines the chaos outside his front door, he steps outside to be attacked by a pit bull, putting the back of his right hand to his ass, flapping it as he growls to denote the dog, his body moving in circles as the animal tries to snap at his ass. Then there is the use of his right hand, fingers extended and wagging above his head to denote Lee Harvey Oswald being flown over President Kennedy by pigeons. Hicks is fond of a hand gesture into the air above, a sweeping move to suggest a headline or sign. His hand wavers for flying saucers, jabs to make a point, is holding a tray as a waffle waitress, or is an open palm in front of him to denote reading a book. Such simple but effective gestures help create the props an audience would expect from a piece of drama.

To qualify the assertion that Hicks physical comedy is less well acted than Pryor's: Pryor was a genius, the best: an artist at physical comedy. The fact that he could make so many middling to dire movies shows that he was the best thing in many of them. Indeed, some of his acting was more than just commendable. In his stage show, Pryor has a character called Mudbone, an old timer whose complete and detailed characterisation shows how refined and skilled he was as an actor. Similarly, his depiction of a junkie is not only funny for its accuracy but also powerful in the way he doesn't seek to punctuate it with cheap laughs. Frequently, Pryor's junkie portrayals are filled with silence as he administers the drugs and feels the disconnected exhilaration of the hit. He plays out the character at length to accentuate the emptiness of the experience, and by implication the hopelessness of drug addiction in the black community. The slow drawl of his speech, the heavy disorientated eyes and the tired rubbing of his face show Pryor as an exceptionally skilled actor.

In contrast, Hicks was using characters as conduits for material, not as entities in themselves. When they were mere comic characters his material was somewhat simplistic; from Elmer Dinkley in his early career to the later Goatboy. Goatboy is a horny Satan and is physically one of Hicks' best-acted characters. In terms of material it is rather one-dimensional, an offshoot of Hicks' rants against bland television and rock stars. What Hicks brings to Goatboy is a sense of largeness and power through the deep voice and physical gestures. He looks down and gestures at crotch level the gentle patting of Vanilla Ice's head to convey Goatboy's size. Similarly, sound effects are used in this way with the swish of air as Goatboy tosses paper away and the exaggerated bursting noise of his zipper opening. In addition, Hicks uses other characters to accentuate Goatboy's power, playing the innocent young girl looking up at Goatboy, biting her lip, pouting, curling her hair, and locking her hands onto his horns. Visually it is a rich presentation, but unlike Pryor's characters, we don't get much of a sense of personality behind the visual representation.

The other two characters from Hicks' early career, Mumsy and Goober Dad, based on his parents, evolved to denote caricatures of all types of Southern rednecks, hicks and generally stupid people. The Dumb Jock character would evolve into young, right wing men, those so happy with their own gratification that they ignored real issues, like those in "hog heaven" in the Gulf War, picking through a weapons catalogue and enjoying the killing. Though not as accomplished as Pryor, Hicks nevertheless would go on to develop his physical comedy very effectively in the late eighties through to the end of his career.

Pryor used body first, then face and was a master of both. He has a routine about deer stalking in the woods in which he uses his body for the deer, bent over in profile, drinking water. When the deer hears a noise Pryor snaps his body up and turns his head face on, his eyes darting back and forth in fear. He uses eyes and eyebrows – alerted, twitching – to show the deer's suspicion. Hicks was more facial; eyes wide with disbelief, squinted with suspicion; mouth gritted, bitten, grimacing. Like Pryor the raising or lowering of eyes creates a sense of space by acknowledging characters, like when he looks up to rednecks who say "Well, looks like we got ourselves a reader," or in his routine about being pulled over by the police whilst tripping. Here, Hicks looks to the left as the cops tap on one car window, and then looks to the right, mouth open, staring at them in the other mirror and believing them to be miniature. These simple gestures create the space of the car before he looks gradually to the left, eyes moving up to create an image of the real size of the cop standing outside the car. From his facial features evolved rednecks and do-gooders with subtle ticks to denote their narrow-mindedness, all expressions imbued with anger and irony, an over emphasis and lack of subtlety which matched the characters he was portraying. Pryor's rednecks employ the same physicality as Hicks' with hunched shoulders, wide eyes, tongue pushing out his lower lip, head nodding, pathetically confrontational.

His body fixed closely to a space on the stage (almost the archetypal stand-up comedian beneath a spotlight), Pryor can also create that sense of presence and space. In one routine, structured around a statement that "The madder I get, the quieter I get," he mimes out his anger gradually mounting, his vocals fading away until it's just physicality conveying his fury. He uses his left hand to create a sense that other characters are in the space around him as it points at himself, at the woman he is addressing directly ahead, and at the space to his side. Sometimes the fingers are extended wide or extended to a point. This variety of expressions gives fullness to the characterisation, perfectly allied to Pryor's lips miming words, his head jolting as sentences are expressed; his eyes low then widening, looking up to a figure in the distance. They convey suspicion, disbelief and anger, faultlessly in time with the staccato body jolts that indicate increasing vexation as his emotions rage out of control. You can read Pryor's lips, but it's not just "Fuck you!" that's discernable; it's a sense of the intervening dialogue, the mouthed rhythms of speech synchronised with the jerks of his body. The strength of Pryor's characterisation shines light on the satellite characters around his body space so that the audience get a sense of many characters interacting. Again it is the quickness of the routine that takes the audience with him, Pryor's miming adeptly suggesting for the audience what other characters are saying to him.

So proficient is Pryor's physicality, it gives his performances a nonchalance which allows him to make the surreal more everyday and employ personification in some of his most original and amusing routines. His routine about dogs imbues with the creatures an aloofness, an insouciant expectancy as the dog reads the ingredients of a food can, " 'Yeh Rich, this'll be good, fix that up for us please.' " He carefully crafts his head into a position looking up as he voices a menacing Doberman looking down to speak to him. Pryor adopts a low, soft voice as a German Shepherd comforts him on the loss of his pet monkey. Physical gestures are interwoven, with Pryor moving as a horse, shitting as it walks, his hand round his back, extended from his rear, flapping to denote shit being released. Then he noises the flies approaching this shit, his vocals in a buzzing whine, his body moving towards then backing off the shit as the whine turns direction too. With personification of animals Pryor again only needs to craft a rounded character to match the audience's preconceived visualisation.

More abstract is Pryor personifying his body parts, as in his dick shouting "Emergency!" as he recounts being on fire. The dick even has an ethos, with self-preservation at heart as it refuses to help the stomach: "Fuck you! I'm protecting the balls!" In a similar vein, Pryor personifies his heart during the heart attack he had, his right shoulder and elbow snapping back as the pain kicks in, intermittent with a vocal change as his heart warns him about a life of excesses. As the heart attack becomes worse he falls to the ground, the routine continuing with Pryor on the stage floor for several minutes.

For a comedian to continue from the stage floor is a dangerous tactic if it cuts off the view and therefore engagement of the majority of the seated audience, but Pryor pulls it off because of his exemplary set up. The audience's minds are already hooked into the routine and they don't need to see Pryor to continue enjoying it. Similarly, Hicks has routines where he drops to the floor, as when he imagines those in marketing sleeping easily at night after making poisonous baby food. After setting up the routine, Hicks is confident enough in the visual he has created for the audience to cut himself off from them and lay on the stage with hands clasped beneath his head like a pillow, relaying the marketing man's explanations of his work to his wife.

Pryor's skill with personification means he has less need for props. Creating shapes from thin air with his physicality is just the start. Pryor adds on layers to open up the space of the stage, his personification detailed and clearly drawn. His coke pipe is simply denoted by his right hand grasping the end of the pipe about a foot from his mouth, sucking in his cheeks for the hits. The routine achieves space as Pryor paces to his stage right and puts the pipe down at a point above the ground to identify a table. This is his 'set' construction, which gives it that theatrical sense. Presence comes with the personification of the pipe, Pryor imbuing it with appropriate characteristics as it tells him what to do: "Time to get up." The voice is pitched impeccably for the insidiously friendly character, all false benevolence in the informality of the address, "Time for some smoke, Rich" and "I know how you feel." The pipe reassumes a smoking position as a conversation ensues between it and Pryor, who then moves to different positions on the stage as the dialogue goes back and forth, gradually exploring aspects of the pipe's character as it becomes more threatening. The pipe is still there as the routine progresses, trying to gee up Pryor before Jim Brown comes around on a mission to straighten Pryor out. In the subsequent dialogue between Pryor and Brown, the pipe is silent, as if cowering in a corner, only re-emerging on Brown's departure with a whispered, "Hey Rich, Jim's gone."

Pryor's performance envelops and mesmerises the audience through its diversity of personification, and though his vocals and words are rooted in stereotypes, Pryor's pacing and seamless changeovers evoke a multi-faceted community existing on the peripherals of society. Because of his sense of space and distance the audience can imagine a performance of many characters linked by a cohesive narrative. With Hicks the effect is the same, though its route is different. His more stationary manner is no less animated. From within him Hicks can create a plethora of characters by simple use of facial and hand gestures. Although less well acted than Pryor, Hicks' material is more open. His spiritual sense, in mind and subject matter, allied to material on God, aliens, space and the connectedness of things means he takes the audience on that ride, opening up the stage. With this, his physical comedy has a resonance that is as powerful as Pryor's. When Hicks is watching a space between his feet and the audience, obviously musing, contemplating weighty issues, the material that has gone before and that is to come will sweep up the audience, getting them to see the bigger picture, on the outside of all creation looking in.

Although Hicks does not have such personification beyond two moths in discussion as they fly to the sun, and an all too infrequently used routine in which pot is personified, announcing, "I am Pot. I am going to meet nicotine and alcohol for a debate about legality," he nonetheless makes more use of mundane objects in the stage's space than Pryor. These 'props' implicitly echoed the personification Pryor used. Pryor has vodka bottles, crack pipes and his heart talking to him, whilst Hicks uses his microphone and it's stand or a stool (generally not rooted in human characters) to create that sense of space. In his early shows, Hicks would use the microphone stand for his impression of a surveyor, holding it to his eye to denote it as the surveyor's guide. From his early Mumsy routines, the microphone stand was also used as a hose as his mother sprays speeding motorists, causing them to crash when really she wanted them to stop speeding dangerously.

Eschewing personification, Hicks finds a myriad of imaginative uses for props about the stage such as a stool, whether it be to denote some kind a table situated in the Gulf, on which rests a weapons catalogue that a U.S. soldier flicks through, or using the stool as a human, being fucked or being blown backwards by an Uzi toting Jesus, Hicks kicking the stool away as he noises and gestures the gun being fired. One time Hicks is leaning back on the stool, legs outstretched, hands miming the reigns of a horse as he gently rocks his body for the motion of being on a wagon train. The use of props, allied to a use of his body, brings these props to life, as when Hicks steps onto a mounting at the back of the stage and wraps the microphone chord around his neck, talking of Wham breaking up, sarcastically saying "How can I go on living?" as he jumps from the mounting. When Hicks uses a cigarette packet it becomes a prop brought in from the real world, such reality giving credence to his turning of other props into different things.

Like Kinison, Hicks' favourite use of the microphone was as a cock, but Hicks took it one step further, engineering it to be Satan's scaly phallus going deeply into the mouths of talentless pop stars such as Vanilla Ice and MC Hammer (accompanied by gnawing, hellish noises). Beyond this somewhat obvious application, Hicks was more imaginative and subtle in finding a variety of uses for the microphone and its stand. Accompanied by sound effects, the mic was a potent tool, from a gentle finger roll on its surface conveying the sound of a door being knocked, to Hicks' crashing it against his forehead to boom out the sound of moths flying into light bulbs (an echo of Pryor's hitting the mic against his forehead to evoke punches about his head). One inspired use had Hicks as a post-tracheotomy smoker, holding the mic to his throat, his growling vocals capturing the garbled communication of a voice box. His cheeks inhaling deeply, Hicks' smoker is unable the give up the habit, drawing smoke through the voice box before descending to other possible orifices about his body, to eventually be smoking through his ass-hole.

When Pryor uses props they are just one facet of his characterisation, as in using the microphone to mime horn playing, perfectly positioning his body for the truest effect, his left hand resting on the lower half of the mic, which is central and beneath his chin. His right hand is below the left as he pushes his fingers up and down to imagine horn playing, rocking his head to the music. The same positioning can be seen when Hicks evokes playing a sitar. Both comedians are not seeking vague gestures but complete and realistic miming with close attention to detail.

In tandem with this physicality and use of props, both comedians use sound effects as another way to create a sense of presence on the stage. It is seen with Pryor mimicking the bleeps on a heart-monitoring machine as hand gestures signal flashes of life, and also with Hicks' sound of windscreen wipers accompanied by the side-to-side motion of his right hand. It is another way for Hicks to bring the real world into his act, to evoke a human society he seeks to analyse. So we have the sound of crickets at night when he mocks TV news portraying a world full of chaos, or the grrr of a lawnmower when a pussy-whipped Satan is mowing the lawn. Naturally, the rock and roller in Hicks also seeks to employ guitar sounds, be it to illustrate the vitality of good music (with air guitar accompaniment to his own hummed interpretations of Hendrix and the Rolling Stones) or more cleverly when he comments on the wah-wah guitar effects used in the music for porn films.

Both comedians adeptly create that extra dimension on stage through all the aforementioned sounds, use of props and physicality, and in this way they can create a dialogue between two characters, like Pryor and his crack pipe or with his animal sketches. For Pryor this dialogue helps embellish the characters' personalities, but is also a comedic end in itself. Though Hicks has dialogue between him, his mother and his father discussing the merits of the "suck your own cock" routine which is purely comic, the more frequent purpose of his multi-character dialogue is to convey a message. For Hicks, the multi-character dialogue was essential to his material, allowing him to play the devil's advocate, to adopt personas of those he disagreed with, then question them and mock them. It can be seen when he questions fundamentalists who believe the Bible is 12,000 years old, the people who believe alcohol is an acceptable part of social interaction, or when he is questioning a man who sold weapons to Iraq, making his argument that he thought it was "farming equipment" ring foolish and hollow. These characters speak to Hicks so that he can point up how ignorant, blind and misguided they are. In his skilful crafting of presence and distance on the stage, Hicks avoids these characters becoming too obvious tools.

Pryor was the last major influence on Hicks' comedy. From the early 1980s he began filtering his own style and material through his influences and gradually transcending them.

Pryor's life, out of control on freebase, took a dramatic turn in 1980 when he set himself on fire (only admitting to it being a suicide attempt some years later). Arduous and painful recovery followed with Pryor undergoing several skin grafts before a return marked by the release of the concert film *Live On The Sunset Strip* in March 1982.

It is easy to see why Hicks was so awe-struck by this performance. Naturally Pryor is taking on stage the baggage of his cocaine abuse and the fire that burned his body, but to actually confront and use it for comedy purposes is as naked as any stand-up performance before or since. Looking back at Pryor in the show, there is a sense of poignancy in the way his facial features have been altered, the sense that despite some impressive facial reconstruction and skin grafting his physiognomy has lost its innocence. Nonetheless, whilst his body is more agitated than ever in the show, the material is as confrontational and perceptive as anything he had done previously and the film was a big box office hit. In many ways it can be seen as Pryor's last triumph, followed as it was by a series of ever more limp and poorly received films that didn't tap into his considerable acting talents. *The Toy* (1982), *Superman 3* (1983) and *Brewster's Millions* (1985) were light and undemanding, whilst his self-directed concert film *Here And Now* (1983) was a somewhat subdued affair.

For Hicks, having followed his turbulent life story closely, Pryor had become almost mythical. To the Bill Hicks who was emerging in the early 1980s, it seemed like true rock n' roll comedy with Pryor's making humour from his turmoil and excesses, giving him a rawness and credibility that few contemporaries could match. When Hicks returned to Houston in the summer of 1982, he too would aspire to rock n' roll comedy through the use of drugs.

7
Just Say Yes

During the late 1970s cocaine usage in America had risen sharply, becoming the drug of choice for people in the entertainment industry during the 1980s. Comedians like Pryor and Belushi were addicts whilst the likes of Robin Williams and Sam Kinison became regular users, often referencing it in their material. Up until 1982, Bill Hicks had steered clear of drugs, but increasingly he had grown to feel his comedy was going nowhere. His material and performances were sharper and more sophisticated, but he seemed unable to make the next step up.

Los Angeles' entertainment community was the centre for drugs and it was whilst in the city during August 1982 that Hicks took a tab of acid. Like all the artists who were his heroes, the drug experience proved inspirational for Hicks, prompting him to write new material, unfettered by any parameters that had previously been around his comedy. The experience brought new ideas to his act and a wider awareness of life, spending tripping hours examining the minutiae of existence and approaching subjects from diverse angles. So exhilarating was the creative surge, it led Hicks into a drug odyssey involving an array of different substances over the next six years.

He moved back to Houston in the winter of 1982, spending a lot of time in Austin, Texas, working with Kevin Booth and David Johndrow on the film *Ninja Bachelor Party* and enjoying a thriving local scene that saw musicians, film makers, writers and comedians rubbing shoulders regularly. As a comedian, he was putting the influences of Woody Allen and Richard Pryor behind him and being more of himself on stage, encouraged by the new and original ideas his drug experiences were throwing up.

Following his appreciation of illegal drugs, Hicks began to enjoy the "socially acceptable" drugs, alcohol and tobacco. As Bill explained, "For years I had been looking down on my fellow comedians as drug-using, alcoholic chain smokers. One night I did a show. It went great but I was miserable. And I'd been miserable for my whole life...I started everything that night. Drinking, smoking and drugs" (21).

A new Bill Hicks was unleashed, his comedy angrier, his sex routines more hardcore, and from the stage he was enjoying heated verbal arguments with audiences, lambasting traditional attitudes, mocking hypocritical beliefs. He went through his hatred of Ronald Reagan and the television shows like *Diff'rent Strokes*, taking broad swipes at American society and its choice of idols.

Alcohol and drugs were making him fearless, his confrontational routines getting him noticed, although some shows - with Bill's excessive intakes - were prone to rambling and unfocused anger. With this came (possibly apocryphal) tales. At one gig there was said to be two Vietnam veterans who took exception to his routine and broke his legs (another version sees a bartender beating him up and breaking one leg). Whatever the truth of these tales, Hicks did actually have his ankle broken at one gig. Yet, for all the unchecked anger there was an insightful perceptiveness, which simultaneously made audiences think and laugh at the absurdity or irony of the state of things. That some people didn't want to think about the issues his comedy raised gave credence to Hicks' developing philosophy about a society made apathetic by consumerism.

1983 saw him back gigging in L.A. New comedians like Jim Carrey were making a name for themselves and the comedy scene (albeit less vital than in its 70s heyday) was still good copy for the media with Pryor's turbulent life, John Belushi's death in March 1982, and *Saturday Night Live* returning to something of its former glory with the emergence of Eddie Murphy. The first wave of the show's stars like Dan Aykroyd, Bill Murray and Steve Martin, after initially choosing offbeat and anarchic movie vehicles, were beginning to make more mainstream choices, whilst stand-up shows were getting released as movies and chat shows were on the look out for fresh new talent. Chat show, *Late Night With David Letterman* was getting the same hip young audience as *Saturday Night Live*, a young, sophisticated audience eager for originality and controversy. Meanwhile, nightclubs adjusting to the end of the disco era and needing to fill empty venues, were putting on more comedy nights, allowing Hicks plenty of opportunities to find work.

Hicks' liberal attitude to drugs can be linked to the decade in which he grew up. The 1960s, driven by rock music, saw a more liberal attitude to drugs, particularly with the use of pot amongst students at universities, with whom drugs were a way to distance themselves from the old fashioned establishment and form a link to the rebellion of their rock heroes, the same heroes Hicks referenced in his material; John Lennon, Keith Richards, Jimi Hendrix. As already noted, Hicks appealed to an audience tuned into a rock and roll culture in which drugs were an intrinsic element, but whereas rock stars may celebrate substance consumption, their hedonism can often seem individualistic. In contrast, Hicks offered the stoners and trippers in his audience (or perhaps, more accurately, those from the chattering classes who had experimented and enjoyed) an articulation of the drug experience, its idiosyncrasies and idealism, its awakening and opening up of the consciousness; to such an accurate and enlightened degree that the routine and its ideas and rhythms are akin to a trip without drugs. Within this there is an ideology – a vibe even – that owes much to mythical images of the sixties (empowerment, freedom, the musings of a philanthropic soul), yet doesn't slip into the mawkish fantasy of stoner rhetoric with its peace and love ethos amid archetypal images of flowers in hair and down the barrels of guns. Hicks allies the decade's optimism with a contemporary realism that makes it all the more irresistible, evoking the possibilities of the decade with the added impact of a reasoned argument. Moreover, the connection is extended to sixties proponents of drugs like Dr Timothy Leary (sacked from his lectureship at Harvard University in 1963 after experiments into the effects of psychedelic drugs) who have a philosophy in tune with Hicks'.

For Leary, like Hicks, the drugs issue was linked to personal freedom. In his *The Declaration Of Evolution* Leary wrote that all species should have the "Freedom to Live, Freedom to Grow, and Freedom to pursue happiness in their own style." Hicks' material focused on the freedom of choice, that he should be allowed to do whatever he liked to his body "as long as I do not harm another human being," a response to the implementation of Nancy Reagan's vile *Just Say No* anti-drugs campaign. Launched in 1984, the campaign was merely a political tool to assuage white middle class fears of the drug threat to their young, whilst doing little to address the spiralling drug problem amongst America's black community.

For Hicks, long interested in the powers of the mind, expanded awareness and Transcendental Meditation, drugs were a means to explore the deepest workings of his imagination, remembering his experiences and using them for routines. His drug choices included LSD, cocaine, quaaludes, ecstasy, marijuana and meth amphetamine, but his favourite drugs were psilocybin magic mushrooms taken from cow fields and experienced in natural surroundings.

The mushroom trips, lasting between five and seven hours, further opened his eyes to the world and evolved his perception, enabling him to see the connectedness of things. The trips took Hicks on a ride through inner and outer space, magic mushrooms invariably producing hallucinations linked to nature, allowing him to see humankind's relationship with the natural world and its importance in life. He was seeing the bigger picture, one that the ignorant masses – placing value on materialism – never could, too preoccupied as they were with buying into the everyday consumer bullshit. Drugs helped Bill explore his expanded awareness and use his intellect and imagination to spiritually travel, seeing Aztec temples, aliens circling the pyramids and Jesus riding a unicorn.

Hicks embraced the power of mushrooms and was fully aware of their importance in humankind's evolution. Contemporary society seemed unaware of the historical significance of mushrooms, that they had been used by ancient tribes as a means to step into the spiritual world, dating back to the Aztecs of Mexico in the 1500s. The Aztecs named mushrooms 'Teonanacatl', which translates as "flesh of the gods" or "divine flesh." With mushrooms growing on cow turds and the Hindu culture seeing the cow as sacred, Hicks viewed McDonald's as "the anti-Christ." Beyond ancient cultures, there is the theory that prehistoric rock art was inspired by magic mushrooms with the discovery of rock paintings dating back tens of thousands of years showing mushroom-like objects being used in primitive rituals.

Such theories appealed to Hicks' sense of the connectedness of history. In this respect he subscribed to Terence Mckenna's view that hallucinogenic drugs had aided mankind's evolution. McKenna's writings and research focused on spiritual transformation, analysing ancient cultures and their use of hallucinogens. Hicks was a big fan of McKenna's book, *Food Of The Gods*, which expounded the theory that the human brain had abilities which were not tapped into, but which were opened up through the psychedelic experience, much like Timothy Leary's belief that drugs "allow us to peer into bits and zones of Chaos."

Hicks' view of drugs as facilitators of evolution can be seen in his early 1980s material, with throwaway lines like giving monkeys at the zoo acid-laced cookies to "watch them evolve before my eyes." As Hicks read more of McKenna's studies on the use of mushrooms by prehistoric man, this routine would grow into the cosmic significance of *Revelations* and the Neanderthal man who picks mushrooms from cow dung, takes them and thinks he can "go to the moon." In then humming the music to the science-fiction film *2001: A Space Odyssey*, Hicks links to McKenna's view that mushrooms could have come from outer space because they open up in the taker such knowledge of the galaxy that they must have been left by an omniscient alien race.

For Terence McKenna, "The future is bound to be psychedelic, because the future belongs to the mind...we are going to discover the plasticity, the mutability, the eternal nature of the mind and, I believe, release it from the monkey" (22). Hicks was never into drugs for their easy thrills, mocking those who use them and want to play miniature golf or go to Astroworld. He took drugs to open his mind, leaving the mundane behind for more enlightened experiences where he could go racing into trains of thought, connecting ideas as he tripped through life's injustices and ironies. Mushrooms gave Hicks a connection to the soul, the soul that had been disconnected from humankind by an emotionless consumer culture. He saw how the denial of this soul created all the problems in the world, made people narrow minded and hateful, governed not by love but by fear and mistrust. It is a view shared with Mckenna, that "our breach of faith with the symbiotic relationship to the plant hallucinogens has made us susceptible to an ever more neurotic response to each other and the world around us" (23).

McKenna's conclusion that "The suppression of the natural human fascination with altered states of consciousness and the present perilous situation of all life on earth are intimately and causally connected" (23) echoes Hicks' belief that governments want to suppress humankind's imagination by not only making the drugs illegal, but also by allowing television programmes that are simplistic, unenlightening and more concerned with keeping people stupid. It's why Hicks' style and language is open, languid and optimistic when musing about mushroom trips and coarse, claustrophobic and frenetic when mocking consumer culture. This is the dominant culture, which for McKenna "has led us up a blind alley" (22).

The fear of the government was that people on drugs would see more of the truth and what was really important in life, for instance a realisation that going to a job is not worth the effort and instead spending time learning something creative, like playing the sitar. Of mushrooms, Hicks said ironically, "I'm glad they're against the law," as he relayed the truth of how the open mindedness caused by drugs was a threat because when he took mushrooms, "I lay in a field of green grass for four hours going 'My God, I *love* everything.' The heavens parted, God looked down and rained gifts of forgiveness onto my being, healing me on every level...And I realised our true nature is spirit not body, that we are eternal beings and God's love is unconditional...It is only our illusion that we are separate from God and that we are alone. In fact, the reality is we are at one with God and he loves us. Now, if that isn't a hazard to this country." He then adopts the voice of those in power, who are exasperated and threatened by this philosophy: "How are we gonna keep building nuclear weapons? What's gonna happen to the arms industry when we realise we're all one. It's gonna fuck up the economy." Governments want to keep people's thoughts limited so that they don't question and keep buying the products.

Though drugs can often lead to the atrophying of an artist's talent, for Hicks the way the drugs opened up his mind led to his comedy becoming sharper. Just as he believed drugs did good things for rock musicians, so it made his comedy more perceptive with truly killer jokes and ironic pay-offs that incisively exposed the mendacity and duplicity symptomatic of Reagan's administration and the culture its measures created. Only too aware that he was improving as a stand-up, Hicks' growing sense of ease with an audience is reflected in the nonchalance of asides such as where he casually asks a member of the audience for a cigarette, adding "I left mine in the machine." He was always quick-witted, able to think on his feet, as an anecdote by comedian Johnny Torrez reveals when he and Bill were watching a juggler in a night-club and Bill turned to Torrez and said, "You know Johnny, why is it every time I see a juggler on stage I think of somewhere in the world there's some poor seal out of work" (24). Hicks' ability to improvise, to draw on a body of ideas and riffs so effortlessly, not only gave his comedy an irresistible fluency (the same fluency apparent in the free association imaginings of drug trips), but also displayed such confidence that his take on issues had the irrefutable air of truth.

His routines were including something of the old uncontroversial stuff about his education and not being able to get up for University, whilst also bringing in his new wild drug experiences with the hedonistic implication of, "I was going to *night* school." Like other comedians, such as Robin Williams, drugs were coming into his material, as in a routine about doing cocaine with people you'd normally run from. "So, how many people have you killed?" Hicks asks a killer as they gleefully share the coke.

The inference that he was living the rock n' roll lifestyle permeated his material, even when mocking army commercials that said "We do more before nine a.m. than most people do in a day" responded to by Hicks with a somewhat puzzled "I go to bed at eight." His Mumsy character was still evident as were the dick jokes, but he was also expanding his act to bring in Eastern philosophy and mankind's evolution.

Despite Hicks favouring mushrooms, much of his drug material concentrated on marijuana. He saw it as a natural drug; that God left pot everywhere (some routines claiming it by accident, some as part of God's plan). Hicks' God felt saddened that it'd been left on the planet, but only because it now meant, "Now I have to create Republicans." It is another prescient view in the light of Chris Bennett and Neil McQueen's recent book, *Sex, Drugs, Violence and the Bible* (Forbidden Fruit Publishing). In it, the argument is put forward that Jesus used a cannabis extract called *kaneh-bosem* in the anointing oils used for ceremonies.

Hicks' take on pot was, unlike those who were anti-drugs, based on knowledge and understanding. For him, pot "serves a thousand different functions, all of them positive." As with mushrooms, Hicks understood the historic origins of pot and its positive uses. Though society liked to connect it with a hippy dropout culture, Hicks understood cannabis was first cultivated in China around 4000 BC; that amongst its uses could be for clothes, paper, food and medicines. In Hicks' philosophy, the best solution for a financial deficit was to legalise marijuana and use the "biggest cash crop in America" to serve its many uses, "all of them positive."

Government lies and misinformation about pot have shifted the emphasis of its threat over the years, yet never found a sustainable argument for its illegality. From the 1930s, anti-cannabis propaganda has seen it linked to murder, insanity, prostitution and death, never once mentioning that President George Washington said, "Make the most of hemp seed. Sow it everywhere" or that the original drafts of the Declaration of Independence were written on hemp paper. The spin that marijuana makes people unmotivated has its origins in 1967 when Henry Giordano, the head of the Federal Bureau of Narcotics, gave the dangers of marijuana angle a new impetus with commercials saying it makes people unmotivated and dysfunctional. Hicks' counter argument was that "you can do everything you normally do, just as well, you just realise it's not worth the fucking effort."

He saw the flaws in the media's presentation of drugs and its employment of subjective language. When asked "Have you ever experimented with LSD?" Hicks retorts, "I used to experiment. Finally had a breakthrough. Found a practical monthly use." The media was more concerned with fear mongering and disinformation, ignoring the pleasures of drugs and the enlightened view they could generate.

When Hicks quit drugs in 1988 he could look back on his experiences objectively, but unlike so many celebrities he didn't then rail on about the hell of drug addiction, a particular trait of 1980s yuppie culture with famous people going into rehab when their careers were deteriorating. Instead, Hicks used his awareness to enlighten: "I've had some killer times on drugs," he would say, promoting their legalisation. "Didn't murder anybody, didn't rob anybody, didn't rape anybody, didn't lose, mmm, one fuckin' job, laughed my ass off, and went about my day. So-rry. Now, where's my commercial?" Hicks sought a balanced view from the media, felt frustrated that its presentation was based on fear rather than education. He saw the holes in the messages being put across and was not only angered that they didn't convey the benefits of drugs, but that in being so one-sided the views they espoused were dangerous. The reasoning was that by being so misinformed these commercials made even the true facts about the dangers of drugs seem false. Amongst a slew of anti-drugs commercials in the 1980s was one particularly inane one from the Partnership For Drug-Free America with its "This is your brain on drugs" conveyed by a frying egg supposedly denoting the effects of drugs. It pompously ended with the rhetorical, "Any questions?" as if the debate had been accurately summarised in the broadcast. It implied there were no questions to ask, typically in line with the narrow minded *Just Say No* campaign.

Hicks went on to mock news coverage that always concerned itself with people's unhappy experiences of drugs: "You never see a positive drug story on the news do you? Isn't that weird since most of the experiences I've had on drugs were real fuckin' positive." Hicks instead hoped for a different perspective with his news report announcing: "Today a young man on acid realised that all matter is merely energy condensed to a slow vibration, that we are all one consciousness experiencing itself subjectively. There is no such thing as death, life is only a dream, and we are the imagination of ourselves. Here's Tom with the weather." A gem of a riff, taking the audience on a ride, its economical use of words helping the audience imagine. It lasts a lifetime, each pocket of the one consciousness he shares.

The media manipulation went hand in hand with the War On Drugs, another of Reagan's ill thought out and populist causes. The 1986 Anti-Drug Abuse Act was a wild stab in the dark at America's drug problem, more concerned with punishment than treatment or education. The Act made at least 1 kilogram of heroin or 5 kilograms of cocaine punishable by at least ten years in prison. Selling 5 grams of crack resulted in a mandatory 5 years in prison. As crack was cheaper than cocaine, the law resulted in more blacks being sent to prison.

Hicks felt disbelief at a strategy that lumped all drugs together, giving the public the view that pot was as dangerous as hard drugs like crack and heroin. The idea of a "War" not only saw Hicks mocking the fact that the government were losing and therefore people on drugs were winning, but also questioning the ideology that went with it. The government saw it as a battle where punishment was the only solution, making an ex-policeman the Drugs' Tsar, the figurehead to oversee the strategy. For all Hicks' celebration of drugs he did acknowledge there was a problem, believing that treatment and education should be at the forefront. For him, it would be more progressive to have a recovering addict as a Tsar, someone able to draw on experiences rather than a narrow-minded policeman who couldn't possibly understand the complexities of addiction.

Hicks' pro-drugs stance would continue throughout his career, developing to include not only its pleasures, but also his indictment of the War On Drugs baton picked up by George Bush. In many ways the campaign worked as a replacement for the Cold War. With the realisation that the Soviet Union was no longer a threat, America needed a new enemy to unify the people; a new enemy that – in Republican thinking – could generate fear and separate people into good and bad. Bush had the same attitude as Reagan, in 1990 proposing another $1.2 billion including a 50% increase in military spending to fight this war. The fact that the cost of putting one person in jail for drugs offences was equal to the treatment and education of 200 people pointed up the absurdity of the whole War On Drugs, a war that ultimately could never be won. In a good year U.S. drug Enforcement agents might seize only 1% of the worldwide drug crop, but successive Republican administrations seemed blind to this and continued their "War", not only because they believed it showed their determination to tackle the problem, but also because it helped them appeal to middle class Americans, those who accepted the whole drug story shock tactics of the media.

More than anything, it was the hypocrisy of the War On Drugs that angered Hicks; maddeningly obvious when anti-drug commercials could be followed by beer commercials. In selling and celebrating alcohol consumption, they seemed gleefully unaware of the mixed messages. To Hicks, they were revelling in the ethos of, "here, let's be hypocritical bastards," as he concluded that the only reason drugs were illegal was because they weren't taxed: "Those are the drugs that are bad. Those *non-taxed* drugs." He pointed out the facts of alcohol and tobacco related deaths being substantially more than those from drugs, figures supported by the National Institute on Drug Misuse Research Monographs, which found that in a typical year there were 390,000 deaths in the U.S. from tobacco, 80,000 from alcohol and 0 from marijuana. Hicks contrasted the effects of alcohol and marijuana perceptively with material about people who are drunk getting into fights. Those on marijuana didn't "because it's fuckin' impossible," as he envisioned the scene where a fight seemed about to break out between pot smokers, only for the threat to recede when, as a result of being high, they realise they are taking life too seriously.

For a time Hicks managed to combine the drug taking and partying with his continuing hectic touring. Rather than drugs blunting his comedy, they were the catalyst for an exploration of ideas as he assembled all the facts and all the angles for the purpose of making his comedy sharper. He felt more than ever as an outsider looking in on what was happening in Reagan's America. His lifestyle contrasted starkly with a country now determined to get fit, a counterbalance to the excesses of the 1980s, some kind of guilt reducer for all the self-indulgence, or as Hicks put it, "trying to make up for all the cocaine/disco bashes." For the stars, there was The Betty Ford Clinic near Palm Springs, opened in 1982 as a private clinic for the famous, for those individuals ruined by alcohol and drugs, the kind of people Hicks so detested because they gave drugs a bad name whilst at the same time their self-pitying, sanctimonious denouncing of drugs exposed them as hypocrites. For ordinary people, there was the tube, with people like Richard Simmons peddling their weight loss programmes on national television (his character hilariously mocked by Eddie Murphy's *Saturday Night Live* impersonation) whilst Olivia Newton John had released her *Physical* album in 1981 and was now doing swift business in exercise videos.

The get fit craze was matched by a proliferation of self-help books on weight loss, love, being happy, getting fit and starting and maintaining relationships, as if people were unwilling or unable to think for themselves. This colourful day-glo boom of happiness was a symptom of Reagan's none-thinking, everything's fine America. Hicks saw through this gloss, most hysterically in the irony of the Jim Fixx story. In 1977 "runner and health nut" Fixx had published his first book *The Complete Book Of Jogging*, which had become a best seller and kick started the get fit craze. A second book followed in 1980, *Jim Fixx's Second Book Of Running*. After recently quitting smoking, 52-year-old Fixx had died of a heart attack in 1984 whilst jogging.

For Hicks, it allowed him to puncture the myth of life somehow being dependent on physical health, the "eternal life fantasy" (though for comedic purposes Hicks ignored Fixx's family history of heart disease). He imagined a baffled Fixx in heaven, wondering how he could have died, contrasting his life of denial with that of actor Yul Brynner (and, at times, Keith Richards still living). Brynner had died of cancer in 1985 after a life of sex, drugs and partying. Hicks imagined Brynner in heaven, happily offering anecdotes detailing his exploits, celebrating a life enjoyed to the full, not one based on fear. Yet, before his death, Brynner had made an anti-smoking commercial denouncing the habit, for in Reagan's America smokers were the new pariahs.

Hicks' use of ironic contrast through the connection of disparate ideas is a feature of his comedy as he points out the difference between the media spin on events and the objective truth of them. The Fixx/Brynner material is a prime example, similar to the drugs coverage with its selective facts, biased language and an apparently moral message all, in reality, clouding the truth. In focusing on Brynner's death, there is a denial of the complexity of his life; an inability to accept that he may well have enjoyed his time on Earth much more than those, like Fixx and all the other Americans eager to get fit, who believe that longevity is dependant on abstinence. Yet it seemed to Hicks that the American public were swallowing the spin quite easily, making them (and for Hicks that meant "we") complicit in the lies. It was therefore left to the few, like Hicks, to expose the truth behind Reagan's America.

8
Republicanism On The Rampage

In February 1984 Hicks got his biggest career break thus far when he was called to be on *Late Night With David Letterman*, a TV chat show garnering plaudits for its left-field style. After opening for comedian Jay Leno in Houston, it was Leno who helped get him on the show, acknowledging Hicks was "still too far off the wall for the *Tonight Show*" (20). Carson's show was now firmly established as a show for a predominantly middle-aged and middle class audience, its satire the gentle kind that even its targets could laugh along with. Letterman's show was its brash successor, its irreverent take on the news and its host's studied nonchalance finding an audience with the young and upwardly mobile.

The show was always on the look out for fresh, original comedians, regularly using the likes of Andy Kaufman and the *Saturday Night Live* crew whilst also seeking to break new comedians to maintain its association with originality and hipness. It wasn't until 5th December that Hicks did his debut show, his routine somewhat tamely focusing on his family and experiences in school. Nonetheless, he went down well with the audience and Letterman liked him enough to want him back.

After his first Letterman appearance there was plenty of work for him, but he was still drinking, partying and taking drugs. Although he never became a sad, pathetic addict, he did give some ragged performances and showed frustration with audiences during and after shows. In places where he angrily mocked audiences, or the times when, out of his head on drugs, he stared emptily at them and struggled to hold down material, he got a bad reputation and found he wasn't welcomed back.

He still enjoyed the special tours the Outlaw Comics were putting on, but as the eighties progressed each member was striking out on his own more often. Alcohol and cocaine reunited Hicks and Sam Kinison during 1985, but this wasn't the same friendship as before. Hicks had a different perspective to Kinison whose comedy could sometimes be intolerant and narrow-minded. Film star Rock Hudson's death from A.I.D.S. in 1985 saw the disease become a major news item for the first time in America. In Reagan's fundamentalist America the disease was seen as God's punishment for homosexuals, allowing evangelists like Pat Robertson to promote their bigoted views. Kinison's comedy in many ways was playing to this ill-informed view, his material becoming less humane in the process. In contrast, Hicks was in touch with his consciousness, though as yet - with partying - he hadn't yet fully channelled it. The Outlaws' themed shows were a bore if it meant re-working familiar material, particularly when Hicks was so in tune with current affairs, always on the look out to work news stories into his act, as in 1984 when James Huberty shot dead 21 people at a McDonald's restaurant in San Ysidro near San Diego and Hicks used it for material he had on the American obsession with guns, mocking the sensationalist news coverage that didn't seem to want to open up a debate on gun control.

At the other end of the spectrum he had a particular obsession with *Houston Light And Power*, due in no small part to having the electricity cut off in his apartment. It was also an early indication of his dislike of the corporate machine. Even his early 1980s routines were looking at language, albeit simply in the form of bills from *Houston Light And Power* which said, "thanks for giving us the opportunity to serve you" as he mocked the lack of options. Such was Hicks' connection to the world around him, so alive to everything that was going on, that anything could inspire him to look at it through the comedian's eye.

22nd August 1985 saw his second Letterman appearance, Hicks beginning to develop his somewhat jaded outsider persona as he talks about not being a team player and the fact that "my career continues to wobble unevenly." His cleverness with language is evident as he talks about his girlfriend contemplating committing suicide, threatening to jump in front of a bus, complaining that Hicks is not being helpful, to which the comedian quips, "So I sent her a bus timetable." In addition, when he points up the irony of Jim Fixx dying and Keith Richards still living, it not only establishes Hicks' sophisticated perception, but also his rock and roll credentials. He does riffs about his family, Southern rednecks and evangelists, but once again, little of Hicks' live show was evident in the routine, but then the Bill Hicks on Letterman was unlike the Bill Hicks outside the studio. This Bill Hicks said "fuck" and "cunt" and took drugs regularly as he gigged and partied.

In December, *Houston City* magazine had Bill on the front cover with 'Is Bill Hicks the Funniest Man in Town?' expressing succinctly the feelings others in stand-up circles had had for a long time. His career in the ascendancy, a third Letterman appearance came on 13th February 1986. On the show, Hicks did a routine about evangelists being more concerned with money than faith. It wasn't particularly controversial, but the show cut a whole chunk of his routine out leaving Hicks very frustrated and more aware than ever of the denial of truth in America.

He wanted away from the Letterman shtick, feeling unable to evolve ideas in tight five to eight minute slots where he was expected to work to a pre-approved script. Hicks was a comedian who worked and developed his material on stage as he went through a routine, and though the routines had a structure he still had the freedom to be spontaneous and digress at anytime, always confident enough to return to his structure and tie ideas up neatly when the mood dictated. His stage shows were unsparing in their attacks on Reagan and extreme right-wingers like Pat Robertson, but they also showed a deeper philosophical coherence, his imaginings able to wander, giving him a rush of energy he was never able to feel amid the constrictions of the Letterman show.

Of more concern to Hicks was the right-wing agenda festering throughout the country after president Ronald Reagan's re-election victory in 1984; the largest ever victory for the Republican Party. The media talked of a "landslide" but that was far from the real picture. Election turnout had been around only fifty per cent of those eligible to vote, giving Reagan only a 29% of those eligible.

Reagan's presidency was a connection to Hicks' youth and the conservatism of Richard Nixon, though Reagan's politics were certainly more reprehensible. Hicks said when "Reagan got elected, I got a fuckin' gun in the mail." Here was a fear-mongering and dangerous man now president of the United States whose immediate concern was to lower taxes for the wealthy, cut benefits for the poor and pour more money into the military machine. By placing right-wingers in positions of power he controlled government like some dictator, thoroughly exploiting traditional American ideals almost as a front for his insidious and decidedly un-American policies, as when his administration destroyed documents rather than allow them to be declassified under the 30-year rule. What freedom meant to the American people was something different to what it meant to the Republican administration, as evidenced in 1981 when Reagan issued an executive order giving the CIA its first full authority to conduct domestic covert operations. Undercover operations and lies were to become the predominant features of his presidency.

Here was a president who claimed, "Our military strength is a prerequisite to peace." He'd even dug up the tired old enemy of communism, referring to the Soviet Union as "the evil empire" and "focus of evil in the modern world." He invoked patriotism in much the same way as Hitler, even joking in a 1984 microphone test: "My fellow Americans, I am pleased to tell you I just signed legislation which outlaws Russia forever. The bombing begins in five minutes." What his anti-Soviet policies actually did was stifle change in the communist block, the Soviet threat no more than a smokescreen, a way to engender patriotism. As Hicks saw it, America needed an enemy and Reagan's anti-Soviet rhetoric fooled people into getting behind him by suggesting that he was the most patriotic, God-fearing politician, one who could protect the country against an imminent danger. Hicks would mock this threat by sarcastically talking about his desire to abolish that part of the world because "Every day I feel the Soviet threat in Houston."

Reagan ploughed billions of dollars into the Strategic Defence Initiative, the so-called Star Wars military programme, maintaining that such spending was necessary because the Soviet Union was increasing its spending on defence. Yet in 1984 the C.I.A. admitted to being "lying cocksuckers," saying that they had "exaggerated" their claims that Soviet military spending from 1975 had been growing by 4 to 5 %. The real figure was actually 2% (25). Nonetheless, such extravagant military spending to counter this illusory threat had to be funded from somewhere, so Reagan borrowed heavily whilst also targeting the disenfranchised.

He cut welfare benefits, stopped the funding of all International Aid that supported family planning, and gave free reign for capitalism to imprint its ethos on American culture and values. Reaganomics had seen the gap between rich and poor grow ever larger after the recession of 1981-1982. The economic boom that followed created wealth not shared by all with 1982 seeing 30 million people unemployed for all or part of the year. Meanwhile, in October of the same year, the White House ordered a set of ivory china at a cost of $209,000. Reagan's belief that the poor were better off without government help created a society in which compassion somehow became a weakness.

Reagan's policies in the 1980s saw corporate America growing wealthier with tax cuts for the rich and the expansion of free markets. As George Carlin noted, "they're against street crime, providing that street isn't Wall Street." An economic boom had been created through consumer spending and Reagan's heavy borrowing. For Americans, material possessions were the answer to their problems, giving them the necessary "feel good factor," thus prompting a political shift, a lurch to the right received with little dissent from Democrats. It was a culture where getting rich was seen as a triumph, giving rise to the "yuppies", the affluent American middle classes who sought material possessions and name brands. Wall Street became the symbol of the decade with the effortless buying and selling of companies allowing individuals to make millions of dollars without thought for the human cost of such corporate machinations.

It is not difficult to agree with Hicks' assertion that Reagan was " a criminal against humanity" (26). In his first year in office he gave $82 million in military aid to the government of El Salvador. This was a country where 2% of the population owned 60% of the land, where those opposed to the regime were ruthlessly killed. Reagan's military aid merely enabled the regime to suppress rebellions and thus maintain U.S. business interests. Similarly, during the Iran-Iraq War (1980-1988), Reagan supported Iraq, supplying them with sufficient weaponry to prolong the ghastly conflict, whilst the technology it received from the U.S. was later used to develop chemical weapons. Indeed, when that wily old hawk Donald Rumsfeld visited Iraq in 1983 and shook Saddam Hussein's hand it was at a time when Iraq was using chemical weapons against Iran (a meeting Rumsfeld became distinctly nebulous about when he was seeking to rally support for the 2003 offensive against Iraq).

The chaos in the Middle East found no balanced or reasoned argument from the Reagan administration, its measures exacerbating the situation when Israel invaded Lebanon in 1982, killing some 20,000 people, able to do so through the support of the U.S. government. And for all Reagan's self-righteous posturing about Christian values and American decency, it had blood on its hands in 1985 when a car bomb exploded outside a mosque in Beirut, killing 80 people, mostly women and children, and injuring some 200 others. It had been meant for a senior Muslim figure, set off by the C.I.A. after authorisation by its then Director, William Casey.

For Hicks, a man acutely aware of the connection between all the world's people, he saw America the superpower as having a responsibility in that world. Yet the American Dream was being soured, degraded by its government's foreign policy, which seemed little more than an endeavour to become the "bullies of the world." An America public, which had never come to terms with the disaster of the Vietnam War, was willingly complicit in this shaping of America as a mighty force, a vocal majority fervent in their support of Reagan's policies. Though Hicks used "bullies of the world" in the context of America's intervention against Iraq in 1991, it is a routine well aware of the previous decade and the Reagan administration's selling of weapons to poor nations whilst at the same time challenging nations substantially weaker militarily. The terminology is particularly appropriate as it is generally accepted that a bully's actions are the result of low self-esteem, and this can be seen with pre-Reagan America, imbued with a deep sense of insecurity after the failures of Vietnam and debacle of the Iranian Embassy siege. The "bullies of the world" angle was particularly pertinent when, on October 23rd 1983, a suicide bomber killed 240 U.S. marines in Beirut, and to assuage the country's wounded pride Reagan picked on easy target by invading Grenada two days later. On the premise of the threat of Cuba gaining influence after a military coup, 7,000 troops invaded the little country for an easy campaign that ended in December and resulted in a pro-West government being installed.

In 1986 the covert sale of arms to Iran was uncovered, revealing that funds had been used to arm guerrillas trying to overthrow the Nicaraguan government. The C.I.A. had organised the Contra rebels against the democratically elected Sandanista government, which had overthrown the previously corrupt, but U.S. backed regime in 1979.

Right from the beginning of his presidency, Reagan had begun a war against the Sandanistas, in 1981 giving $19 million to the Contras, covertly via the C.I.A. The Sandanistas aimed to work for the country's poor and gained praise from worldwide health organisations for the progress they were making. Democratic elections were held in Nicaragua in November 1984 involving seven different political parties, yet Reagan continued to demonise them as a dictatorship, ably assisted by an unquestioning media. Even when the Sandanistas won with 67% of the popular vote, the U.S. papers called it a fraud and Reagan continued diverting funds to the Contra rebels.

In the hearings that followed, dubbed 'Irangate', it was shown that key documents had been destroyed and that both Reagan and vice president George Bush were shown to be complicit in illegally getting funding to the Contra rebels in Nicaragua, rebels who had committed murder and torture throughout the country. Between 1981 and 1985 the Contras murdered 3,346 Nicaraguan children and teenagers and killed one or both the parents of 6,236 children (27). Both the World Court and the U.N. Security Council condemned the U.S., only to be dismissed by a Republican party as insular as it was narrow-minded. Hicks was enough aware of the truth of what was happening to call events in Nicaragua and other South American countries a "genocide" and label Reagan "a mass murderer." Much of the money that went to the Contras came from drug trafficking, which the Reagan administration knew of, but didn't seem to feel impinged on the

Just Say No campaign. Yet there were no consequences for Reagan; riding on patriotism's stupefacient enchantments and seemingly oblivious to criticism, he became known as "the Teflon president" (he had even survived an assassination attempt in 1981 by the Jodie Foster obsessed John W. Hinkley).

For Hicks, Reagan was creating a soulless America: " 'Conscience'. Look it up in a pre-Reagan dictionary" (3), he advised. This was an America going against everything that Hicks stood for, going against the ideals of the American Dream, projecting an image across the world of an uncaring, bigoted and unimaginative country. For Hicks it was frustrating that very few people seemed to share his view, even when it wasn't difficult to see the foolishness of Reagan's policies, like relaxing gun laws in 1986 when the country was seeing more and more incidents of individuals going on shooting sprees. But the right wing National Rifle Association had found an ally in Reagan whose view of American gun culture was wrapped up in some kind a mythical John Wayne vision of guns righting wrongs rather than killing innocents.

Undoubtedly, the Reagan-years shaped Hicks' comedy, allowing him to expose ironies with skill and perception. He saw through the façade of consumer spending and technological innovation, a façade exposed in 1986 with two dramatic events. In January the space shuttle exploded on take off, scattering the debris of billions of dollars that could have been spent feeding and clothing the poor of the world. Then in April the nuclear reactor disaster at Chernobyl saw radiation spread over Europe. It was indication of the smallness of the world, of how we are all sharing the same space on Earth and therefore are responsible to each other for it. In October 1987, "Black Monday" saw stock markets around the world crash, uncovering the fragile foundations on which Reagan had built America's economy. Though the repercussions even impacted on the self-absorbed yuppie culture, there seemed to be no accountability in corporate America (perhaps a blip in profit forecasts, whereas for some it meant the loss of a job).

The entertainment industry, vibrantly driving the culture in the 1970s, now offered no challenge to Reagan's presidency or his ideology. Hicks had cited 1980 – quite deliberately, being the year Reagan was first elected - as the beginning of "a certain anti-intellectualism" in America. Intellectualism is, if not to be feared, to be mistrusted, for it is the foundation for independent thought and self-awareness, leading to a situation where – God forbid – people might actually question what they are told. Thus, popular culture becomes not a theatre for edifying debate and reasoned argument, but a mesmerising narcotic, its ephemeral hits characterised by over simplification and gratuitous pleasure, and predominantly tied to a right wing agenda.

The Republican ideology was prevalent in the types of movies being produced throughout the decade. Indeed, films such as *First Blood* (1982), *Missing In Action* (1984), *Rambo* (1985) and *Top Gun* (1986) played up to it with jingoistic re-writing of America's involvement in the Vietnam War and subsequent conflicts. *Top Gun* was the type of empty no-brainer gloss that represented the 1980s. Directed by Tony Scott after a career making adverts, it amounted to little more than an expensive commercial for how great America was. These films chimed in neatly with Reagan's bullying of small countries around the world, offering a re-assertion of America's might, tagged with an easily digestible moral standpoint and a clear distinction between good and evil. So, when terrorists exploded a bomb in a nightclub in Germany in 1986, killing one U.S. serviceman, Reagan decided, without evidence, that Libya's Colonel Khadafi was responsible and sent planes over to bomb Libya, killing one hundred people. It's a neat and plausible cause and effect scenario, but one that is superficial and highly dishonest, yet it generally goes unchallenged in the anti-intellectual climate of Reagan's America.

As the decade progressed the feel good factor switched to a slew of baby movies like *Three Men And A Baby* (1987), *Baby Boom* (1987) and *Look Who's Talking* (1989). Hicks would answer these films with routines mocking the joys of childbirth: "it's no more a miracle than eating food and a turd coming out of your ass." These films linked in with Reagan's religious conviction that the family was everything in American society, celebrating the joys of parenthood despite the problem of the world's growing population. Once again, Hicks swims against the tide with his, "There's too many people in the world. Someone needs to say that, *by the way*…Let's work out this food/air deal." For Hicks, an attitude that promotes children as the most important things in life is dangerous because not only does it ignore the bigger environmental picture, but it also becomes a convenient emotive tool for governments. Thus, the ideology of placing children first allowed Reagan to campaign against drugs because they were a danger to children, giving him a reason to spend endlessly on the military in order to save the nation's progeny from an apparent Soviet threat.

Television wasn't going to change anything either, and certainly stand-up wasn't offering a fight with comedians doing predictable jokes about Reagan the former actor, but rarely tackling his policies. The Republican

102

agenda was infiltrating television too, dominated by a happy all-American perspective that ignored the problems of the world. First it had been NBC's *Diff'rent Strokes* (1978 - 1986) with its saccharine charm and moralistic political correctness. In it, a wealthy, white, single parent takes in two black children, a premise for subsequent episodes centred on family values and good Christian morals. The distance between television and the real world was never more apparent in the ironic fate of the cast of *Diff'rent Strokes*. Todd Bridges, the older brother, Arnold, got into drugs whilst cutesy Gary Coleman, the show's Willis, found little work after the show had finished, sued his parents and punched a fan who asked for his autograph. Dano Plato, who played the wholesome white daughter Kimberley, went on to appear in *Playboy* magazine and in 1992 tried to hold up a video store, eventually dying aged 34 from a drugs' overdose.

Hicks hated *Diff'rent Strokes* for its falseness, some of his most vicious drug fuelled rants distracted by his lambasting of audiences for making the programme so popular. One 1983 episode even had Nancy Reagan making a guest appearance in an anti-drugs plotline, pushing her own *Just Say No* campaign, sanctimoniously supported by the main characters.

The same family values were apparent in its generic successor, the number one hit, *The Cosby Show*, which had begun in 1984. It fitted right in with the Reagan years, its middle class black couple enjoying their affluence amid homely tales, shows ending with a warm, everything's going to be all right feel, completely ignoring the realities of African-American life with its institutionalised racism and crack problems. Similarly, there was the yuppie wet dream of *Thirtysomething* (1987-1991); for Hicks a collection of "whiney white people" whose trivial life problems were elevated to big issues through sentimental contemplation.

These were shows wholeheartedly towing the conservative ideology. Some had pretensions to addressing issues like single parenthood, as in *Who's The Boss* (1984-1992) in which widower Tony Danza and his daughter moved in with a divorced woman and her son. Danza's character was a celebration of stupidity, the American male still into football and chicks but with a sensitive, caring side, making him a regular guy and an upstanding citizen. It was okay to be like him, okay to be dumb as long as you were anti-drugs and pro-children. In effect the show said, 'Aren't we all just like this really?' It fitted in with Reagan's presentation of himself as an ordinary citizen, one of the people. Of course, shows always ended with an affirmation of family values, the same white Christian morals as the comparative *Full House* (1987-1995). Another of Hicks' pet hates, *Full*

House concerned a former sports reporter, Danny, who'd turned to hosting a morning talk show. His wife had died, leaving him with three young girls to raise, a task aided by a musician and a comedian, as well as Danny's girlfriend; all congregated under one roof (hence the deliriously clever title, *Full House*). These characters all represent role models set against corny, preachy plot lines oozing with self-satisfaction.

Similar in concept was *My Two Dads* (1987-1990) an execrable exercise in new man sensitivity, the kind that made comedians like Hicks and Kinison want to go the other way, to offend in the worst ways possible regardless of political correctness. Here we have two men who could both be father to an orphaned girl whose mother had been seeing both males. Plots generally involved the men meeting women before deciding that the little girl was the only female they needed. Again, we have the dumb honesty, the idea that as long as you're a good family person it's okay to not be engaged with real issues.

If it wasn't the ostentatious affluence of shows like *Dallas* (1978-1991), television served up dumb, escapist adventures with tough heroes like *T.J. Hooker* (1982-1987), *Hunter* (1984-1991), *MacGyver* (1985-1992) or *The A-Team* (1983-1987), whilst *Miami Vice* debuted in 1984 and became an instant hit. This macho show was a paean to consumer culture, filled with expensive cars, clothes and synthetic music. Guns, car chases and explosions substituted intellect and the good guys always won.

The trend continued with Bush carrying on Reagan's policies in the late eighties/early nineties. Though they would see themselves as dealing with social issues, shows like *Beverly Hills 90210* (1990-2000) and *Blossom* (1991-1995) used stories on racism, homophobia and drugs as mere window dressing, their political correctness coming up with the obvious conclusions that racism was bad as well as still pushing the idea that drugs were unquestionably wrong. The former concerned the lives of rich middle class kids and had token gestures to liberalism, the kind of self-satisfied liberalism that doesn't involve doing anything about social problems other than saying its bad. *Blossom*, starring Joey Lawrence – an actor Hicks called "that little Tony Danza wannabe" – concerned a divorced father with three children, one a former drug addict. In one vomit inducing anti-drugs episode a small amount of marijuana is found and there is suspicion it might belong to the youngest child, Blossom, or the former drug addict, Anthony. The plot develops predictably with both children eschewing and condemning drugs, and Anthony offering a little morality tale about a friend whose marijuana use led to heroin addiction (implying that it always does).

Television seemed to reach the bottom of the barrel with the baffling success of *American Gladiators* (1989-1996); a show in which individuals go into 'gladiatorial' combat with weapons such as padded sticks. Hicks found much amusement in this show with its "pituitary retards" and its bewildering appeal to Americans. It seemed to him to exemplify everything that was bad about America, using it as a prime example of people not wanting to think: "Go back to bed America. Here, here's fifty-six channels of *American Gladiators*." It was another show where Americans could indulge in a fantasy mock-heroic world and leave the real one outside of their living rooms.

Music was equally atrocious during this period, to Hicks some "kind of Reagan wet dream". On the one hand there was the bubble haired soft rock of bands like Bon Jovi and Motley Crue competing with the equally anodyne synthetic music arriving from Britain and the happy bright world of Wham's *Wake Me Up Before You Go Go* (see Chapter 10).

Music had a fake conscience in 1984, the famine crisis in Ethiopia prompting Band Aid's *Do They Know It's Christmas?* charity record and USA For Africa's *We Are The World* in 1985. The American one is perhaps more offensive with preening pop stars all glammed-up in the video. 1985 also saw rock and roll being branded "the devil's music" with people like Pat Robertson and Jimmy Swaggart criticizing rock music and Ronald Reagan invoking the founding fathers as people who would not believe that "the violent and malevolent would be given free rein to prey upon our children." It was also the year that the parents of John McCullom attempted to sue Ozzy Osbourne claiming that his song *Suicide Solution* had inspired their son to commit suicide. A similar case followed in 1986 when two families sued the band Judas Priest over their 1978 album *Stained Glass*, claiming it had encouraged their sons to commit suicide. Hicks' would wonder at the logic of rock stars wanting their fans dead as he sarcastically took up the voice of a rock star saying he'd had enough of the money, sex and drugs and devising a plan to get the audience to kill themselves. It was a logic ignored by the media as it wrapped itself up in analysis of song lyrics to debate whether they were violent and dangerous. Hicks coldly concluded from the suicides that there were now "two less gas station attendants in the world." A harsh verdict, but it was the stupidity of the suicides he was targeting, the way they were unable to think for themselves: the lasting trait of the entertainment industry in Reagan's America.

Enough moral panic was caused for Tipper Gore to form the Parents Music Resource Centre (P.M.R.C.). This organisation campaigned for warning stickers to be placed on albums that contained swearing and adult themes, successfully forcing the music industry to adopt the practice from November 1985. Yet for all this outrage, the music making the charts was cheery and harmless. Perhaps the anthem of the era was Bobby McFerrin's 1988 hit *Don't Worry, Be Happy*, which could almost be re-titled "Go back to bed America."

Hicks, raging against the tide of popular opinion, was deeply critical of this "Lying b-actor dickweed," bewildered at the level of good will Reagan received, dumbfounded that "this b-actor fucking illiterate bozo looking fuck can't be the president of the country can he?" For Hicks he was "a liar...cocksucking fascist" and to the public call to have him put on Mount Rushmore, Hicks returned "Let's put him *under* Mount Rushmore."

Here was a new Hicks emerging, one that had undergone a drug fuelled catharsis and was now on a mission to expose the machinations and self-interest of those in power, not just for laughs, but also to empower those who came to see his shows, to empower them with the truth that he hoped would accelerate social change.

1987 saw further progress with a short appearance on Rodney Dangerfield's *Nothing Goes Right* TV special. Dangerfield had moved in Lenny Bruce's circles, and had given career breaks to Sam Kinison and Andy Kaufman. Although something of a wife and mother-in-law comedian, he possessed intuitive comic instincts and was always on the look out for an opportunity to give exposure to young comedians. The Dangerfield special offered Hicks a chance to be more of himself than his previous television appearances on Letterman had allowed. Though his subsequent segment mainly, and rather inoffensively, mocks Southern culture, Hicks is allowed to swear, smoke on stage and do his rant against non-smokers. Despite not being the big break he would have hoped for, it did show television audiences a darker side of Hicks, cast as the unrepentant smoker in a country subservient to health and cleanliness, the contrast getting him good notices and more work.

As the gigging and partying continued there was an increasing power about Hicks' performances, involving apocalyptic visions with a gun-toting Jesus, the mocking of Jimmy Swaggart and Reagan and his violent routines about killing talentless celebrities like Barry Manilow. The more angry he got, the more Hicks accurately skewered targets, emerging as a fresh voice and gaining critical praise if not mass popularity.

The Houston Post magazine had Hicks on the front cover of its September 20th 1987 issue with the headline *Bill Hicks Houston's king of comedy*. The article shows just how far Hicks had come, and how he had gained the admiration of his peers with John Farnetti commenting, "There is Bill Hicks, and then there is everybody else." He is sat on a chair, leaning forward, mouth open and poised, as if a barking preacher intent on telling the truth. The photograph shows everything about Hicks' confidence and intent. He was about to embark on his quest to slay the Republican beast.

9
Out Of The Whirlwind

Hicks was on a mission, 1988 a turning point as his anger became more focused, channelled increasingly towards exposing the deceitfulness of those in government and the way the media works for those in power, continually puzzled by the lack of questioning from his countrymen. In an interview early in the year he asked, "Aren't people frustrated by the lies they are being told daily in the name of God and country?" (26). He saw those lies and felt it his mission to enlighten others: "As long as I'm going to live in this world, I might as well make it the most enjoyable and fun and fair place I can make it." More than ever he was the cowboy hero from his youth, the Kwai Chang Caine seeking to right injustices.

Despite finding increased exposure through a preponderance of television shows devoted to comedy, he remained fearless, making no attempt to manufacture a cuddly persona so he could land a TV sit-com or movie. His dark poet wasn't going to conform, but he was beginning to question his reliance on drugs and drink. After moving back to New York, he quit drugs and alcohol in January 1988, leaving chain smoking as his only vice.

Post drugs saw the most productive period of Hicks' career, adding to the sustained gigging with several minor television appearances. Amid this, in the summer off 1988, Hicks had an opportunity to appear in his first film, albeit one – *Comedy's Dirtiest Dozen* – which involved a short slot alongside various other stand-up comedians. The makers wanted 'dirty' in the sense of swearing and blue material, amply supplied by the majority of the featured comedians. Looking at the finished product, Hicks seems somewhat incongruous amongst the likes of Tim Allen doing lame jokes about the differences between men and women and the male interest in burping, shitting and grabbing their crotches. Otto and George is an act where the dummy, George, substitutes wit for frequent reference to blow jobs as the ventriloquist moves his lips. At the bottom of the barrel is the show's last act, Jackie "The Jokeman" Martling, whose traditional gag telling style of getting the punch lines out with minimal set-up is reminiscent of adolescents in schoolyards. His material is not much better, merely a collection of juvenile sex gags and innuendos.

It's a pretty lame film, notable only for Hicks and an appearance by 21-year-old Chris Rock, who does some socially conscious and funny material on the possibilities of Jesse Jackson becoming president and the fears of white America. Hicks stands out from the other comedians. There is no sunny side to his performance, no attempt to use false warmth to get on the audience's side. Introduced by host Ben Creed as "a comic, a poet, a revolutionary" Hicks immediately has his sights set higher than dirty sex jokes as he criticises the media's coverage of drugs stories before attacking Ronald Reagan, pondering what it would take to kill him: "A syringe of A.I.D.S. shot in your eyeball? I'll do it. A trident missile shot up your fascist, evil, mean-spirited, corporate puppet, devil, cock-sucking ass? Where's the button?"

We find the more political, revolutionary Hicks emerging in the short interviews which feature with the closing credits as he talks about the film being "a great opportunity because I want to say some things that capitalist networks won't allow me to say." Ever the idealist, this is the mission statement of a stand-up more and more taking the role of a social commentator.

After a campaign coloured by negativity and cynicism, the election of George Bush in 1988 only compounded Hicks' anger and determination to speak the truth. Figures show that from 1968 to 1988 the average length of a TV news soundbite allotted to a presidential candidate fell from 43 seconds to 9.8. Meanwhile, pictures of candidates with no words tripled (28). The political debate came second; it was image over issues, a continuation of the "anti-intellectualism" Hicks cited, the culture and its media pandering to people unable or unwilling to think about ideas. A survey before the election showed the American public's disillusionment with politics, revealing that two thirds wanted candidates other than Bush or his Democrat rival, Michael Dukakis. This lack of faith in the political process was reflected in another turnout of only about 50% of those eligible to vote. The country saw no use in the electoral system. It didn't seem to change anything. Hicks recognised this, the feeling that his views and those of millions of other Americans were being ignored. Other comedians seemed more inclined towards the safe option of mocking vice president Dan Quayle, particularly after he had participated in a spelling bee at a school in New Jersey and spelt potato with an "e" on the end. Quayle was an easy target, regularly delivering nonsensical comments like "I believe we are on an irreversible trend toward freedom and democracy, but that could change." Though Hicks too mocked Quayle for his stupidity, it was only a small part of his anti-Quayle/Bush material and he was more concerned with exposing the way Bush continued with Reagan's evil policies whilst the American public took it unquestioningly up the ass. Hicks' rants continued to alienate audiences, but it didn't bother him. At least he was eliciting a reaction to contrast with the general apathy of Americans.

Hicks was anything but apathetic, his hectic touring schedule seeing him play small backwater towns all across American, doing what he would call his "flying saucer tour." In addition to the touring he began recording material for his first album, *Dangerous*, material that would see him more than ever identified as a social commentator and mark his separation from the humour of Sam Kinison and the Outlaw Comics.

Bush, for Hicks "a child of Satan", was to carry on with Reagan's right wing agenda. As a former director of the C.I.A. his hands were already dirtied by his involvement in the Iran Contra affair, his policies and interventions in central America making him, in Hicks' view "a mass murderer". What made Hicks dislike him even more was his willingness to maintain the status quo of the Reagan years with the War On Drugs, the anti-abortion pro-family stance and the use of American strength in interfering with events in other countries. He had no time for environmental issues, an attitude as insular as Reagan's seen in 1992 when Bush wouldn't sign a treaty protecting endangered plants and animals, saying it would "retard technology" despite 172 other nations agreeing to the treaty. Continued spending on the military did not address the failing domestic economy or the rise of inner city violence, but by creating enemies in Central America and the Middle East, Bush's military expenditure was justified as protecting the good Christian people of the United States.

The ideology was wrapped up in the same patriotic fervour as Reagan, as seen in June 1989 when the U.S. Supreme Court decided in favour of the rights of U.S. citizen Gregory Johnson to burn the American flag. President Bush announced he wanted to amend the constitution to prohibit flag desecration. Much national debate ensued with ruminations on what the verdict meant, along with outrage from those who argued that people had fought in wars and died for the flag. Hicks saw the whole debate as a smokescreen, an elevation of something trivial in order to ignore urgent and important issues. It revealed to Hicks the "retarded nation that we are" noting that "No one has ever died for a flag...They might have died for freedom, which by the way, is the freedom to burn the fucking flag." Beyond the obvious irony of "My daddy died in the Korean War for that flag...What a coincidence, mine was made in Korea" is an indictment of an

American Dream cheapened by consumerism and distorted by false patriotism. A flag that should represent belonging and the aspirations of its people (as when it was planted on the moon) has been reduced to a political tool and a means to manipulate opinion.

The Flag Protection Act of October 28th 1989 saw many protests involving rituals of flag burning, many including Vietnam veterans, individuals who'd suffered most in the name of the flag. Arrests followed, wasting time and resources as, when the cases were brought to prosecution, courts threw them out, citing the Act as being unconstitutional. It wasn't to end there though. This petty issue continued throughout the 1990s until June 24th 1999 when the House passed the constitutional amendment outlawing flag desecration.

Hicks had been doing the comedy club circuit relentlessly since the late 1970s, yet his exposure in America had been minimal. He hadn't added to his three previous Letterman show appearances since February 1986 when his routine had been cut. Though this had left him frustrated and vowing never to go back, *Late Night With David Letterman* had allowed Hicks to tap into his natural audience of hip, young liberals. Subsequent short television appearances had reached only a small audience and he had never been given a chance to show his full repertoire to a viewing public. Moreover, other comedians such as Eddie Murphy had moved passed Hicks after finding success on *Saturday Night Live* in the early eighties. Like Hicks, Murphy was born in 1961, but his rise to stardom was certainly more rapid with his first album *Eddie Murphy* released in 1982, his film debut in *48 Hours* the same year and a concert film, *Delirious*, released in cinemas in 1983. Murphy's physical comedy and material on the black experience saw him as a natural successor to Richard Pryor, though there was something about Murphy that was too in tune with the affluence and glossy self-interest of the decade, not only in homophobic and sexist material, but in garish clothes and arrogant delivery. He certainly wasn't as controversial as Pryor, making him much sought after by television shows and movie producers.

It wasn't just Murphy who had seemingly leap-frogged Hicks. Richard Jeni, featured in the Hicks Channel 4 documentary *It's Just A Ride*, and a clever observer of the human condition, used physical comedy, sound effects and a frenetic delivery, and after starting in 1982 had secured a half hour special in 1989 with *Richard Jeni: The Boy From New York* (though he threw away artistic integrity with his commercials for Certs the same year). Meanwhile, Billy Crystal, who'd featured at L.A.'s Comedy Store in the 1970s, had progressed from the TV series *Soap* and a successful appearance on *Saturday Night Live* in 1984 to movies and his own TV special *Midnight Train To Moscow* in 1989.

Jerry Seinfeld, another comedian who'd been starting out with Hicks at L.A.'s Comedy Store in the early 1980s, was also taking off, winning the American Comedy Awards' Best Male Stand-Up in 1988 before his hit show *Seinfeld* debuted in July 1989. Roseanne Barr, who'd started on the comedy circuit in the early 1980s found her niche when her show *Roseanne* debuted in 1988. The show was a feminist, liberal sit-com based on a blue-collar family and its struggles to survive in Bush's America. It subverted the genre, fearless in its exposition of the reality of family life, tackling issues in a non-portentous way, a million miles from *The Cosby Show* and its reassuring warmth. Hicks had no wish to find a sit-com like Seinfeld or Barr, but within the genre's confines, these two comedians were at least pursuing their own vision without compromise and being recognised for their originality.

Nonetheless, Hicks' time gigging in New York, Los Angeles, San Francisco and a multitude of other places across America had honed his skills. He was supremely confident in front of audiences of all types, his mind – from hours spent travelling between gigs and staying in hotel rooms – sharply aware of the minutiae of life; rich with experiences and ideas. From out of the whirlwind of his drugs' years was emerging a new Hicks, more focussed than ever on waking people up to what was happening in the world.

A realisation that television wasn't going to offer him the exposure his contemporaries were enjoying created the need for Hicks to do it himself. On 14th July 1989 at The Laff Stop, Austin, Kevin Booth and David Johndrow filmed Hicks' stage performance, for the first time with a view to broadcast and release. The show sees Hicks at the crossroads, a point where he is marginalizing the dick jokes and becoming more political. Filmed for Austin's public access station ACTV, *Sane Man* begins with a montage of grainy footage of Hicks shuttling between venues, his voice-over wearily saying, "God help me. I'm so tired. I need my sleep. I make no bones about it. I need eight hours a day, and at least ten a night." It seems to acknowledge the point Hicks is at in his career and perfectly captures a hard working, relentlessly gigging Hicks about to unleash his most explosive comic moments to date.

He enters the darkened stage dressed in black shirt and jeans, indicative of the little dark poet persona, the truth teller he had been developing, emerging to Bob Dylan's *Subterranean Homesick Blues*, playfully and confidently strumming along. Through his waffle house routine, we see Hicks attacking the prevalent "anti-intellectualism" in America as he confronts a waitress astonished that he is bothering to read when he could just "flip on the tube." She is symptomatic of the Reagan/Bush era, of a culture metaphorically waiting to be *given* direction via the easiest option: television. It's not that she views reading as uncool, it is that she *really* is baffled by Hicks' desire to read, so inebriated is she by an apathetic culture where no questions need be asked, therefore knowledge is redundant. Hicks is equally baffled by the waitress' attitude, needing to contemplate his response to the seemingly overwhelming and profound question she poses, "Why read?" But whereas she cannot fathom his purpose, her inertia conveyed by a repetitive chewing of gum, Hicks determines to reach a conclusion, albeit one that is meant to bludgeon her senses awake: "I guess I read for a lot of reasons, but the main reason is so I don't become a fuckin' waffle waitress."

As an antidote, Hicks smoothly moves on to poking fun at his own Southern background, talking of road signs that say, "speed limit enforced by aircraft", able to see the absurdity of life - a thread that ran throughout his career, perhaps a driving force. Humans take life too seriously and invest too much time being concerned with unimportant things. When introducing the topic of smoking he seems to be whipping up the crowd to mock smokers, like some PC comic as he talks about coughing up a "flim". He questions how many non-smokers there are in the audience, getting them to cheer before altering perceptions with " what a bunch of whining little maggots," nonchalantly pulling out of cigarette. This is the dark little poet, a man on a mission to change the way people perceive things.

The performance shows the various influences on Hicks coming together cohesively. The free-flowing association of Sahl, Bruce and Allen is evident as Hicks paces the stage, scanning the audience, linking material on waffle houses and dirt for sale, returning to the riffs in later routines, reciting parts of the Dylan lyric in pauses. Here is a confident Hicks, transmitting his ease to the audience, warming them up to let them in.

The use of props and the physical comedy of Kinison and Pryor can be seen as Hicks recounts being pulled over by cops and made to prove he isn't drunk, walking then skipping a straight line, miming getting his dick out and putting it into an exhaust pipe and using the stool as the driving seat of a car.

His drugs routine has evolved into a political statement of freedom, mocking George Bush's assessment that "we are losing the war on drugs," by taking up the implication that the creative, high people must therefore be winning. Keith Richards still living shows the grey area in the government presentation of drugs, seamlessly leading into his material on rock stars with a scathing attack on George Michael and other manufactured, corporate musicians. From the stupidity of Southern types, Hicks has moved onto the stupidity of the masses buying into the music of people like George Michael.

There is a joy in this performance with Hicks back in familiar territory after two years, perhaps most obvious when he goes into his Elvis routine, wiping his brow with objects from the stage and from the audience, drawling "Brand new Cadillac" and wiggling his hips.

Hicks perfectly builds the crescendo, using pauses, asides and throwaway riffs as he moves towards attacks on Reagan and new president George Bush, using his bent over body to show the Reagan/Quayle/Bush axis fucking the country. Despite running on a campaign of not raising taxes, Bush, another of those government "lying cocksuckers" called for them to be raised in the first year of his presidency.

During the Reagan years, with Hicks partying and not quite getting his ideology into a sharp enough focus and with his lack of exposure on television, there is a sense that Hicks didn't say enough of what he wanted to say about his hatred of Republicanism. Now that he had found his political voice and the possibilities of his ironic perspective, it was as if Hicks were a comedic sniper constantly targeting the Bush administration and waiting for evidence of its evil. There was plenty.

Like Reagan, Bush was to employ America's military strength in bullying smaller countries. He ordered the invasion of Panama in December 1989 to arrest General Manuel Noriega and take him to the U.S. for drug trafficking offences where he received a 40-year prison sentence. Noriega, a brutal dictator, had been a friend of the U.S. during its support of the Contras in Nicaragua. Over 2,000 people were killed in the invasion, including 23 Americans, which resulted in a pro-American government being installed.

Sane Man sees the birth of the new Hicks, a collection of life experiences and observations to draw from, unfettered by distractions as he focuses on what needs to be said. The show is tied up beautifully with "You know all that money we spend on nuclear weapons and defence every year. Trillions of dollars, correct? Instead, *instead*, just play with this...." He convulses, to shake the rage against apathy from his body, to plead desperately that humanity will evolve and see his vision: " If we spent that money feeding and clothing the poor of the world – and it would pay for it many times over, not *one* human being excluded – we could, as one race, explore outer space together, in peace, forever." One stark figure from the Reagan years illustrates Hicks' point perfectly, that according to Ruth Sivard's *World Military and Social Expenditures 1987 - 1988*, the $1.5 billion spent on the Trident nuclear submarine programme was enough to finance a five-year programme of child immunization around the world, preventing five million deaths from deadly diseases (25). It's a theme that has continued to resonate long after Hicks' death, with the United Nations' annual Human Development Report (June 1997) estimating the wealth of the world's richest seven countries could be used to end world poverty and provide socials services for the quarter of the world who need it.

Hicks' final words in *Sane Man* are a powerful summary of the policies of Reagan and Bush. The defence budget remained high and tax cuts were only being made to make the rich even richer. By 1989 the chief executive officers (C.E.O.s) of corporations were making 93 times as much as the average factory worker. In 1980 it had been 40 times as much (25). This is what it all meant, what ties the performance together: All the pettiness of humans, all the self-centred, blinkered and bigoted outlooks, all the little ironies we miss each day. If we could cast this aside, we could make a better world.

10
<u>When Music Had A Soul</u>

Now sure of his purpose and resolved to enlightening people, Hicks was putting on some awesome performances in 1989. Once more the Letterman show was drawn to him, and Hicks, acknowledging a need for his message to have greater exposure, agreed to appear on the show on 12th September, over three years since his segment had been cut. Coming out to The Rolling Stones' *Jumpin' Jack Flash*, Hicks strolls on nonchalantly, a leather jacket aligning himself to the bad boy history of rock and roll.

Hicks' segment shows how far he has developed as a performer since his last Letterman appearance. The six-minute slot had always been constricting to the digressing Hicks, but here he manages to touch on playing small towns on his UFO tour, smoking, bums and housekeeping in hotels, but still keeps it tied together with a theme of "anti-intellectualism" giving the routine the same cohesion as *Sane Man*.

By this stage in his career Hicks was known predominantly for his routines on smoking, drugs and rock music. His political material, now fully developed, was beginning to permeate more of his shows, and though the rock music riffs were decreasing, they were to remain as some part of his shows until the end of his career.

Bill Hicks has often been described as a rock n' roll comedian in that his comedy was fearless and anti-establishment, addressing issues relevant to a younger generation. Indeed, his constant use of the microphone and its stand (see Chapter Six) is something akin to the way rock stars use both them and their guitars as totems of individuality and snarling anger. As well as this, Hicks performed in two bands with Kevin Booth, the first being Stress in his high school years, and later, Marblehead Johnson (named after the biggest fish in a pond at Kevin Booth's family ranch). Not only did Hicks sing and play guitar on the film *Ninja Bachelor Party*, but Marble Head Johnson also recorded songs in early 1991 and released an eponymous album. He always had a desire to fuse comedy with rock music, using the track *Chicks Dig Jerks* on the *Relentless* album and employing mood music on both *Arizona Bay* and *Rant In E-minor*, giving the albums an hypnotic, dreamy feel. Though he appealed to the same audience demographic as that attending rock concerts, his inclusion of music was more due to seeing comedy as something beyond the traditions of a stand-up under a spotlight. He wanted the same sense of connection that music engendered, a bond between performer and audience that allows the sharing of ideas.

Hicks' love of rock music had its origins in his interest in Elvis Presley, moving on to blues rock guitarist Rory Gallagher and the theatrical, overblown rock of 1970s groups like KISS. Yet when he did routines on rock music, it wasn't the 1970s stars he cited but those from the 1960s.

For Hicks, that decade was a time "when music had a conscience and a soul", when music was original and potent and had a purity of spirit. He saw music as a universal language; able to connect people, as in The Beatles live broadcast of *All You Need Is Love* in 1967 connecting 400,000,000 people. In referencing the icons of 1960s music he bought into the mythology of heroes like John Lennon, Jimi Hendrix, Keith Richards and Bob Dylan, heroes who exemplified everything he loved about the medium.

In both Dylan and Lennon, Hicks saw the same idealism and revolutionary spirit he saw in his own viewpoint. As Dylan was the lone troubadour with protest songs aimed at the establishment, so Hicks was the lone voice of reason raging against the government and media. But it was Lennon he most often cited, the Lennon who in his Beatles career had told Maureen Cleaver in 1966, "Christianity will go. It will vanish and shrink. I needn't argue that; I'm right and I will be proved right. We're more popular than Jesus now." The strength of conviction is apparent with Hicks telling audiences, "You're wrong, get over it" whilst the idea of religion becoming unimportant is seen with Hicks' assertion that it is merely made up of "quaint superstitious and beliefs" that are "no longer relevant." Lennon's statement angered many Americans, particularly in the South where there were protests involving the burning of Beatles' records and Klu Klux Klan demonstrations at concerts; the same kind of over-the-top outrage that Hicks frequently mocked in his routines on Southern fundamentalists. The response to Lennon's statement revealed a narrow-mindedness and denial of freedom of expression that didn't want to debate the argument, but instead just dismiss it out of hand.

Hicks became more aware of Lennon with his listening to music in the early 1970s, at a time when Lennon had left The Beatles and was producing music as naked and open in its self-analysis as Hicks' comedy was in opening up the American psyche, leaving himself alienated from popular opinion. It was a period when Lennon became ever more political, a revolutionary hero for America's youth. He supported CND, protested against America's involvement in Vietnam and performed a song about

John Sinclair at a rally in support of Sinclair, manager of legendary rock band MC5, who had been given a 10-year prison sentence for possession of two marijuana joints. Songs like *Attica State* in protest at Governor Nelson's Rockefeller's brutal response to riots at the prison and *Angela*, in support of jailed black activist Angela Davis, added to Lennon's revolutionary credentials. He even contributed $75,000 to a group planning to disrupt the Republican National Convention of 1972. As almost a spokesman for a generation disenchanted with politicians, he was constantly harassed by the Nixon government; considered so subversive and influential that the F.B.I., fearing he could become the focus of left wing agitators seeking a popular and charismatic leader, opened a file on him. As well as closely tracking his movements, the F.B.I. attempted to have his visa terminated and use an old conviction for drugs as reason to deport him.

Lennon's belief in peace and his desire to spread an optimistic, idealistic vision of what humanity could aspire to were central parts of Hicks' philosophy. The timing of Lennon's death sealed Hicks' bond with Lennon, coming at a point when Reagan was moving into office and extinguishing the liberal voice of reason and all the hope that went with it.

In this respect, Lennon's death left the legend generally untarnished. Though critics could point up Lennon's arrogance and self-indulgence, for Hicks' he remained a pure and free spirit whose music was about enlightenment and progress. He didn't go on to become a caricature of himself, unlike KISS who hopped onto the 1980s soft rock, permed-hair bandwagon with dire songs like *Crazy Crazy Nights*.

Similarly, Jimi Hendrix's legend remains in tact due to his early death. Hendrix's appeal for Hicks is different to that of Lennon. To a dedicated guitarist like Hicks, Hendrix was *the* guitar God, a creative genius able to produce awesome, innovative sounds with his instrument: "Playing the guitar like no one else ever played it since. Fuck Eddie Van Halen, fuck Steve Vai, fuck these phoney soulless piece of shits." Hicks attacked contemporary guitar heroes because these musicians were from the bouffant-hair soft rock school that substituted long-winded, fast picking guitar solos for soul. At least Hendrix's elaborate and intense playing reflected the hedonistic, rock and roll lifestyle he led. It was the showman in Hendrix that most appealed to Hicks, the unfettered celebration of life through music. Playing guitar with his teeth, setting fire to it, wielding it like a phallic symbol, Hendrix had the power and stage presence Hicks aspired to. It is why Hicks so often references Hendrix in comic contrast to modern vacuous music, and why *Ninja Bachelor Party* includes a Hendrix clip as well as being dedicated to him.

In the great tradition of rock music, Hendrix had an insatiable appetite for sex and drugs, as if outside the law and unconcerned with popular opinion. In not being defined by hypocritical morality, Hendrix had that sense of rebellion perfectly in tune with Hicks' belief that his lifestyle was of no concern to anybody else, as it didn't hurt anybody else.

The same ethos is why Keith Richards is so often celebrated in Hicks' material. As guitarist with The Rolling Stones, Richards suffered the same establishment hounding as Lennon with frequent drug busts and harassment throughout the 1960s. Just as Hicks never went on to deny the pleasures of drug use, so Richards never grew into the old mature grandfather figure in rock, the one who would painfully and superficially regret his vast intake of drugs. Richards is the ultimate rebel, like Hendrix celebrating life through excess, separating him from the more pious and preening Mick Jagger. He is an icon in rock and roll mythology, synonymous with drugs and the freedom to do as he pleased. He's the man who pushed boundaries, went over the edge and found "there's a ledge beyond the edge." By not dying prematurely, Hicks could use him to poke holes in the arguments against drugs and smoking, his stamina celebrated by Hicks with a riff that after a nuclear war all that would be left is "Keith and bugs."

The fact that all Hicks' heroes took drugs and produced great music allowed him to contrast them with modern pop stars. He had little time for modern trends, although he did appreciate a wide range of different styles from Beethoven and Miles Davis to Frank Sinatra and John Hiatt. What riled Hicks about modern music was that it had no spirit or genuine feeling, yet just because the singers were upright and clean-living, many promoted them as good examples for the young, leading him to question, "since when did mediocrity and banality become a good image for your children?"

His love of rock music had grown at a time when it was still innovative and dangerous, but as he grew as a comedian music began its assimilation into the mainstream with the introduction of MTV on August 1st 1981, a channel devoted solely to music and music videos. It's first video, tellingly, was Buggles' *Video Killed The Radio Star*, heralding the dawn of an era when music became about image over content, with artists more concerned with ever-expensive videos like Michael Jackson's *Thriller* and Duran Duran's *Hungry Like The Wolf*, whereas for Hicks' heroes the music was what was important and any image engendered came from being themselves, not by design.

The 1980s was filled with vacuous pop artists and the regurgitation of old ideas, exemplified most succinctly by the early eighties medley craze like *Stars On 45*, where segments of old hits and musical genres were shamelessly cut together. The so-called "new British Invasion" began in 1982 with the Human League's *Don't You Want Me Baby*, bringing the synthesiser-pop then dominating the British charts across the Atlantic to clog up those in America. One of Hicks' earliest targets was Wham, whose *Wake Me Up Before You Go Go* arrived in 1984, Hicks responding to such manufactured happiness by imagining waking them up with gunshots at their sleeping bodies. Their songs and videos were a ghastly bright concoction, all jovial choruses and narcissistic responding to the camera. The antithesis of what Hicks believed music should be about, their phoniness was apparent in their empty-headed t-shirt slogans urging "Choose Life" (as detestable as the "ain't life keen" brigade Hicks mocked), and when they split in 1986 Hicks sarcastically mourned their demise by wrapping a microphone lead around his neck and feigning suicide. Hicks' anger was only further raised with lead singer George Michael's solo output. Michael sought acknowledgement as a serious artists, using some fake controversy like his song *I Want Your Sex* (1987) to stir this up. In December 1987 he introduced his new image with the song *Faith*, appropriating the leather jacket rock look and marrying it with stubble like some extra on *Miami Vice*. But he wasn't fooling Hicks who lambasted him as "a girl", and to the lyrics "You gotta have faith," retorted, "No, you gotta have talent." Yet *Faith* became the biggest single of 1988 in America.

It was an era of megastars in pop music, the likes of Michael Jackson and Madonna selling millions with their albums, part of a kind a rock royalty as seen at the Live Aid concert for Africa's starving where the appearance of performers like of Phil Collins and Queen resulted in increased record sales and the kudos of being seen as caring. For Hicks, the music and musicians merely had a "fake conscience" that betrayed the legacy of his 1960s heroes. If these stars really wanted to help the world's starving, then giving up some of their vast wealth would have gone a long way.

1987 also saw the emergence of 16-year-old "mall creature" Debbie Gibson with her first hit *Only In My Dreams*. Meanwhile 15-year-old Tiffany had made her first album, promoting it by performing in shopping malls, achieving a number one hit with the cloyingly coy *I Think We're Alone Now*. It wasn't just the music that offended Hicks, but the image these teenagers put across. Unlike the unforced innocence of teen acts from the 1950s, these juvenile stars carefully manufactured their image and music for commercial gain (pretty obvious with Tiffany placing herself alongside products in the consumer nirvana of malls). Both Tiffany and Gibson were wholesome, girls-next-door types, who denounced drugs and trumpeted family values, seemingly perfect products of Reagan's America.

From this teen music scene emerged New Kids On The Block, their *Hangin' Tough* of 1989 a laughable attempt to present themselves as rebellious. But this was a rebellion born out of image rather than attitude, one concocted only for the sake of sales. New Kids On The Block were just as eager to denounce drugs and lay on the family values angle with 1990's sugary ballad *This One's For The Children*.

The infiltration of these teen pop stars saw Hicks produce some of his darkest material in routines laced with violent imaginings. In many ways he was taking from the darker aspects of the music he loved; the reckless abandon of his heroes and their unrestrained kicking against the pricks. The "music with soul", as Hicks labelled it, did not seek to fascistically convert audiences to an upstanding life of virtue and conformity, more often than not employing lyrics which were a celebration of individuality and immorality (or, more pertinently, they joyously proclaimed their disdain for the constraints imposed by a hypocritical society). In opposition to Hicks' tastes were supposedly "moral" organisations like the P.M.R.C. making claims that such music was "the devil's music", a concept laughed at by Hicks as he announced a preference for good music and "surfing on the lake of fire" over an eternity in heaven with anodyne pop music. Once again, Hicks employs contrasts. Against the power of Hendrix standing "next to a mountain, chop it down with the edge of my hand" there is Debbie Gibson frivolously shaking her love. In Hicks' dark visions he has Hendrix's dick as "a buzz saw" either cutting Gibson in two, or raping both her and Tiffany and administering gunshots to other pop stars he finds offensive. It's a routine that sees Hendrix elevated from rock icon to avenging angel, becoming almost a deity through Hicks' suggestion of immense size and power. His role as a violent arbitrator of taste is akin to another Hicks routine where he has Jesus returning to Earth and blasting away hypocrites with an Uzi.

It seemed like there was an endless stream of one-dimensional pop acts seeping into the music charts. Rick Astley, another dark shadow in British pop history, had come to prominence by producing a series of number one hits that were difficult to separate in style and lyrics; each one backed with a monotonous, computer generated beat courtesy of ubiquitous producers Stock, Aitken and Waterman. Undoubtedly these were easy targets, but

Hicks felt the need to ridicule performers like Astley because their popularity seemed to him to suggest everything about the lowering of standards, and with his "one consciousness" perspective that meant that as these standards became the norm, it affected us all.

This pop music was false, seen most obviously in the rise to prominence of Milli Vanilli in 1989. After number one hits and awards it was uncovered that the duo had never sung on the records in the first place, an encapsulation of Hicks' belief that these artists were not interested in the music but in the fame and money that stardom gave them. These artists were manufactured for profit, "ball-less, soul-less corporate little bitches, suckers of Satan's cock." They had none of the artistic integrity of Hicks' heroes, no purpose other than to seek fame and fortune.

Beyond this there was something more insidious about their prevalence, Hicks seeing them as "demons set loose on the Earth to lower the standards for the perfect and holy children of God." This music didn't want to question or offend, but to reassure that everything was all right, to make people "happy consumers," like the state sponsored music in Orwell's *Nineteen Eighty-Four* with its "sentimental songs which were composed entirely by mechanical means" in order to keep the proles content. For Hicks, contemporary pop music was every bit as dangerous as governments in that it came with a shiny happy face, mendaciously suggesting it offered spiritual enlightenment. In denouncing drugs, this new generation of pop stars even had the gall to see themselves as social commentators, but they didn't seek the freedom of choice and conveying of injustices like Lennon, instead they were merely making statements that would gain them more record sales. They were tools of the government – "We're rock stars against drugs because that's what President Bush wants" – with no real convictions of their own, leading Hicks to link the New Kids On The Block with Nazis in that Hitler used the arts to convey his own ideology.

The endless conveyor belt of these pop stars and their subsequent financial success connected to a mall culture where people were happy consumers made indifferent to the world around them by the happy pop being offered, creating a situation where Hicks identifies Earth as "the third mall from the sun." From 1960s artists railing against the establishment, "The Man", this new breed were whoring for The Man, showing their true selves by doing adverts, "hawking" products to enlarge their bank accounts. Pepsi Cola had sponsored Madonna before it withdrew its support after the controversy of her 1989 *Like A Prayer* video whilst George Michael was selling Diet Coke. Meanwhile, Phil Collins and Eric Clapton, musicians with pretensions to artistic integrity, were hawking for Michelob.

Whereas the music of Hicks' heroes was about truth and honesty, these pop stars were aligning themselves with a medium that told lies. He couldn't imagine true rock stars doing commercials, conveying the absurdity of "It's Keith Moon for snickers" or "John Bonham for Certs." Again, Hicks calls on mythical rock rebels with Led Zeppelin drummer Bonham and The Who drummer Moon. Both played their rock star parts with their predilections for orgies, alcohol and drugs, smashing up hotels and throwing televisions out of windows, dying young from their excesses. These were anarchic individuals whose ethos may have been about self-interested hedonism, but who nonetheless would never have countenanced marketing that image – and thereby making it false – for advertising purposes. But then, contemporary trends suggested for Hicks that "we live in a backwards universe" one where Lennon can be murdered whilst the real villains like Barry Manilow are allowed to continue.

Over the years Hicks kept up with trends and changed those he targeted. When radio-friendly rapper MC Hammer (hawker of Kentucky Fried Chicken) emerged, Hicks saw through the argument that he was a good dancer, "The guy's got a sand crab in his knickers. He's not dancing; he's having a fit. That's Satan's sperm eating its way through the lining of his stomach." Vanilla Ice and Marky Mark, despite their pretensions to be something else, were in the same league, two white boy rappers seeking to project an image of themselves as dangerous, deep and edgy. For them, rebellion was not about challenging the establishment, but rather it meant moody photo shoots or getting drunk and fighting.

In contrast to the teen market was the adult middle of the road rock of such performers as Michael Bolton, who had a hit in 1990 with *How Am I Supposed To Live Without You?* In glossy videos he looked into the camera with big deep eyes in some kind of egotistical masturbation of his own looks, but for Hicks he could be tagged as nothing more than a "rodent appearing human." Such macho posturing was again evident with one Billy Ray Cyrus, the "jar-head, no talent cracker asshole." In the annals of rock music there is little to compare to the nadir that was his *Achy Breaky Heart*. Like some backwater hillbilly he strutted onto the world stage with his "fruity little ponytail" and found millions of adoring female fans. For Hicks, his appeal to women was similar to that of serial killer Ted Bundy, an appeal based on superficiality.

Hicks' fiery rant against corporate musicians on *Relentless* is one of the darkest and most passionate routines he ever did, a showcase for his detestation of music that regurgitates, blanderises, mollifies, and suffocates the visionary, the talented artist. Conformity and inoffensiveness are the results of a music industry only out to exploit and make money.

Hicks' shows often saw his appearance on stage accompanied by music, most frequently The Beatles, Jimi Hendrix and Bob Dylan. In subsequent years the link with rock has been reciprocated with many bands dedicating material to him or using samples. Tool cited Hicks as an influence on their *Undertow* album in 1993, whilst on *Aenima* (1996) they sampled his material and included a painting of him on the inside cover. He introduced Tool at the Lollapalooza tour in 1992, telling the audience to stand still as he'd lost a contact lens. The band Pitchshifter also sampled Hicks on their song *You Are Free* whilst Hamell On Trial's 1999 album, *Choochtown* includes a song, *Bill Hicks*, with lyrics wishing that Hicks were still alive. Other bands have included dedications, amongst them Super Furry Animals, Radiohead, Rage Against The Machine, and The Bluetones, whose lead singer Mark Morris does Hicks' "Brand new Cadillac" line at gigs, complete with Elvis' Southern drawl.

Despite not being particularly involved with contemporary music, Hicks did like bands such as Metallica and Nirvana and the angry anti-establishment stance of Rage Against The Machine, particularly the latter's *Killing In The Name* and its lyrical attack on those who kill in the name of religion (towards the end of his career, Hicks closed his shows with the last lines of *Killing In The Name*: "Fuck you, I won't do what you tell me"). His distance from music outside of the 1960s and 1970s is due to the way music can never really be as challenging as in those decades. Such is the dominance of MTV and its ilk that any modern trends are assimilated into the mainstream quickly, their potency subsequently blunted. Such is the corporate rush for money that innovative bands are signed up in their infancy and given little time to establish themselves before being dropped for commercial reasons.

Though Hicks' material at the end of the 1980s was more concerned with politics and humanity's evolution, his continued use of rock music as a comedic source fitted into his sense of anger that the public so easily bought into these terrible musicians. If the species to which he belonged chose these pop stars as its role models then he too was being denigrated by that society. Thus, audiences were ushered in to his comedy of hate and forced to undergo a catharsis, which he hoped would expel "all the shitty shit."

11
<u>The Comedy Of Hate</u>

There was to be no post-drugs, mellow incarnation of Hicks. After Reagan's departure from office he felt a profound sense of disbelief that the country could then vote in George Bush as successor. His abject disappointment and anger with America can be seen in a now notorious show at the Funny Firm in Chicago. When a female heckler shouts "You suck" Hicks launches into a fearsome tirade, his gravel-vocals burning with rage as he confronts the woman: "You fuckin' cunt, get out of here now...Fuck you, you idiot. You're everything that America should be flushed down the toilet...Go see fuckin' Madonna you fuckin' idiot piece of shit...I want you to go find a fuckin' soul."

During his alcohol and drug years there were many instances of Hicks verbally attacking audiences, but this wasn't just because he was loaded, as the Funny Firm gig shows. With this show there is little rest for Hicks as the heckling continues, becoming almost the main focus of his performance. When a male heckler interrupts, Hicks rifles back, "You come-sucking piece of shit," the only apparent sophistication being his ability to devise outrageous and original obscenities. It's a rage at America, at the way comedy audiences seem to be uninterested in the message, as if they are expecting the kind of performance they have seen on television where anger is tempered by warmth (more so with the plethora of other comedians on shows, but still true to a certain extent with Hicks' appearances on Letterman).

As a performer Hicks often commented on being part of the audience, so that when it seems they are ignorant to his message he is tarnished with the same complacent attitude. It creates a conflict between Hicks' intentions and the audience's expectations, what Will Kaufman identified as "the conflict between the urge to tell the truth and the comedic requirement of the playful untruth" (29). This urge to tell the truth, to put forward ideas society ignores or finds unpalatable, leads him to the darkest places where he can assert "People suck and there's too many of them and they're easier to kill when they're foetuses than when they're grown up." For Hicks, a population explosion that places a strain on the world's natural resources is something that "needs to be said", but rather than re-treading an argument that has seemingly provoked only an apathetic response, he seeks to shock audiences into an awareness of the message with the most brutal comedy. Yet this nihilism becomes a burden when Hicks feels audiences expect it to lead to some crude sexual image, another element of the aforementioned "conflict." In essence it's Hicks' desire to be more than just a dick joke comedian, hammering this home at the Funny Firm when he sarcastically sings, "I've got hours of dick jokes, I've got hours of come jokes." The heckling continues and Hicks seethes with "You've lost the ability to think, so fuck you! Go back to Gallagher…You fuckin' yuppie piece of shit." When an audience member asks, "So what's your point?" with a certain tone of superiority, quick as a flash Hicks is back with "Well, you're proving my point…The whole point is about mediocrity, but as I look around me I understand that some of you aren't going to get it." He mocks them as "fuckin' goat people" making goat noises, telling them that the reason the French like Jerry Lewis is because he's a typical stupid American. He detests their mediocrity because he sees it as conformity; an acceptance of a societal status quo that is at best self-satisfied, at worst complicit in allowing governments to carry out policies unchallenged, policies that extend to terrorism and genocide.

Hicks had to generalise with audiences and not just attack the minority of bigots because in all being "one consciousness" everyone was complicit, the narrow-minded views of the minority being given credence by the apathy of the majority. The only way for Hicks to wake them up was to rage against the audience as a whole, to provoke a reaction by whatever means necessary, be it through his dark imagery or the audience alienating invitation to lighten the mood by introducing the subject of abortion. It is method most succinctly pinpointed by writer John Lahr's assertion that "Hicks makes unacceptable ideas irresistible" (6), so that laughter – give or take those train wreck shows - shines light into his darkened world.

The climax of Hicks' anger at the Funny Firm reaches a darker level than even the incendiary last album *Rant In E-Minor* as Hicks' throaty vocals seem almost set to burst with "Hitler was right, he was just an underachiever! Kill them all Adolf! All of them! Jew, Mexican, American, white, kill them all! Start over! The experiment didn't work!" his desperation evident as he says, " I pray to God to kill these fuckin' people!" It seems to Hicks that reason no longer works and humanity cannot evolve because it has somehow got locked into an existence based on the lowest common denominator. For him, the only hope for the planet is to remove its most detestable creatures: "some people *need* to fuckin' die…they are riff raff: Thoughtless, mindless fuckin' herds of people, squandering this planet's valuable resources." His desperate fascistic proclamations are playing with an ideology at some distance from his own, but the idea nonetheless crops up in routines where he advocates the extermination of the musicians and TV stars he hates. It is also apparent when he responds to the possibility of aliens abducting rednecks: "Maybe we'll be lucky and it's some kind of sterility/dentistry program they've got going. Maybe they come down here, castrate you, straighten your teeth and split. Sort of a Clean Up The Universe pact." In this and "Kill them all Adolf!" Hicks is submitting a method to rid the world of those "that are tainting our collective consciousness," that are so dominating the culture that they are gradually subordinating the thinkers, liberals and "voices of reason" who could aid humanity's evolution. Of course, it's a joke, but Hicks is so exasperated by people's inability to see where an apathetic response to the lowering of standards is leading that castration and genocide are invoked to prompt a response; some kind of engagement with issues and questioning of his motives that will serve to counter complacency.

With Hicks, the anger is not superficial, not the kind employed by Denis Leary to create an edgy image. Nor is the anger merely used as a tool to shock audiences for the cheap laughter that derives from discomfort, but instead it emanates from a personal hurt that others are not willing to share his vision. As fellow comedian Riley Barber said, "What Bill is doing on stage is a direct reflection of what Bill is. It isn't derived from anywhere else" (30). The nakedness of his comedy, like the 1970s music of John Lennon, leaves open his soul. He has a beautiful vision of what life could be, but when audiences won't even let him get passed dick jokes and take them on that idealistic ride, he feels slighted. More than that, it is impotence, his purpose and readiness to prompt change suffocated at birth.

Although he had a big following in Austin, Chicago and San Francisco, generally in America he remained an anonymous figure during his lifetime. After years of tireless touring all across the country, playing to unresponsive audiences, Hicks can't help but feel angry and jaded, which is why there are performances where he begins with saying he is "tired of staring out at your vacant faces looking back at me waiting for me to fill your empty lives with humour" or prefaces shows by asking for time to "plaster on a fake smile and plough through this one more time." He is not acknowledging any failings of his own, but rather those of the audience and the way they seem to want to be detached from the performer, as passive as if they were watching TV.

It has been argued that the reason Hicks didn't find more receptive audiences in America was because he was anti-American. This couldn't be further from the truth. Hicks believed in traditional American values of justice and freedom of expression, but saw how politicians, the media and a voracious consumer society were denigrating these values: "Everything I talk about is true freedom and true democracy. It so happens that we've swayed so far from the true values of this country that to right wing, fundamentalist reactionaries...I'm talking about the opposite" (16). That audiences attended his shows for an easy fix of gags only compounded Hicks' frustration and accentuated the conflict.

A disinclination to compromise also created the conflict. Indeed, like Andy Kaufman, Hicks sought to go against expectations with requests for familiar routines being met with responses like "I'm not a fuckin' jukebox." He was prepared to alienate audiences with his material on children, mocking the Republican ideology of putting the children first and indulging in dark fantasies such as a child being sucked out of plane with Hicks gleefully watching as it splatters on the ground. Hicks had as much affection for children as anyone, he just wanted to challenge the way people indulged and elevated the idea of children above all else. He saw that people who presented themselves as loving and caring regarding children didn't seem to care as much about the environment, the problems in society or the dangers of right wing politics. Therefore, in being confrontational he is seeking to steer the audience to a more open view of the world.

Stand-up comedy is a social thing. It requires an audience response. Audiences validate the comedian with laughter, unlike a theatre performer where an audience generally sits for around two hours as silent witnesses. This therefore leads some stand-ups to just do gag after gag and get the laughs out. There is no need for cohesion, no need for a moral or a message. The bottom line is laughs. Yet, just as Hicks is not particularly concerned about audience validation, he also contradicts the archetype by shaping his material cohesively and making sure there is a point to it. In tying material together and re-introducing riffs, the structure of Hicks' material always leads to a point, held together essentially by freedom of choice and a view of an alternative, better world. Like the acts of a play, his performances see a narrative link so that mockery of Southern rednecks leads to the stupidity of the masses accepting what they are told by television. Television links to its use by the government for control, then to commercials, which lie, then to the lies about drugs, then to rock stars against drugs.

That there is a message perhaps makes audiences uncomfortable because they aren't allowed to just take away the laughs, but must also think about the issues. In effortlessly using words to create visual images for an audience, Hicks seeks to take them with him on his ride, but he is also creating an illusion, undercutting images with ironic twists that shift the audience's perspective and makes them look at things from a different angle. Though it keeps the audience alert, in some ways it is making them see their own ignorance. Hicks doesn't want to set himself up as being better than the audience, but they could perceive it that way and take offence, missing the point of Hicks being there to illuminate rather than mock (them).

Hicks' hope was that by the end of the performance audiences would have expelled all the meaningless trivialities of day to day life, leaving them clear to see the bigger picture: "It's supposed to be a fuckin' catharsis man, a fuckin' release from the daily grind. I wish it worked for me." Almost the martyr, the last line is said only half-jokingly, for in his endless touring Hicks found himself time and time again coming up against a reactionary and blinkered viewpoint. In these instances there is no purgation, no healing the anger, because in Hicks' "one consciousness" there needs to be a shared perspective, otherwise – as he recognised – he is just a bitter curmudgeon. Referring to his "Comedy Of Hate" was apt in that its violent fantasies and blistering rage seemed anything but love. It is also a title somewhat in tune with a growing interest in shows like that of Jim Rose, a touring contemporary carnival famed for its body piercing exhibitions and contortions of the human frame. Yet for Hicks it is an ironic reference to the way his shows might be perceived if audiences only look on a superficial level.

Nonetheless, it would be disingenuous to paint a picture of Hicks constantly battling with audiences. His particular skill was to be able to connect so easily with the mood of an audience, always aware of their reactions and able to respond. It is seen with his quick retorts to hecklers, as at the Funny Firm where he challenges a heckler by asking if he takes a guitar to play at Eric Clapton concerts. It is also seen in his asides whereupon he takes the voice of an audience member commenting on his show. The comment is usually one of shock at Hicks' material, but is employed to acknowledge their presence, show he is conscious of their mood and to put them at ease. In acknowledging their possible discomfort he also points up their responsibility to listen to his ideas. Amid the elaborate and subtle use of pitch and cadence, the presentation of complex issues, and the intensity of Hicks' emotions, these asides work as a kind of detour from the main journey. They function as a pause, a way for Hicks to join his audience, on the outside looking in, encouraging their participation in his imaginative ride. In addition, his ideas can detour, travelling on the path least travelled, but remaining in control of the audience, intent that they should catch up when he judges the comic moment to be appropriate; the moment when they are in effect at their most vulnerable – through their ignorance, through not seeing the connection he is about to make as he returns from the detour. This is what sweeps them up majestically. He did therefore find many receptive audiences who shared his vision, but such was his commitment that whenever an audience didn't get it he felt that his previous achievements were diminished. It is again a part of Hicks' feelings of sharing in a performance and being connected to an audience, of taking some of the responsibility for the hatred and bigotry of people.

Those comedians who have made a career from stand-up, those who have developed a loyal following, are able to connect with audience perspectives and ideologies. You like a comedian in no small way because he or she connects with your perspective, gives voice to and articulates an idea or aesthetic (or even a prejudice) you have long shared. The comedian offers a more precise and infectious articulation of the absurdities and frustrations felt by his or her audience. Thus, those who constitute the audience of someone as execrable as Andrew Dice Clay are unlikely to find Hicks' perspective amusing. Yet, what binds Hicks to his audience is not a shared hatred of the world. Hicks' ability to tap into an idealistic perspective and articulate the frustrations many feel about the neglected potential for change, define his comedy as not that of hate, but one where he seeks a coalescence of laughter and embracing of possibilities. It is why, many years after his death, Hicks attracts new fans, whilst the implications and imagination of his material still has a profound impact on existing ones. In essence, his words offered hope, the laughter his routines prompted suggesting everything about the possibility of laughing at hatred and bigotry, selfishness and greed, his dark imagery and acerbic visions conversely showing how beautiful the world was and how enlightened humanity could be.

As 1989 drew to a close, in November the Berlin wall came down, and though the Bush administration were bewilderingly cautious about the meaning of this historic event, for most of the world it seemed the dawning of a new era of hope (albeit one which was something of a false dawn with the subsequent conflicts that arose). From the frustration of playing to unresponsive audiences, 1990 was to be a hugely productive and successful year for Hicks, seeking further diverse audiences to convey his message to. After another Letterman appearance in December 1989, he kicked off 1990 with a gig at the Adult Video Awards in Los Angeles. That he would, unlike mainstream comedians, play such places (he even did a gig at Disney World in 1993), shows Hicks' desire to connect with all kinds of audiences and not play it safe.

His first album release, *Dangerous*, came in spring 1990. The growing prevalence of rap music, particularly the brand known as "gangsta rap" pioneered by Niggers With Attitude's *Straight Outta Compton* album in 1989 had seen Tipper Gore's P.M.R.C. increasingly busy in trying to ban and dilute what music Americans were allowed to listen to. If Hicks' was "The Comedy Of Hate" then gangsta rap might be deemed "The Music Of Hate," certainly by organisations like the P.M.R.C. who didn't see the social criticism in the gangsta rap genre and didn't see the idealism in Hicks' material, seeking to silence the messages of both.

Gore's campaign saw more and more albums having to put on warning stickers. Ironically, rock stars were using them as some kind of badge of honour, a celebration of alienation from a mainstream that ignored real issues. *Dangerous* also had a warning sticker, although there was an edited version for radio play. The album does not diverge significantly from the traditional comedy album, its collection of routines able to stand on their own and not being wholly cohesively linked. Therefore, the album comes across as somewhat tentative, not really capturing the effortless movement within and between subjects that was characteristic of Hicks' live shows. Despite some inspired routines on smoking and drugs, *Dangerous* only did moderately well in terms of sales, even after Letterman gave it a plug when Hicks did another spot in June.

Despite some disappointment, Hicks saw that his comedy was heading in the right direction, aware that his words had power, and hopeful that "the next revolution is going to be a revolution of ideas. A bloodless revolution. And if I can take part in it by transforming my own consciousness, then someone else's, then I'm happy" (31). It echoes Lennon's belief in fighting the establishment not with their own weapons of violence, but with ideas and reason. Despite a frustration and lack of fulfilment from his constant gigging, he continued to be busy, growing at ease with audiences, his sobriety allowing a more thoughtful and sophisticated Hicks to emerge. His clever use of irony and dissemination of accepted truths, crafted onto a

131

narrative that explored many facets of existence, could be nothing short of dazzling.

His appearance at the *Just For Laughs* festival in July 1990 caught the attention of British critics and producers who were well aware that his sophistication and irony would go down well with British audiences. Perhaps American audiences were more easily offended by his confrontational style than Britons whose theatrical history, dating back to Shakespeare, had involved violent language and watching in discomfort amid filthy environs.

Further exposure came when he filmed *One Night Stand*, a television special for HBO in October. Even though its viewing figures were low when it broadcast the following year, Hicks had at last been allowed to show television audiences more of what they hadn't seen on Letterman. *One Night Stand* shows Hicks evolving further into the self-titled "dark poet." This is a progression from "The Comedy Of Hate" in that Hicks' dark ideas are now being raised to a literary level, aligning himself with the dark language of Jonathon Swift and William Shakespeare. Hicks was about to make his most significant comedy step and find his natural audience when in November 1990 he was booked for a show, *Stand Up America*, in London's West End.

12
Billbo Hicks In Hobbiton

The popularity Hicks enjoyed in the UK has many strands to it. The American comedy boom of the late 1970s was dying out by the end of the 1980s and early 1990s. Stand-up had developed a smugness and self-satisfaction in America, where too many poor comedians were being hired whose material was either copied or poorly conceived, seeming to focus on unimaginative observations like meals on aeroplanes and Chinese drivers. These comedians saw stand-up merely as a platform to greater fame and fortune through television and the movies. In addition, cable TV in America had brought stand-up shows into living rooms on a regular basis, making what was once original and often shocking seem rather mundane and conventional. Moreover, the charismatic major players of the 1970s comedy boom were either dead or had moved onto sit-coms, talk shows and some lame movies, replaced by a slew of nondescript journeymen.

Some critics have labelled Hicks anti-American, which is a rather lazy accusation because what he really hated was the unquestioning love of America that bordered on nationalism: "I fuckin' hate patriotism. It's a round world last time I checked." Though he addressed the masses in general, his vitriol was aimed at the vocal minority of bigots who seemed to get heard the most, whereas voices criticising the institutions with power were marginalized. Britain had more of a history of satire, poking fun at the establishment not only in literature but also in the satirical television shows that began in the 1960s. Hicks acknowledged this when saying, "They are an older culture that have been screwed by their government longer and have a very healthy sense of cynicism" (3), seeing it as a place in tune with his own perspective.

The satire boom of the 1960s in America had been a response to the prevailing atmosphere of mistrust towards politicians after Kennedy's assassination. In Britain it evolved from the complacency and self-satisfaction of the 1950s and England's nostalgia for its waning world power. The *Beyond The Fringe* show had debuted at the Edinburgh Festival in 1960 with Peter Cook, Dudley Moore, Jonathan Miller and Alan Bennett. Moving to London in 1961, the show was a great success and paved the way for a long tour of America the following year (with one show attended by the Kennedys). When Peter Cook opened *The Establishment* club it gave exposure to an array of young comedians unafraid to satirise the elitism and racism of British society. *The Establishment* attracted the same *Guardian* newspaper reading liberals as Hicks did when he broke through in the U.K., young audiences of the 1960s rather embarrassed by the outdated ideas of Prime Minister Harold Macmillan and his Conservative government. The club even managed to secure a month long engagement for Lenny Bruce in 1962 (though a further engagement never materialised as Bruce was hounded out of the country by an hysterical British tabloid press).

The movement soon infiltrated television in the autumn of 1962 with David Frost's *That Was The Week That Was*, the kind of show never before seen on British television with its breaking down of the medium's artifice, a sense of reality created by performers speaking casually as if there were no cameras. It attacked the sacred cows of religion and politics, puncturing pomposity, and mocking Britain's status in the world much as Hicks mocked U.S. perceptions of itself.

Comedians of the 1960s like Peter Cook and others from *Beyond The Fringe* took comedy to a new level, growing more surreal as the decade progressed with Cook and Dudley Moore in the TV show, *Not Only...But Also* (1965-1966) and *Monty Python's Flying Circus* (beginning in 1969), but still maintaining a satirical edge with the hard-hitting *The Frost Report* (beginning in 1966).

The satire boom in England celebrated intellectualism, the kind of sophistication with language that appealed to Hicks. Hicks enjoyed playing with words in much the same way as Shakespeare, Jonathan Swift, George Bernard Shaw and Oscar Wilde. He liked witty turns of phrases, the sophistication and cleverness of language seen with a cannon of English writers and with his American literary heroes like Twain. During his career Hicks also cited his admiration for writer and comedian Robert Benchley, who was adept at clever turns with language, and actor W.C. Fields, well know for his cynical and sharp wit and turn of phrase. Hicks was un unashamed reader, proud of his intellectualism and eager to promote the pursuit of knowledge as a means to enlightenment. A voracious reader, his love of books is evident in the way his eclectic favourites list was ever expanding, from J.R.R. Tolkien's *The Hobbit*, to Martin Amis' *Money*. Although a somewhat unrealistic perception, he saw the British as cultured and felt at home in a society that would acknowledge the value of his extensive reading, whilst in contrast he felt embarrassed that America exported to the U.K. shows like *American Gladiators* and *Beverly Hills 90210.*

In the 1970s satire in Britain gradually died out, partly due to television becoming so popular that more family orientated entertainment dominated, thus attracting safer comedians and non-confrontational comedy shows such as *The Two Ronnies* and *Morecambe & Wise.* By the end of the decade, comedy in Britain grew broader. Pioneers like Peter Cook were marginalized (or too busy drinking) whilst Eric Morecambe's death (1984) seemed to be the end of a more innocent era. The new comedians coming through, particularly in stand-up, were harking back to "seaside humour," merely a euphemism for dirty jokes that were sexist and frequently racist.

From the mid to late eighties, 'alternative' comedy began making inroads into the UK mainstream. This comedy was, unlike its American counterpart, more seriously politically correct. American comedians like Sam Kinison, Andrew Dice Clay and Eddie Murphy could be deeply sexist, racist and homophobic, and as stand-ups, these comedians never crossed over to find mass appeal with a U.K. audience. Their machismo proved something of a turn-off for Britons with a more healthy need for self-deprecation, something born of a society which cheered the underdog and celebrated heroic losers. Both the wacky humour of *Saturday Night Live* and Steve Martin's stand-up never found an audience in the U.K. either. *Saturday Night Live* was rooted too much in American culture, its comedy seeming somewhat self-indulgent and unsubtly knowing. Though Martin's humour is similar to the surreal craziness of Monty Python, Monty Python was more in tune with British society, exaggerating characteristics and archetypes British audiences could relate too whilst Martin's comedy was rooted too firmly in American society, particularly that of California. Undoubtedly, the British alternative scene shared with its 1970s American counterpart a sense of anarchy, but what really lay behind both the comedy booms was a willingness (and need) to mock the establishment.

It was a visit to L.A.'s Comedy Store that persuaded former disc jockey Peter Rosengard to open a similarly named comedy club in London's Soho district. The venue quickly established a reputation for promoting bright young comedy talents like Alexei Sayle and Ben Elton, comedians who were left leaning and politically correct. This new generation of comics were lumped together under the label of "alternative comedy" in that they were an alternative to established nightclub acts that employed mother-in-law gags and racial stereotypes. The subsequent comedy boom had its roots in the rise to power of Margaret Thatcher and the Conservative government

135

in 1979, only a year before Reagan, the two leaders sharing something of a mutual appreciation society, both vigorously pursuing a right wing agenda. Thatcher's ideology seemed to be summed up in her statement, "There is no such thing as society, only individuals," a philosophy contrasting starkly with Hicks' "one consciousness." The comedy Hicks brought to the U.K. in the early 1990s had evolved as a reaction against the ideology sweeping America throughout the 1980s, and because the trends in America were mirrored in Thatcher's England, his targets were generically similar, thus allowing an easier connection with audiences.

Like America's Moral Majority movement, Britain had Mary Whitehouse's National Viewers and Listeners Association denouncing most television programmes and films as offensive, eagerly pursuing censorship as a means to halt a supposed decay in society's values. Bafflingly, the enemy in early 1980s Britain was the so-called "video nasties" which were basically gory, but poorly made and laughably acted Italian zombie movies and American slasher films. Reagan's appeal to family values was mere guff to promote his ultraconservative agenda, as he showed no time for families on welfare or families with drug problems. Equally, Thatcher's appeal to family values was undermined by a government filled with "lying cocksuckers" and hypocrites like Conservative Party Chairman, Cecil Parkinson, having an affair with and getting his secretary Sara Keays pregnant, and extreme right winger Harvey Proctor being arrested in 1987 for "gross indecency" concerning the spanking of young men.

Similar to Reagan using conflicts around the world to bully small countries and engender patriotism, so Thatcher found a convenient enemy when Argentina invaded the Falklands in 1982. It was during the Falklands War that the pool system for journalists first came to prominence. The system, later successfully used in the Gulf War, allowed only news of the war that the military wanted to show, restricting information and – through selection of images - generating a feeling of patriotism. In comparison to Reagan's use of talk show hosts to help convey his message, Thatcher's media ally was the vile newspaper *The Sun*, a paper often filled with anti-gay and racist propaganda, demonising any figure with left-wing leanings. Most obvious was the paper's vilification of miner's union leader Arthur Scargill during the coalminer's strike of 1984/1985, presenting him as an extremist and (wrongly) suggesting an involvement in the embezzlement of funds. Hicks' deep interest in the power of the media, its ability to distort and present rumours and lies as facts, was certainly a concern of Britons who recognised Thatcher's use of newspapers to influence opinion, not only

136

through the obsequious *Sun*, but also more surreptitiously using M15 to prompt the *Daily Mirror* to claim Scargill had used miner's strike funds to pay off his mortgage (a complete lie, but one which effectively marginalized Scargill as a political figure).

The Sun put itself at the forefront of the patriotic fervour and jingoism the Falklands War generated, one crass headline, "Gotcha!" plastered on its front cover when an Argentine ship, The General Belgrano, was sunk, killing hundreds. It chose to ignore the fact that the ship was outside an agreed exclusion zone and should never have been attacked, but then Thatcher's government and her allies were as much "lying cocksuckers" as Reagan's administration. Victory in the Falklands swept Thatcher to a massive victory in 1983, giving her a platform from which to move her policies even further to the right.

Thatcher began a programme of reducing spending on welfare and public services and giving tax cuts to the rich, funding these cuts by selling off publicly owned industries, beginning with British Telecom in 1984. Ordinary members of the public bought shares and got rich quickly whilst bosses gave themselves pay raises, sacked workers to cut expenses and generally took what they could get from the industries. She had the same aim as Reagan to reduce the power of government, pushing through privatisation and deregulation and giving power to private corporations. As in Reagan's America, the rich got richer and the poor got poorer. In the 1980s the richest 20% of earners in the U.K. increased their share of post-tax income to well over 40% while the poorest 20% of the population saw their share fall from an already meagre 7.4% to only 6% (32). Like Ronald Reagan, Margaret Thatcher led the country through recession and high unemployment levels with over three million unemployed in Britain in 1986, the dissatisfaction of those not sharing in the economic boom manifested when riots erupted in Brixton and Toxteth in 1981 and Handsworth and Tottenham in 1985.

Hicks targeted the hypocrisy behind the façade of family values. Though he focused on American culture, British audiences could relate to the same targets. They had had the same experiences in the 1980s, his liberal *Guardian* newspaper reading audience feeling the same sense of disillusionment, that despite all the mean-spiritedness and sleaze of the Tory party they – like the Republican Party - won successive elections throughout the decade. Hicks was alive to the comparison, referring to people "voting with their wallets" and a population, in the U.K. and U.S., seduced by the promise of tax cuts, right-wing governments shamelessly appealing to and promoting self-interest and financial accumulation as a viable moral choice. The British alternative comedy scene had grown throughout the decade, an energetic and occasionally haphazard response to Thatcherism, moving into television with the caustic satire of the puppet show *Spitting Image* in 1984 and Ben Elton hosting Channel 4's *Saturday Night* in 1986, a show that gave exposure to more left leaning comedians.

By the time Hicks was making an impact in Britain in 1991, Margaret Thatcher had been ousted, replaced by John Major - a rather insipid and bland politician. Subsequently, the satire was rather domesticated and inoffensive, whilst the alternative comedians – having successfully moved the focus of stand-up away from racial and sexual stereotypes – were falling into the trap of substituting anarchy and "toilet humour" for wit and invention. Their humour was controversial only in the sense that it offended polite sensibilities, and even this 'edge' was being eroded as the 1990s saw what was once "alternative" being more generally accepted as the norm. Though talents were emerging – Mark Thomas, Jeremy Hardy, Mark Steel – at the beginning of the decade, popular stand-up lacked political bite and social comment, leaving an opening for Hicks to gain a following, particularly with comedy's branding as "the new rock and roll" in the U.K.

The timing of Hicks' 'arrival' on the U.K. comedy scene was an important factor in helping to quickly establish an audience and reputation. The U.K government was wholeheartedly behind the U.S. in the Gulf War of 1991. Indeed, Margaret Thatcher had strengthened Bush's resolve to go into battle. She needed a war as much as he did (though her resignation in November 1990 saw John Major benefiting) and left leaning liberals were, like Hicks, unhappy about involvement in the conflict. Thus, Hicks' material on the war rang true with British audiences, the comparative actions of both countries meaning there were no cultural boundaries to hinder Hicks' voice. After the U.S., Britain was the second largest exporter of arms around the world and just as the U.S. government had sold arms to Iraq, so in the mid-1980s the Conservative government had encouraged the sale of machine tools to Iraq (which everyone involved knew could be used to make weapons).

At the beginning of 1991, President Bush's poll ratings were low and there was widespread unhappiness at his handling of the economy. Iraq had invaded Kuwait in August of the previous year; its president Saddam Hussein believing the U.S. would not intervene as it had supported Iraq in the Iran-Iraq war, but he – like so many tin-pot dictators – would soon realise that the U.S. government will only support oppressive regimes for as long as it is in their interests to do so. In 1991, Bush needed to find what Hicks would call a "distraction" from his domestic policies, and that meant convincing the American people of the need for a war against Iraq.

Fifteen-year-old Nayirah al Sabah told Congress about how Iraqi soldiers were taking babies from hospitals and leaving them to die on the ground. Six witnesses testified to the U.N. that Iraqis were taking children from hospitals in Kuwait. This was used by Bush to drum up support for the Gulf War, yet it later transpired that the women had been sent by the public relations firm of Hill and Knowlton who had been paid $10 million to present the Kuwaiti case. Moreover, the fifteen year old who had tearfully relayed her story to Congress was the daughter of the Kuwaiti ambassador to the U.S. No evidence was found to support the claims she had made, but by the time that these falsehoods were exposed, the emotive story had been repeated relentlessly in the push towards war. Hicks' view that governments were lying cocksuckers is again evident, and it is true of both the U.S. and U.K. governments with their complicity in arms dealing to Iraq and their manipulation of the media. Subsequently, in 1992, a Congressional inquiry reported that President Bush had ordered a cover-up of the Republicans' secret support of Hussein and selling of illegal arms.

Bush described Saddam Hussein as "another Adolf Hitler," keen to play up the dangers Iraq posed to national and world security. The U.S. government claimed that there was a threat to Saudi Arabia from Iraq, that there were (classified) satellite pictures showing a quarter of a million Iraqi soldiers amassed on the Saudi border. This was not true, as, according to respected Florida journalist Jean Heller, who got hold of independent satellite photographs, "We could see empty barracks where you would have expected to see thousands of troops billeted, but they were deserted" (33).

Voices of dissent found little opportunity to present their arguments in the predominantly right wing press, television and radio, the relentless push towards war culminating in Operation Desert Storm beginning with a US led attack on Iraq on January 16th. Iraq's leader Saddam Hussein became the latest international demon; the media colluding in presenting him as the new Hitler, citing his killing of the Kurds as evidence, yet making no mention of Turkey killing Kurds. Again we see a misinformation of facts, an obfuscating of the truth and disinclination to see anything other than in terms of black and white: a perfect breeding ground for Hicks' comedy.

The war lasted 41 days, the ground war a mere 100 hours. Hicks watched the news avidly and saw how flawed the coverage was. Media manipulation and conspiracy theories had been a mainstay of his act, with JFK, Elvis

Presley, and now the lies being told in the news about the Gulf War. His material was assembled with an immediacy that other comics couldn't or didn't dare match. As Eric Bogosian noted on the *It's Just A Ride* documentary, there were well known comedians who "wouldn't put their neck on the line. They were against the war and they wouldn't say anything, because they basically felt that they'd watch those little bags of money just float away. It was like, kiss your career goodbye." It again saw Hicks as the lone warrior and speaker of truth, his growing sophistication continuing to receive critic's praise. His material about the Gulf War was telling people things they really hadn't been allowed to be aware of because of the state's careful management of the media. He altered people's perceptions of events, made them see things from a different angle and certainly wasn't chasing easy targets.

1991 had also seen the release of the film *Ninja Bachelor Party* after ten years in the making, and another appearance on Letterman in April, on which he did some of his Gulf War material. He had been nominated at the American Comedy Awards as Best Male Stand-up, along with Tim Allen, Will Durst, Richard Jeni and Dennis Wolfberg. Wolfberg won in April. He was a comedian who'd started in 1979, appearing on *The Tonight Show* and ploughing on with his facial contortions and amiable observations before a HBO special in 1992 (dying of cancer in October 1994). He was another safe winner of the award, which Hicks would be nominated for two further times without winning (1993 and 1994).

It was at the *Just For Laughs* festival in Montreal that Hicks unleashed his most damning material about the Gulf War. The taping of one show on July 15th, *Relentless*, was to be Hicks' biggest break in Britain when transmitted unedited on Channel 4. In the show, one of Hicks' finest performances, he is wearing glasses, dressed in black, his hair slicked back, his "dark little poet" persona now fully developed. His criticism of the Gulf War from Letterman was expanded, touching on the attitude of both the soldiers and the public as well as offering a hilarious indictment of government spin and media misrepresentation. The bottom line was that the war, as well as boosting President Bush's popularity, had been embarked upon to maintain U.S. control of oil in the Middle East, a debate lost in the media's frenzy to create a picture of Iraq's might and the threat therein, when in truth the U.S. had total control from the start. The conflict did only last 41 days. During the war media coverage was subject to censorship, the government only allowing information which helped the public get behind the war or feel good about it. There was talk of "smart bombs" which were supposed to be so accurate that they avoided civilian casualties, yet 40% of these bombs missed their intended targets. In fact, under 10% of the bombs dropped on Iraq were "smart bombs", the rest were conventional – and by implication even less accurate - bombs.

The Gulf War presented Hicks with another example of how the media manipulates information, seemingly to lend credence to government lies, a theme apparent throughout his career. Here was a war in which the news remained strictly controlled by the government. Any reporters who didn't join a pool assigned to them by the military did not get interviews. The system worked by selected journalists within the pool being taken by the military to wherever they deemed the story was, then the journalists reporting back to the rest of the pool. It resulted in sanitised news, carefully managed to avoid a repeat of the Vietnam War where shocking images of America's dead and injured swayed public opinion against the war. The cinema verite style of CNN's coverage suggested honesty and immediacy, but beneath the high drama of wobbling cameras and panic there was very little close analysis or reporting of the conflict. Breathtaking images following missiles to their targets and the careful management of information led philosopher Jean Baudrillard to venture that the war had never even happened (perhaps inspiration for Hicks' quip that "there never was a war. A war is when *two* armies are fighting"). It was an unreal war, seemingly following a Hollywood script, one that the military wouldn't allow anyone to diverge from.

Thus, the media were not allowed to report anything that didn't help the public get behind the war effort, as in mid-February when the U.S. dropped a bomb on an Iraqi air raid shelter killing some 500 civilians. News pictures of the effects of the bombing were heavily censored so as not to show its horrific consequences, including the burned bodies of at least six babies.

Towards the end of the war, with a ceasefire about to be signed, U.S. aircraft attacked Iraqis reatreating on the Basra road. They fired missiles and dropped Napalm B, which sticks to the skin whilst continuing to burn, leaving a scene of carnage in their wake. As a symbol of the war, it said everything about an aggressive attitude at some distance from the ostensible aim of freeing Kuwait. The Basra "turkey shoot" seemed to suggest soldiers consumed by careless abandon and the destructive power of their weaponry, the type Hicks referred to as being "in hog heaven out there." It's a line used to convey the idea that these soldiers view the war as some kind of adventure, a view supported by an interview with a fighter pilot in the war's first week: "I was going gung-ho the whole way. It was kinda neat," whilst another said, "I feel like a young athlete after his first football match" (35). It's also a term with deliberate connotations of college jocks and beer monsters engaged in a brainless orgy of excess, used in the context of the Gulf War to convey the soldiers' lack of control and ignorance of the human costs of their actions.

The sense of a cheery, alcohol-fuelled adventure subtly links to Hicks' points about news misinformation, as if after the party only sketchy (and convenient) details remain. So we have reporting where American soldiers are heroes, with no mainstream attention given to incidents such as that where several thousand Iraqis were buried alive in trenches as U.S. bulldozers ploughed through the sand. And it wasn't until 1994 that the Defence Department admitted that U.S. Marines had dropped 489 napalm bombs on Iraqis in trenches (33), whilst the use of depleted uranium (a real weapon of mass destruction) has subsequently led to deformations and cancers in babies. Such occurrences were barely conveyed to the public so that the anti-war feeling could be easily managed and marginalized, if not suppressed; once again, a lesson learned from the effect on the American public of horrific television pictures of the Vietnam War.

Some 88,500 tons of bombs had been dropped on Iraq and Kuwait by the end of the war. In Bush's victory speech he said the war had "freed America from the memory of Vietnam," a quote which says everything about Bush's motives for starting the war. As a result of the destruction of Iraq's infrastructure, tens of thousands of children died, and when the war ended there was no U.S. support for those within Iraq who wanted to overthrow Saddam Hussein. As a result of the war, a quarter of a million Iraqis had been killed whilst the "new Hitler" was allowed to remain and become a useful tool for successive U.S. governments seeking an enemy.

TV anchorman Dan Rather told audiences at the end of the war "There's one thing we can all agree on. It's the heroism of the 148 Americans who gave their lives so that freedom could live" (34). His use of "we" with the emotive "heroism" and "gave their lives" is a deliberate swaying of public opinion, a way to vilify and cast out those who don't agree. He made no mention that the allies, as a result of so-called "friendly fire", killed a quarter of those Americans.

In response to the end of the war, and allied to the break up of the communist block, Bush made his "new world order" speech, talking of a "peace dividend." Yet, subsequent years were to see an escalation of the number of conflicts around the world, statistics relating to wars between 1991 and 1992 showing the highest number of deaths since the Vietnam

War. As Hicks so precisely noted, "Didn't you think with the Cold War over, things should have gotten better? Wrong! Now twelve different countries have nuclear weapons – it just got twelve times as bad," a particularly prescient view with all the conflicts arising from the collapse of the Soviet Block.

Hicks' Gulf War material tapped into Britons' sense of injustice and their desire to question the establishment. In this he had the same rebelliousness as his British rock heroes, The Beatles and John Lennon. In addition to this, the contrast between his successes in England, further enhanced when in July 1991 he won the Critic's Award at the Edinburgh Festival, and his virtual anonymity in America, reflected the career of another rock hero, Jimi Hendrix, whose career had taken off only after success in England.

Hicks brought a sharpness to comedy, a cleverness and sense of irony that appealed to UK audiences, who liked jokes that played to and complimented their intelligence. As Hicks saw it, British audiences didn't have a problem with his routines on American society, "They just know so much about Americans…stuff I have to explain, they give the time to explain it…If you're on stage I think the English feel you've earned it somehow, let's give him a chance to explore any ideas" (36). It's in keeping with Britain's theatrical tradition and the sense of theatricality in Hicks' performances that U.K. audiences were more in tune with the developing narrative of his shows.

His performances were shown unexpurgated in the UK, on mainstream channels, unlike in the USA, thus allowing audiences to see the full routine and appreciate his sophistication. In this sense he also seemed distant from a stereotype of Americans the rest of the world often sees. The American people and the ideals of its society have been tarnished by the actions of its governments, particularly with aggressions against smaller countries. This has created an anti-American feeling all over the world (and despite the sympathy the September 11th attacks provoked, George Bush Junior seems intent on further alienating America from the rest of the world). So we have the figure of a fat American, eating burgers, watching TV, driving a gas-guzzling car, patriotically celebrating as smaller countries are brought to their knees. It's an American stereotype insular in thinking, disengaged from real issues and ignoring the murdering of innocents in foreign lands. It's a view acknowledged by Hicks with "is it any wonder we're hated the world over?" when he ponders the success of comedian Gallagher and his routine of smashing fruit when there are so many starving in the world. It's not an accurate view of Americans, but undeniably it's a perception a large proportion of the world's population accepts. By mocking such types, British audiences warmed to Hicks, seeing him as one of their own, perhaps doing more than his complacent countrymen to challenge the stereotype by being so engaged with world events and using a sense of irony not often associated with Americans.

The irony Hicks' employed was part of a wider enjoyment of language, a desire to play with it and look at its contradictions. Not only was his use of language sophisticated in the way it opened up its meanings, but also in long routines it could be beautifully poetic, rich in imagery and attention to detail. As well as his dark and prolonged visions of laying waste to the fevered egos of the famous, the seamless ebb and flow of his dialogue, setting up multi-faceted situations with such finesse as to seem effortless, gave his performances an irresistible rhythm and depth that elevated them to a literary level.

Hicks' *Revelations* show at the Dominion Theatre, London, epitomises the literariness of his material and perfectly illustrates why he was so highly regarded in the U.K. Almost immediately, Hicks employs contrast when doubting the appeal of a perennially "hot and sunny" climate in Los Angeles, conveying his love of a cooler environment with a series of images suggesting vitality and cosiness: "coats, scarves, cappuccino and rosy cheeked women." Alliteration of the 'c' sound quickens the sentence's pace, suggesting energy and an eagerness to engage in life's rich pageant, a stark contrast to the insipid (and brainless) repetition of "hot and sunny" that had preceded it.

From a somewhat parochial observation, Hicks moves on to the L.A. riots, to a world seemingly in chaos, one where it is "Not a time to quit smoking." We have the imagery of a cigarette being so tempting that it appears to have been produced through divine inspiration, "made by God, rolled by Jesus" (with a little help when "moistened shut with Claudia Schiffer's pussy"). As a piece of throwaway bathos, the routine succinctly punctures pomposity, but also offers -in typically literary fashion – several interpretations. Superficially, both God and Jesus can be seen as corrupted by modern society, each merely workers on a production line before the *piece de resistance* performed by a woman whose success has been based mainly on her looks. Yet the real essence of the piece is to present each as ordinary individuals, perhaps fallible, but more tellingly – for Hicks – eager to indulge in life's pleasures without hurting another human being.

Hicks continues with religious imagery when moving on to President George Bush, describing him as "a child of Satan here to destroy the planet

144

Earth." Prevalent throughout his career, such Biblical allusions serve as a backdrop, a clear mechanism to allow rough definitions of good and evil when seeking to get to grips with the often complex truth behind issues. Thus, with Bush clearly established as evil, Hicks can then explore the deceit of the Gulf War, once again employing a quick succession of images to convey the vapidity of the arguments for war: "for God and country and democracy and here's a foetus and he's a Hitler." There is a poetic quality about this collecting of disparate images, one where each is somehow abstrusely intrinsic to the whole. A routine built on the hypocrisy of selling arms to Iraq, then bombing them because they are a threat is effectively summarised in this line. For pro-war Americans, God is now sanctioning killing; yet Hicks is pointing out the contradictions when those seeking to prevent abortions invoke this same God. Equal to religious convenience is patriotic convenience, "country" and "democracy" as moral anchors, cited as justification for war in the same way that Hitler engineered the support of the German masses.

The culmination of this routine sees Hicks' use of simile and personification with America being "like Jack Palance in the movie *Shane*." It's effective in illustrating his "bullies of the world" routine, but through personification he also seeks to point out that America is more than just a landmass, it is an entity whose culture and actions affect those beyond its borders. For Hicks, this necessitates a certain level of responsibility towards the rest of the planet (we are *all* one consciousness). However, the dominant outlook is insular, becoming an effective breeding ground for fear and hate and a need to bully those that might, just might, be a threat.

Making a deliberate contrast between corruption and honesty, Hicks moves from President Bush to the Kennedy assassination, once again making religious reference with a retort to those who tell him to cease debating Kennedy: "alright, then don't bring up Jesus to me." It becomes a springboard to mock fundamentalist Christians, Hicks employing an image of needing to be strapped into a seat as he hears an absurd argument about the existence of dinosaur fossils being down to God merely testing humanity's faith.

It is not necessary for a stand-up comedian to link routines or seek to develop material from established themes, but Hicks – reader, thinker, intellectual and satirist – is so used to the narrative of novels (and indeed, films) that there is always a sense that each routine is a significant and inseparable part of the whole performance. From God and the Bible, Hicks moves to Christians wearing crosses, then back into the Kennedy assassination, the routine's passage as cohesive as well crafted prose or poetry. And then, consumed by anger at the American public's disinterest in the ramifications of the assassination (they are more concerned with watching inane television fodder like *American Gladiators*), Hicks delves into his dark poet with "kill", "chainsaws", "spike" and "pistols" introducing brutal, contemporary language, his sentences pithily short: "Is it really good for us to watch? Is it too violent? No! Fuck it! Give these guys chainsaws! Let them fuck each other up good!" From the fluently elaborate sentences dealing with the Kennedy assassination, we now have an abrupt, stop start delivery to suggest a society motivated by instant gratification, one where prolonged thought, or even just independent thinking, requires too much effort.

Hicks makes a link between *American Gladiators* and his idea for using terminally ill people in movies, his novelistic attention to detail apparent when he describes a grandmother with "translucent skin so thin you can see her last heartbeat work its way down her blue veins." It is apparent too with his vision of a dangerous world where "you're going to be raped by some crack-addicted, AIDS-infected, pit-bull," assonance of the "i" employed to heighten the stabbing rhythm of his comic exaggeration.

There is no let up from the dark poet, his restored equilibrium when beginning a routine "By the way, if anyone here is in advertising or marketing…kill yourself" merely reflecting the rationality of his violent proposal. Hicks uses the metaphor "I'm just trying to plant seeds" to align himself with what is free and natural, whilst at the same time suggesting advertising and marketing are unnatural professions. There is also an inference that his radical ideas will take time to find acceptance when set against the overwhelming influence and control of consumerism. This is emphasized by the clichéd metaphor of being "caught in a fucking web" when he seems unable to escape from those "putting a goddam dollar sign on every fucking thing on the planet!"

Those in advertising and marketing are "Satan's spawn", whilst Hicks' following routine describes the film *Basic Instinct* as "Satan's shit," continuing to use religious imagery in a contemporary context and providing a lead into Randy Pan, the Goatboy. Goatboy is a lascivious Satan, motivated by a boundless carnality, initially used by Hicks to mock the coyness of British pornographic magazines. The *Revelations* show, as with many others, sees Hicks diverging from the routine, improvising around the character with riffs of dark poetry. From an image of genitals conveyed by "my purple wand," and "my hairy sack of magic" Hicks is as playful and unfettered as his persona, a decidedly non-PC simile used when describing a young girls' genitals: "it's like a wisp of cotton candy framing a paper cut" whilst her anus is "like a little pink quivering rabbit nostril."

British humour's long tradition of bawdiness goes some way towards explaining how such explicit description was accepted by his U.K. audiences, but it is also the sheer majesty of his language that sets him apart from mere shock comedians such as Andrew Dice Clay. Indeed, in some of his most graphic material, Hicks' inventiveness with sexual imagery can quite easily be described as Shakespearean, with "women licking up semen like kittens under a cow udder" and "Arcing ropes of gissum" hilariously evocative, amongst many that go some way towards justifying the "dark poet" literary tag.

It is evident then that Hicks was particularly skilled at choosing the right words and being aware of how those choices had many connotations, a defining characteristic of great literature. When *Revelations* moves on to Hicks mocking the miracle of childbirth his skill is apparent in his subtle choices of words: "Humans are so neat," uses "neat" to mock, effectively summarising the empty-headedness of that argument with all its connotations of self-satisfaction and hippy-dippy simplicity. "Neat" is oblivious to reality, its very banality implying that no consideration has been given to the problem of over population. Then we have a torrent of pictures to challenge this "miracle", Hicks pluralizing with a series of mundane images, intent on throwing some reality into the argument: "mewling cabbages...like frogs laying eggs...like a sardine can...fucking flies." Each phrase is calculated to create not just a sense of ordinariness, but also a feeling of unease. There is something slimy about the images, emphasized by repetition of the "s" and "g" sounds and intrusive activeness of the "-ing" suffix.

Revelations is offered here merely as a convenient example to show Hicks' adroitness with language. A mastery of words is characteristic of his material and shows, even those that turn into rants against the audience, and this goes some way to explaining why Hicks found success in the U.K. Not only does the show's conclusion capture the essence of Hicks' ethos, but also his consummate skill with words. With a ride at an amusement park symbolising the world, Hicks captures the ride's movement, a sense of up and down in the rhythmic repetition of "and" allied to the description's melodic assonance: "And the ride goes up and down and round and round. It has thrills and chills and it's very brightly coloured and it's very loud and it's fun..." Similarly, the second segment of this climax, more concerned with offering hope in the face of adversity, calls on repetition in a form typical of rhetoric: "No effort, no work, no job, no savings and money" whilst "the eyes of fear" are contrasted with "the eyes of love" and extensive use is made of the inclusive "we." Pitched perfectly, pauses suggest contemplation and possibility, sentences structured in such a way as to accentuate the passage's fluency by linking seamlessly to the next: "It's only a choice. No effort, no work, no job, no savings and money. A choice, right now, between fear and love. The eyes of fear want you to put bigger locks on your doors, buy guns, close yourself off. The eyes of love, instead, see all of us as one." It becomes an irresistible, mesmerising vision, like shattering light into darkness, taking the audience on his ride until a climax that feels like flight: "Here's what we can do to change the world, right now, to a better ride. Take all that money that we spend on weapons and defences each year and instead spend it feeding and clothing and educating the poor of the world, which it would many times over, *not one* human being excluded, and we could explore space, together, both inner and outer, forever, in peace."

Though cultured and intellectual, on a more mundane level, Hicks enjoyed the quaintness of British words like "brilliant", "ruffians", "hooligans" and "knackered" but avoided the easy gag of so many American comedians of making jokes about such cultural differences. Other than some rather obvious gags about how bad the food is – "You don't boil Pizza!" – when Hicks made jokes specifically about British culture he was brave enough and informed enough to seek out targets like John Major and the Conservative government's selling of weapons to Iraq. Unlike a lot of America comedians, he didn't play to the idea of being separate from British culture, for his universal themes of freedom and reason applied to all societies. British comedians who attempted a take on the Gulf War didn't have the depth of Hicks' opening up of the debate; his perceptiveness showing the British truths those native comics could not manage, so that in a way he could be tagged "one of our own." Further to this he could still pick up the minutiae of British life as he did material on "miles of red cones" (a peculiar British spectacle, so predominant were they on British roads that a "cone hotline" was set up for members of the public to report them) and the ubiquitous television coverage of snooker matches (and name-checking player Jimmy White). His take on the British obsession with chips had him imagining "hookers on London streets going 'head and chips!'" as an enticement to potential punters. Meanwhile, as someone who joked that he watched television news "twenty-three hours a day," Hicks was well aware that the national sport of football (which, in keeping with his fellow Americans, he referred to as "soccer") had come to be associated with violence and death. Several incidents where there was substantial loss of life were tragic accidents, but at the same time, throughout the 1980s, hooligans more interested in fighting than watching the game had dogged the sport. Hicks' peculiar perspective had the English soccer ball as deadly as the American gun: "Does a guy walk into a bank: 'Give me all your money! I've got a soccer ball!'"

He did have a somewhat romanticised view of Britain, saying of London in 1990, "It's like New York only it was clean and civilised and friendly" (3), playing to stereotypes in joking that his appeal in the U.K. was due to his pale skin and that there was "nothing like being surrounded by pale nervous people. I was right at home" (3).   Such a stereotypical view can be seen in his attempt at an English accent, a kind of eloquent cockney, used for all manner of Britons, from ordinary folk to rock stars. It's also seen in his quaint view of himself as "Billbo Hicks" amid the green fields and meagre crime of England as "Hobbiton." It certainly was a marked contrast with his most hated place, Los Angeles, with its "hot and sunny" weather all the time, something of anathema to Hicks and his predilection for archetypal images of warm coffee and "rosy cheeked women."

Britain was alive to his viewpoint as he played packed out venues and received praise in highbrow papers, as well as writing columns for British satire magazine *Scallywag* and rock journal the *New Musical Express*. As he said in an interview with Dennis McLellan of the *Los Angeles Times* (June 10th 1993) "People in the United Kingdom and outside the United States share my bemusement with the United States that America doesn't share about itself. They also have a sense of irony, which America doesn't have, seeing as it's being run by fundamentalists who take things literally." Hicks saw the contrast between the willingness of the British to come to shows with an open mind whilst audiences in America brought the societal baggage of patriotism and fundamentalism, reared on a diet of multi-channel television. Britain was awake whilst America was sleeping.

13
<u>Go Back To Bed America</u>

Hicks had long been aware of the way the entertainment industry manipulates the public, beginning with routines about pop stars selling out. There was a similar strand in his mocking of crass Hollywood films and their stars. Hicks referenced films a lot throughout his career, although his mockery was less acerbic than that concerning television. Perhaps this was due to television being a medium that supposedly relayed factual news, with endless commercial interludes forcing audiences to view the world in terms of products. Films were generally just stupid and though they didn't have the same place in his heart as rock music, they generally didn't pretend they were anything other than inane entertainment fodder.

Hicks had long been a fan of films, eager to see even the most brainless ones such as those starring Chuck Norris, Steven Seagal and Sylvester Stallone, as well as C-grade actioneers like *Action Jackson* (1988). He created material from such asinine features, using them to point out the stupidity of Americans who chose muscle men like Arnold Schwarzenegger as their heroes and believed that they exemplified the American Way.

With television, Hicks would often imagine how shows could be improved, as in giving the contestants of *American Gladiators* chainsaws for their combating and believing the show *COPS* would be better if "you get the *COPS*' camera and shine it up your pussy and film the little criminal coming out." Such re-writing is taken to its logical conclusion with Hicks' own idea for a TV show, *Let's Hunt And Kill Billy Ray Cyrus*, which would involve chasing people with no talent around the globe before killing them. Similarly, in referencing films, Hicks also had ideas on improving their content. The most famous example is Hicks citing the special effects of *Terminator 2* (1991) and then proposing a way to top this by putting terminally ill people into movies, using them for stunts, but in essence advocating a snuff movie.

He referenced the horror film *Scanners* (1980) in the mid-eighties as he mused on how sick he was of horror films and the stupid people in them who'd go to investigate obviously suspicious noises. He had an idea for a better horror film where he would hear spooky noises in an attic, but would choose not to investigate it. Instead, he would get on a plane to Alaska, get in a kayak and row into the Arctic Ocean, building up a vivid picture of his escape from the terror as at the same time the monster gets on a plane to follow him. Hicks' film climaxes with him in the tranquillity of the Arctic Ocean before the monster then appears. It's a routine influenced by the surprise endings of horror films such as *Friday 13th* (1980).

The horror genre featured in much of Hicks' film related material. The 1970s had seen a resurgence of interest in the genre with an influx of gory movies involving teenagers being stalked and killed, so called "slasher" movies, of which *Friday 13th* was a prime example. After President Reagan survived an assassination attempt and then cancer, Hicks likened him to the *Friday 13th* series' invincible killer, Jason Vorhees, who, despite apparently fatal conclusions, managed to rise again for several sequels. Similarly, President Bush's vice president Dan Quayle is likened to the demonic child, Damien, from *The Omen* (1976). Hicks frequently acknowledged the pivotal scene of this film, where the mark of the devil – 666 – is uncovered beneath the hair on Damien's head. When his comedy routines gleefully ventured into the dark territory, Hicks would often pose a question to the audience: "How many of you think I'm the anti-Christ right now?" If there was a response, Hicks might announce, "that's not enough," before parting his hair to assure the audience that his only markings were "two sixes and a nine."

The violence of the genre is also apparent in Hicks' dark fantasies, as in a routine serving to illustrate the crime and violence in American society, imagining a newspaper headline, "boy beheads teacher, named best student in class." He finishes the routine with a visual familiar to contemporary horror, using his physicality to show an image of the boy with his arm out, holding the severed head by its hair. The violence of the genre can even be seen in quick asides, as in the infamous Funny Firm show where he battled hecklers, but did find a transient moment when he seemed to be getting back on a comedy track, likening it to "Nick Nolte in T*he Deep*," his relief like the actor's aquatic emergence in said horror film.

On a more lateral level, Hicks' routine about a mall culture has him imagining "that by the year 2000 all malls in the world are going to be connected. There's going to be a subculture of mall people who have never seen daylight." The routine alludes to George A. Romero's zombie flick *Dawn Of The Dead* (1979) in which carnivorous zombies overrun society, the film's main action taking place in a shopping mall. For Romero it is a metaphor for consumer society, a society of brain dead people seeking satisfaction in material possessions and not questioning why they are doing this. These zombies are not in touch with either inner or outer consciousness, but are merely representatives of a society bludgeoned by voracious consumerism.

Although Hicks' film referencing is playful there are times when he feels the need to more angrily deride movies, in particular those movies which provoke debate in the media. As with the debate on "is *American Gladiators* too violent?" this is a fallacious hysteria that suggests the films are more important than they actually are. 1991 saw the release of *Silence Of The Lambs* and the return of a debate about violence in movies. To Hicks, this film (about a serial killer who skins his victims to wear) was laughable, the best comedy of the year, concluding that a better movie would be one where Chevy Chase gets skinned. Chase, one of the original pioneers from *Saturday Night Live*, had pursued a movie career producing films in which he was a smooth, self-satisfied character delivering oh so clever one-liners.

Hicks had more to criticise with 1992's big box office hit, *Basic Instinct*, a story of sex and violence "titillating to middle America," which again sparked a media debate (and protests from women's groups and gay groups). The main selling point seemed to be that its star, Sharon Stone, opened her legs in one scene and revealed her pussy, as if that was "the hallmark of art." Again Hicks saw through the "phoney hysteria" of how it was presented as some kind of radical, explicit sex movie when really it was "a piece of shit." Selling the film as being "by the writer of *Flashdance*" (an all gloss no substance 1983 movie about a female welder and exotic dancer) only added to the way it insulted people's intelligence. Hicks saw a better plot for *Basic Instinct* in which all the dialogue is cut out and the only problem is actor Michael Douglas demanding his part be re-instated, Hicks answering him with a plot summary of the film he envisioned: "Gee Mike, the movie started, Sharon Stone was eating another woman for an hour and a half, then the credits rolled."

Basic Instinct was a film for people too afraid and hypocritical to rent real pornographic movies, Hicks bewildered that people were getting so excited about a brief shot of Sharon Stone's pussy when it is so easy to view "films with nothing but pussy" by going to a video store and locating the pornography section. Hicks employed a similar riff when his routine turned to Madonna's book, *Sex* (also 1992), and its collection of pseudo-arty soft-porn photographs, which was selling for £25 in the U.K., to which Hicks noted, "for twenty-five pounds you can actually *have* sex."

Porno was another genre Hicks was particularly fond of. Porno movies were a mainstay of his routines, his love of them again influenced by another 1970s trend for such movies. "Porno chic" had been coined in that decade by *New York Times* critic Vincent Canby to denote a surge in interest for hardcore sex films, a trend ignited by *Deep Throat* (1972). Its star, Linda Lovelace, became a household name and the subject of many comedians' routines, including Johnny Carson's opening monologues. The film specialised in fellatio, the surreal plot device being that Lovelace could only achieve orgasm through giving oral sex, because her clitoris was in her throat! It's the kind of absurd idea found in much of Hicks' sex material, much of it concerned with oral sex. The film kicked off a trend that saw hardcore films being shown in mainstream movie theatres, attracting couples and the middle classes and being talked about on television and newspapers. *Deep Throat* became the subject of legal wrangles over the next three years, allowing the trend to remain in the media whilst further hardcore films were released to cash in on its success.

Hicks enjoyed going to see sex films, beginning in high school when he and friends had to dress in suits and ties to appear older, his interest not waning when those films returned to flea-pit cinemas during the 1980s. He celebrated them in his routines, but was also keen to point out the way that - like Hollywood films - they often deceived. One such example was *Sex Kittens*, "a pornographic movie, but the pornography is cut out of it." It is again the false promise, the eager selling of something as more than what it actually is; on a base level the titillation of *Basic Instinct*, on a political level the media presentation of the Iraqi army's might.

Though terrible films gave Hicks material, quality films also made an impression on him. He'd been amazed by Richard Pryor's first two stand-up films and enjoyed The Beatles' *Yellow Submarine* (1968) with its animated psychedelia. He'd also envisioned his own movie venture, *Ninja Bachelor Party*, as "The *Tommy* for the nineties" (3), referencing Ken Russell's extravagant, mystical rock opera of 1975. With his interest in expanded awareness, another of Russell's films, *Altered States* (1980) also fascinated him with its plot of a man using sensory deprivation and hallucinatory images, which take him back to the beginnings of human evolution. This is similar to the theme of Stanley Kubrick's *2001: A Space Odyssey* (1968) which charts evolution from Neanderthal man to space scientist, its wild visuals something akin to a trip, a view shared by Hicks with his reference to it on the *Revelations* video when detailing the power of mushrooms. Kubrick is also referenced in a routine about imagining the New Kids On

The Block's Donnie Wahlberg having his head squashed by cars on a freeway and Hicks gleefully watching along with Wahlberg's mother whose eyes are "open like Malcolm in *Clockwork Orange*."

Such clever assimilation of cultural reference points is also seen when Hicks compares the movie *Shane* (1953) to the way America sells arms to poor countries before bombing them. In this routine, the movie's villain, Jack Palance, represents America, encouraging poorer nations (represented by the sheepherder) to take up arms so that it can then have an excuse to kill them. The western genre is particularly pertinent for Hicks, the introduction to the *Revelations* show noting his "growing up on a steady diet of Westerns, I always wanted to be the cowboy hero." Generally, Hicks' comedy compares to the genre's chief attributes, in that it is about a fight between good (honesty, freedom) and evil (prejudice, hypocrisy, government). Moreover, whilst Hicks' extensive travelling sees him very much as the archetypal lone figure of the genre, almost riding from town to town to fight injustice (fellow comedian Dan Vitale said supporting Hicks was "kinda lika riding with Jesse James") it is no coincidence that when he performed with fellow Southern comics they dubbed themselves "The Outlaws."

The western genre, unlike horror and pornography, is accorded some reverence in Hicks' routines. For him, it is representative of another era, a time when American values were clearly defined, uncluttered by consumerism and self-interest, and those motivated to fight injustice (such as Kennedy) were accorded respect because they had earned it. It is why Hicks' routine on Yul Brynner doesn't really take him to task for his preaching against cigarettes. Instead, there is a celebration of his hedonistic life, perhaps in no small part due to Brynner's lead role in genre classic *The Magnificent Seven* (1960), Hicks' frequent stage attire of black shirt and jeans paying homage to the dress of Brynner's character.

Cinema then was a medium Hicks could tolerate more than television, for despite his performances being shown unexpurgated in the U.K. he still found television in America seeking to dilute his message. In many ways, with the brevity of his slots, Hicks' appearances on Letterman offered only a narrow view of what he was really about, yet they remained a foot in the door, appealing to Hicks' sense of subverting from the inside as he agreed to do an eighth assignment on October 4th 1991. The night before, CBS programme *48 Hours* filmed a segment called *Comedy Mission*, following Hicks as he did two gigs in preparation for Letterman. The programme interviews the show's producer, Frank Gannon (for seven years an assistant to Richard Nixon) about his "judgement" of comedy on television. The programme shows Hicks' approach to TV work and his awareness of how a necessary compromise meant the Letterman show was basically using him: "They tell you 'Oh, we like you on our show 'cos you're edgy or you're point of view, but when you come on our show could you not do those.'" Hicks is readily aware that he gives the show credibility and a hint of controversy, whilst at the same time not being allowed to go too far. Gannon's assertion that an appearance on Letterman is "the ultimate achievement" for a comedian was certainly not a view shared by Hicks.

Television had influenced culture heavily since Hicks' birth. From the Kennedy assassination to the moon landing to horrific images of the Vietnam War, TV had filtered the world into the homes of Americans. But as it became omnipresent and more channels became available it began to permeate the culture, the public increasingly looking to it for answers.

For Jack Boulware, Hicks was "the antithesis of TV-friendly material" (37). Not for him the cuddly persona that left audiences believing everything was all right with the world, Hicks had to be radical, had to be shocking so that, according to Will Kaufman, "the shock would need to be ferocious enough to cut through the passivity engineered by complicit – or at least, compliant – television programming" (29).

As discussed in Chapter Eight, television's output in the 1980s and 1990s gave Hicks much material to criticise. There was some shift into the nineties as he looked at the pornography that was chat shows and the ubiquity of talk shows in which famous people or ordinary members of the public discussed "serious issues." Hicks would criticise such TV in America, seeing programmes like *Geraldo*, *Oprah*, and *The Arsenio Hall Show* (1989 –1994) as lowest common denominator television, their false sincerity conveying an idea that fifteen minutes of TV therapy could rid individuals of their problems and set the world to rights. For Hicks, the trend for celebrities to reveal childhood trauma on national television was nothing more than a marketing tool, used to give the impression that these stars had some depth. Hicks effectively satirised such egocentric soul bearing with his idea for a one-man show, the content of which is: "Good evening everybody. Mama never beat me and Daddy never fucked me." Whilst *Geraldo* and *Oprah* offered the voyeuristic thrills of emotional evisceration through pseudo psychoanalysis, Arsenio Hall's show offered a sanitised version of rap culture, thus playing perfectly to white Americans wanting to seem hip but who were too scared of the socio-political rap of groups like Public Enemy. To Hicks, Hall was "a smarmy, untalented goofball" (5). He could not believe that much respected stars like Robert DeNiro went on the show, leading him to wonder if Jesus would be next.

Though shows like *Roseanne* conveyed a more realistic picture of America, its antithesis, *Beverly Hills 90210* (debuting in 1990) was more popular, its relentless banality also apparent with former stand-up Tim Allen's move into television on the sit-com *Home Improvement*. Debuting in 1991, it harked back to the gender stereotypes of Lucille Ball and Jackie Gleason as it basked in its own inanity.

1990s television shows were more concerned with stupidity, substituting originality with garishness and freakish intrusion, the zeitgeist effectively summarised by Carl Bernstein's assertion that "the weird and the stupid and the coarse are becoming our cultural norm, even our cultural ideal" (38). Hicks saw this with his routine about getting work on television and the producers only concerned about "will there be titty?" Television didn't want talent or intellect, but rather the brain dead fodder that appealed to audience's basest, most voyeuristic instincts. *Love Connection* (1981-1993) had a bachelor and three prospective dates with one chosen by the audience to go out with him. For Hicks it was a show that "makes jerking off look like a spiritual quest." To a comedian who wanted people to think and develop intellectually, the crassness of television seemed to mirror the anti-intellectualism of society. It was nothing short of a prelude to the coming apocalypse: "I can't watch TV longer than five minutes without praying for nuclear holocaust." His frustration is with the lack of questioning from the public, the way that they seem to accept what's happening, somehow reassured by banality's omnipresence. He sees such apathy as a natural breeding ground for knee-jerk fundamentalism, for with such simplicity debate becomes obsolete; it's just black and white, good and evil, and in this climate fear and hate become easy impulses, leading Hicks to conclude: "Everyone has a voice of reason inside them and I believe that's been quelled to a large degree by our multi-media society" (2).

He hated the way television dominated lives, to such a degree that many Americans looked to it for opinions rather than thinking for themselves. As Hicks' waffle house waitress says, "Why read when you can just flip on the tube?" Television's purpose seemed to be to keep people dumb: "Go back to bed America, your government is in control...Watch this, shut up!" Those who populated the TV screens of America were the "fevered egos", those people wrapped up in their own self-importance, stars whose egos were so inflated that what they produced was all about them, elevating their 'art' to levels which dwarfed all that was really important in the world.

Television dealt with the trivial, got into an excitable state over such inconsequential things as flag burning.

The media worked itself up into a frenzied state over two sex scandals in 1991. In July actor Paul Reubens, best known for his role as Pee-wee Herman in the children's TV show, *Pee-wee's Playhouse*, was arrested for "indecent exposure" in a Florida porn theatre whilst watching a movie called *Nancy Nurse Turns Up The Heat*. The media lapped it up and paid little attention to local citizens voicing their opinions about wasting manpower in raiding a porno theatre.

There was another media scrum when George Bush wanted to appoint Clarence Thomas, a conservative African-American, to the Supreme Court in October 1991. Media interest began when Anita Hill, a law professor at the University of Oklahoma, not only accused Thomas of sexual harassment when she had worked for him, but also of enjoying pornographic films. Although there was a serious issue to be debated, the media mostly concentrated on Thomas' predilection for pornographic movies before a senate of 98% males voted him in.

Both the Reubens and Thomas incidents saw the media focusing on the pornographic films angle amid familiar cries from the moral majority about civilisation's imminent collapse because of these skin flicks. Hicks lamented the fact that "pornography's got a really bad name," and felt no shame in announcing "I love pornography," before proudly admitting that he had an extensive collection of tapes, from "*Clam Lappers* volume one through ninety" to "*Rear Entry* volumes one to forty," his tapes being nothing short of "pure fucking art." At least pornography didn't pretend to offer any false soul-searching, marginalized sufficiently for its viewing to be a matter of choice for the public.

Hicks felt compelled to watch the show *COPS* like it was some kind of car wreck of what America represented, an insight into the mentality of its people. Sordid sensationalism was apparent in this show's fly-on-the-wall filming of arrests and also the way the news focused on serial killers. Similar to his fascination with assassination and gun culture, Hicks also uncovered the violence in American society with his material on infamous serial killers Henry Lee Lucas, Ted Bundy and Jeffrey Dahmer. When Dahmer was arrested in July 1991, in his Milwaukee apartment police found pictures of dismembered bodies, a human head in the refrigerator and a skeleton in the filing cabinet. Eventually charged with killing seventeen men, amongst the videos found at his apartment were *Cocktales* and (something akin to Hicks' *Clamlappers* series of pornographic films), *Hard*

157

Men 2 and *Hard Men 3*. Interestingly, there was also a copy of The *Return Of The Jedi*, which kind of punched a hole in the moral majority's argument about violent movies inspiring violent acts. In addition, there was a video including a lecture on evolution and an episode of *The Cosby Show*, and several religious books (39).

Though Hicks referenced Dahmer in a re-working of his putting terminally ill people in movies riff, this time offering prison sentences where Dahmer would be sentenced to appear in a Wes Craven film, of more relevance to Hicks' serial killer material was Ted Bundy, found guilty in 1980 of killing over forty women. Defending himself, Bundy drew out the court proceedings before finally being executed in January 1989. During this lengthy process the media fascination with Bundy elevated him to the celebrity status he so obviously craved, drawing many women to him who sent gifts and offered marriage proposals. Hicks would mock their behaviour in his routines, dumfounded that a sensitive intellectual like he was could not find a date, whilst the wife-beaters and people like Bundy seemed to attract scores of females, inspiring the Marblehead Johnson song *Chicks Dig Jerks* with lines such as, "What do I have to offer you baby, poetry and true love. That's not enough I know for sure, you need someone to throw you through the door." Bundy's notoriety showed everything about the dominance of television and its ability to influence the culture, whilst also seeming to suggest that in America, the most abhorrent crimes can be forgotten if the perpetrator manages to achieve the societal aspiration of fame. It is why we often find in Hicks' material on television stars and pop icons such violent imagery, as if Hicks is the serial killer, albeit one with a morality based on taste.

Hicks was a fan of television programmes such as *The Larry Sanders Show*, *Seinfeld*, *Northern Exposure*, *Roseanne* and particularly *The Simpsons*, once unequivocally declaring *"The Simpsons* is all we've got" (40). This animated show had begun as a segment on *The Tracey Ullman Show* in 1987, and then after a Christmas special of its own in 1989, the series debuted in 1990. It soon became a critically acclaimed and hugely popular series, its subversive spirit impeccably annoying the same kind of people Hicks' comedy offended, leading George Bush senior to announce, "we need a nation closer to The Waltons than The Simpsons."

In some ways the characters in this nuclear family mirror Hicks' own family. It is most obviously seen in Marge, always seeking to be upstanding, mothering her family with a warm yet exaggerated innocence. Hicks' Mumsy character, with its tone and homely phrases is similar.

Homer perhaps is a dumber version of his father; both careless of fashion and ignorant of the embarrassment they cause their children. Hicks' sister and brother were as well educated as Lisa, and perhaps Hicks saw in Bart some of his own anti-establishment fervour. Though there is a reference to the series when Hicks does a routine on pro-lifers and comments, "Suddenly I'm adopted by the Flanders" (citing the Simpsons' pious neighbours), the connection between the two is generally more implicit.

In a 1986 show at Comix Annex, Hicks' "I think TV's for stupid morons who have no imagination" has the same ethos as Bart Simpson's acknowledgement that "thanks to television I can't remember what happened eight minutes ago" (from *Homer's Barbershop Quartet*). Satirising television is a frequent theme of *The Simpsons*, be it parodies of commercials that mock the gullibility of the masses or Kent Brockman's news show, which mocks reactionary, sensationalist news coverage. Another episode of *The Simpsons* sees Homer volunteering for the medical testing of commercial products, one of which is a perfume that burns him. Its makers say, "We'll call it Desert Breeze," a mockery of the kind of marketing thinking Hicks often targeted, as with a routine about poisonous baby food being sold as an aid for sleep. More explicit satire is seen through the TV clown, Krusty, and his merchandising, which encompasses everything from pregnancy testing kits to *Krusty's Sulfuric Acid*.

Similarly, the inhabitants of Springfield are mocked frequently for their mob mentality and the ease with which they are easily swayed by trends or the populist rhetoric of politicians. It is seen in the episode *Bart Gets Famous* when Bart becomes famous for a catchphrase "I didn't do it," so that thereafter – like audiences seeking Hicks' dick jokes – it is all the public want him for. This jumping on bandwagons and superficial looking at issues in terms of black and white dominates Hicks' routines criticising cultural consensus, the world where everyone is pacified by watching *American Gladiators*. In *Itchy & Scratchy & Marge* violence in a cartoon sees Marge organising protests and picketing to censor the cartoon, yet the episode ends with Michelangelo's nude, *David*, being exhibited at a museum and Marge refusing to campaign against it. It's an episode that perfectly mirrors Hicks' belief that his swearing and dark imagery have an artistic purpose and that censorship is selective and aligned to a somewhat fascistic ideology. *The Simpsons* mocks the same anti-intellectualism, not only through the dumb muscle bound action film star Rainier Wolfcastle (a parody of Arnold Schwarzenegger), but also in episodes like *A Star Is Burns* where Springfield holds a film festival and Homer (representing

159

Hicks' "bovine America") selects *Man Getting Hit by Football* as his favourite over more intellectual entries.

Such sophistication was little seen in mainstream television. For Hicks, TV was about exploitation and brainwashing, merely a means of preparing the masses for adverts, leading him to refer to the USA as "The United States Of Advertising." TV required no thought or involvement, unlike Hicks' routines, which raged against such passivity. Television is merely there to be consumed, treating viewers as commodities, parading materialism with a contemptuous dishonesty, prompting Hicks to joke that every commercial should be forced to have on the end "Come on, you're stupid, buy it."

Hicks saw that commercials were a cloak for the dumbing down of the nation. As George Carlin said, "When fascism comes to this country, it won't be wearing jackboots; it'll be wearing sneakers with lights in them, and it'll have a smiley face and a Michael Jordan T-shirt" (41). For Hicks, this is the "T-shirt nirvana" where attitude and rebellion are marketing tools, where when he tells those in advertising to "kill yourselves" they will take it as a useful marketing angle.

Though the Supreme Court had defined pornography as that which has "no artistic merit and causes sexual thoughts", Hicks saw adverts as the real pornography, using sex as a means to sell products, referencing sexually alluring female twins on a double mint commercial and musing on what advertisers would like to do if they could: having a naked woman fingering herself with the message being "Drink coke." He pondered how far commercials would go; would it one day be "It's Jesus for Miller!" He saw that television was just about selling, so that the public "buy their horseshit products that we don't fuckin' need and become a third world consumer fuckin' plantation, which is what we're becoming." In this warped world everything has a price and nothing has real feeling or soul.

Hicks' depth on the subject of commercials can be seen in his routine on smoking when he talks of Yul Brynner's commercial, screened after his death in an attempt to shock people into giving up smoking. He contrasts this with the runner Jim Fixx dying whilst jogging, showing how adverts only present one side of the story and beyond that how life isn't predictable, doesn't fit any neat structure, death being more open to chance than anything to do with being healthy.

When radio show host Len Belzer hypothesised about Nike phoning Hicks to offer him $750,000 for one year of promotion, Hicks responded unequivocally, stating that he would answer Nike's proposal with, "You have the wrong number" (3). For him, commercials were propagating untruths, selling illusions and anyone who did them was "off the artistic roll call and everything you say is suspect." From rock stars doing commercials to Jay Leno hawking Doritos, for Hicks fame gave individuals a responsibility; either to pursue an artistic vision or tell the truth, not sell out to corporate entities. He had been offered a commercial for Orange Drink in England, mocking the way the advert might have been with, "You know, when I'm done ranting about elite power that rules the planet under a totalitarian government, that uses the media in order to keep people stupid, my throat gets parched. That's why I drink *Orange Drink*." It's a routine that correlates to his view that those in the commercial world can and do put a price on everything, as if that is what life is about, as if that is the sum total of humanity's evolution.

He attacked marketing and advertising with vitriol, although there was the concession of looking the other way for struggling artists. Hicks was not naive though and realised he would need exposure, which accounts for his appearances on Letterman and brief segments in a variety of less significant other shows. Yet there is no denying that mainstream TV in America successfully denied Hicks a voice throughout his career, and with that it denied the many who shared Hicks' vision and ideas a voice too. Hicks was more at home on Public Access TV in Austin, appearing several times and enjoying the opportunity to air his views free from the restrictions imposed by networks.

Only in Britain did his voice remain undiluted, as when Channel 4 screened the *Relentless* performance in January 1992, garnering Hicks further accolades as he became the talk of the U.K. It was to be a year to blow away cobwebs, Nirvana's *Nevermind* album going to number one in the charts and in one sweep making all the glossy soft rock of Bon Jovi and their ilk seem irrelevant (Hicks showed an affinity when appearing on Letterman to the band's *Smells Like Teen Spirit*). Hicks too had his own new album to promote with *Relentless*. It is certainly a more sophisticated album than its predecessor *Dangerous*, with Hicks more at ease with the format, his routines seamlessly interwoven around his thought processes.

Hicks too, with his growing appreciation in the U.K., felt more confident with his progress, illustrated by a playful interview with Missouri disc jockey Zoë Taylor in March, joking about his promise to name an album after Zoë but saying he'd met a girl called Relentless, adding that when smoking gets him his next album will be called Speechless. He even makes a promise to come to Missouri just for Taylor. His appearance on the

Dennis Miller's TV show was another success, before arriving in England on April 29th 1992 to find that Los Angeles had erupted in violence. Quick as ever to assimilate new material, Hicks incorporated the L.A. riots into his act as he did seventeen UK dates in less than 3 weeks.

The L.A. riots link back to the Watts riots of 1965, an explosion of black anger at a racist society, triggered by the arrest of black man for drunk driving. The story had begun on March 3rd 1991 when Rodney King had been pulled over for speeding. Four L.A.P.D. officers, Sergeant Stacey Koon and officers Lawrence Powell, Theodore Briseno and Timothy Wind, then set about beating King, striking him over fifty times with metal batons and hitting twice with an electric stun gun. From a nearby apartment, George Holliday had videotaped the beating, which was subsequently broadcast on national networks. On 29th April 1992, a jury of ten whites, one Hispanic and one Filipino American acquitted Koon, Wind and Briseno and were unable to reach a verdict on Powell.

After the verdict, a symbolic indictment of the corruption and racism of not only the L.A.P.D. but also the American legal system, widespread riots erupted in Los Angeles, eventually leaving 54 people dead. One of the most shocking images from the news coverage was that of truck driver Reginald Denny being pulled from his truck, beaten with a claw hammer, and having a block of concrete dropped on his head, leaving his skull smashed into over a hundred pieces (42). Denny provided much material for Hicks' routines on the riots, bewildered as he was that Denny didn't just "step on the gas" to escape. As ever, Hicks sought to look beyond a surface reading of the story to find the comedy, tying the absurd to a known reality to come up with a hilarious routine about life for Denny after the attacks, where he never again gets out of his truck, speeding everywhere and being regarded as a great employee. Hicks finished with a comparison, imaging how Denny might fill up with gas when not being prepared to stop, comparing it to the re-fuelling of aircraft. In terms of language and image, it gives the routine a kind of "take-off", similar to other routines in Hicks' "ride." Denny himself was forgiving of his attackers, even filmed later on hugging the mothers of two of the men who had attacked him.

It wasn't until April 1993 that a federal jury convicted Koon and Powell, giving them what many considered a light sentence of 30 months in a federal correctional camp.

Returning to America after experiencing the more liberal attitude of the British, Hicks continued his mission to disseminate the supposed facts presented in the news. With the presidential race in full swing he honed in on the polls that seemed to support President Bush; questionnaire's producing results like, "How many people disapprove of George Bush's handling of the country? Seventy per cent. How many people will vote for him again? Seventy per cent." Hicks likened the public's answers to the pain and pleasure of S & M, insightfully noting that opinion poll responses were merely used to propagate untruths by asking leading questions, such as Hicks' example of "Do you think George Bush, a good Christian white man, should send troops to Iraq to end the brown Islamic tide coming over here and fucking your daughter?" It's an assertion backed up by a New York Times/CBS News poll in early 1992, which when using the word "welfare" in a poll found that 44% of those questioned thought that too much was being spent on welfare. However, when the question used the phrase "assistance to the poor" only 13% thought too much was being spent (25).

On Friday 22nd May 1992 Johnny Carson hosted *The Tonight Show* for the last time, signalling the end of an era, although in truth guest hosts like Jay Leno had been taking over from Carson regularly over the last five years. It was more of a symbolic end, the final bow of a performer whose show had so influenced Hicks. Whatever the implications, television in America had been moribund for some time. Hicks found that his opinions were more in demand in Britain where shows like *TV-AM* and *The Jonathon Ross Show* sought him for comments on the American elections, whilst his regular writing for music publication the *N.M.E.* offered his undiluted slant on political events.

The Republican Party Convention in August 1992 saw Pat Buchanan making a hate-filled speech attacking minorities, homosexuals, the pro-choice campaign, and feminists, referring to a "cultural war" for the "soul of the American people." He even claimed, "Ronald Reagan won the Cold War." The old guard were there – Reagan and Pat Robertson – spouting their right wing rhetoric, railing against liberals like Hicks.

At the end of the year, U.S. marines were sent into Somalia in 'Operation Restore Hope', the government calling it "humanitarian intervention." The spin was that it was going to help feed the country's starving and depose its demonised leader General Mohammed Farah Aidid. Yet the reason Somalia was so lacking in food was a consequence of the previous brutal regime of American backed Mohammed Siad Barre. Journalist John Pilger saw the conflict for what it really was: "to distract attention from frantic attempts by President George Bush Senior…to pardon those who might implicate him in the crimes of the Iran-Contra scandals" (43). At the end of this intervention close to 10,000 people were dead. Of the U.S. interventions in Somalia and Haiti, Hicks called them, "spreading democracy at gunpoint" (2), such interference an extension of his view of America as "the bullies of the world."

When Hicks quit smoking in September 1992, audiences at first found it difficult to accept, Hicks likening their reaction to the outrage that greeted Bob Dylan going electric. But, as with his drugs material, he wasn't going to now lecture audiences about how bad cigarettes were, maintaining that it was still an issue of personal freedom. Cut loose from his addiction, which he had grown to associate with corporate greed, Hicks' withdrawal saw him continuing to rage fiercely against the American right and so called moral majority, his perspective made all the more compelling by his adept comic execution. Of course, when an argument is presented so well and the opposing view so efficiently mocked, it leads to a situation observed by one emcee, Linda Dion, who said, "We actually would take bets to see how many people would leave" (44).

Audience reaction would be of concern to a comedian who measured success in terms of fame and money, the kind who chooses topical material as nothing more than a reactionary connection to audience concerns. Hicks, always the revolutionary, was determined to innovate, which is why he began putting together *The Counts Of The Netherworld* with Kansas City comedian, Fallon Woodland. The proposed television show, commissioned by Channel 4 in England, was to have Hicks and Woodland playing Victorian-era counts chatting and philosophising with guests, people such as Noam Chomsky, John Hiatt and Terence McKenna. It would be a show where ideas evolved through discussion, analysis and comedy, enlightening audiences in a way television – which Hicks referred to as "Lucifer's dreambox" – often neglected. The show would demand people think, approaching subjects from new angles and exposing television's lies.

Left wing dissident Chomsky was perhaps the perfect guest for the show, and in many ways the template, his lecture tours exposing the lies of the media, underpinned by an urbane sense of irony. Chomsky's *Manufacturing Consent* (co-written with Edward S. Herman) was a great influence on Hicks' perspective and material, particularly in the late 1980s when his routines underwent an evolution, becoming more incisive in their take on the media, and more socio-political as they shifted from mocking individual celebrities to confronting how those celebrities were a facet of the whole media machine. *Manufacturing Consent* shares many of Hicks' ideas, dealing as it does with how government, and the corporate entities that support it, control the information people receive. The authors pinpoint this as the creation of "necessary illusions", a phrase of similar intent to Hicks' "Lucifer's dreambox". For Chomsky and Herman the "necessary illusion" is the way the rulers treat people as stupid, oversimplifying things for ordinary citizens, just as Hicks portrays a media keen to simplify arguments on drugs and pornography. The necessary illusion may be, for Chomsky, sports programmes, which he sees as having an adverse affect on the audience, serving to "reduce their capacity to think" (44a) whilst also distracting them from real issues. This is the same as Hicks seeing *American Gladiators* as appealing to the lowest common denominator, but also distracting the masses from issues on which they might have to think (in the case of Hicks' routine, it is thinking about the implications of the Kennedy assassination). Chomsky points to it as a means "to manipulate and deceive the stupid majority and remove them from the public arena" (44a) whilst Hicks, in a similar vein, refers to it as keeping the masses "docile."

Chomsky's take on the media is that there are only a handful of companies that own all the media outlets, thus allowing a very uniform viewpoint to be presented, a viewpoint that is generally conservative and controlled. In the light of the Waco siege, it was a perspective picked up by Hicks with an assertion that there are "eleven companies who own all forms of entertainment in the country." It would certainly have been fascinating to see Hicks and Chomsky in debate, and its not too fanciful to suggest that with the depth of Chomsky's research and his knowledge of world affairs he could almost have worked as a perfect straight man, setting up Hicks for some improvised riffing.

On Friday November 6th 1992, Hicks was back in the UK for the *Revelations* tour, packing out venues in between low key slots on a variety of television shows, the most prominent being an uncomfortable appearance on Channel 4's youth TV programme, *The Word*. The show's host, Terry Christian, fumblingly seeks to ask Hicks questions about his comedy, but he is so banal and frivolous that Hicks is unwilling to offer insight, instead using Christian's prompts to offer excerpts from his routines. *The Word* was aimed at the post-pub audience, at the drunkards returning home after a Friday night out. Littered with gimmicks and cynically playing to an audience's basest instincts, the show on which Hicks appeared also included a hidden camera spying on actor Oliver Reed whilst he prepared in his dressing room. Hicks is obviously embarrassed as Christian and co-presenter Katy Puckrick gleefully encourage the audience to laugh at Reed, plying him with drink in the hope that his behaviour will become more outrageous. As the show progresses, Hicks becomes increasingly disinterested and unimpressed by the parade of grotesques, his feelings adequately summed up by his comment to Christian, "I don't remember a lot of what happened before this moment." *The Word* was a show as crass, vulgar and intellectually offensive as those television programmes in American that Hicks frequently denounced. Equally, it's sordid sensationalism spawned generically similar television in Britain with a slew of shows where ordinary members of the public debased themselves for a brief moment of fame. Happily, Hicks' 1992 tour of Britain and the way audiences warmed to and engaged with his ideas reaffirmed his belief in the country's cultural sophistication.

The tour climaxed with a performance at the prestigious Dominion Theatre in London where he played the 2,000-seat venue to rapturous applause. Filmed for broadcast on Channel 4, the *Revelations* show saw Hicks' ideas and philosophy coming together faultlessly, marrying not only rock music and comedy, but also visuals as it begins with him moving through some apocalyptic wasteland where buildings and cars are on fire. Hicks is at one with the audience, drawing them in, puncturing hypocrisy with his sharp humour. The accumulation of years of touring is evident as he masters the large crowd, connecting to and working off them, confident enough to digress, undaunted by the imposing venue.

His routines about media manipulation were at the forefront, from its presentation of drugs to its coverage of the Gulf War, gleefully showing how its version of events was false. Though he believed "news is supposed to be objective" Hicks perfectly understood the machinations of the media and its manipulation of facts. At the centre of this manipulation is the media's use of language. On the one hand, there was the dumbing down of language, be it through crass television shows or the likes of new versions of the Bible, which are meant to be "more palatable". More significantly, it was the way the news media uses language to mask the truth and to shape uninformed opinions. It's the language that tells America to go back to bed because everything is fine.

The Mark Twain influence is obvious in the way Hicks plays with language and its ironies. For example, from his smoking days when he nonchalantly reads a cigarette packet warning: "smoking may cause foetal injury or premature birth" before adding "Fuck it. Found my brand. Just don't get the ones that say lung cancer." In his ironic exposing of the manipulation of language, Hicks' comedy is linked to George Orwell's writing. Orwell maintains a contemporary relevance because, as with Hicks, his work explores themes like freedom and power, timeless themes that will resonate in any era, their use of irony exposing truths that will never lose their pertinence. In his essay *Why I Write*, Orwell's assertion that "I write because there is some lie I want to expose, some fact to which I want to draw attention" conveys his role as England's moral conscience. It is very much in keeping with Hicks' taking material, which "offends my sense of reason", and offering a previously unacknowledged perspective based on a more detailed analysis of the facts. In a way he is America's moral conscience, saying of himself "To me, the comic is the guy who says 'wait a minute' as the consensus forms" (6). He too believed in exposing truths, saying "The best kind of comedy to me is when you make people laugh at things they've never laughed at, and also take a light into the darkened corners of people's minds, exposing them to the light" (5). But in the same piece Orwell also addresses the need for his writing to be more than just political, the need for "an aesthetic experience." He recognised that "my work…contains much that a full-time politician would consider irrelevant." This is similar to Hicks and his "dick jokes," the way his routines are punctuated by things like his frivolous Elvis impersonations. The same contradictions and complexities are seen in each artist's political leanings, both being left wing but both sceptical enough about politicians to distance themselves from what would appear to be their natural homes. For Orwell it is a lack of faith in the British Labour Party, which he saw as only interested in its own power and exploiting the idealism of the masses. Hicks feels the same distaste for the Democratic Party, viewing the Clinton era's idealism as phoney, his policies without substance and liberal admiration merely the result of appraisal applied through rose-tinted spectacles.

There is also the front of being a comedian, the sense that jokes are Hicks' main purpose; that he is there to entertain, and that all detours and rants must at some point return to their comic instincts. Through being the stand-up on stage Hicks can draw the audience in, allowing him to make political points, the comedy being, as Thea Vidale says, "a spoonful of sugar" (20). For Orwell, this mask is best seen in *Animal Farm*, in which the animal fable allows him to simplify things and coat the message in an accessible narrative, just as Swift does with *Gulliver's Travels*.

Both then use irony as a subtle tool to make the readers/audience aware of that which they were not hitherto aware. This engenders a bond between the writer/comedian and the reader/audience, as if they are uniquely in on the joke and sharing the experience. Thus we have the animals puzzled when the milk disappears in *Animal Farm*, yet the reader is very aware that it is their greedy leaders who have done it. With Hicks, this is seen in the character that sells "farming equipment" to Iraq and is then puzzled to learn it was used for weapons. In *Animal Farm*, the reader knows the truth through the narrative that has gone before, whilst with Hicks it is the preface to his material, the way he creates a sense of disbelief mingled with outrage.

Much of Hicks' material aligns itself with *Animal Farm*. The novel deals with the corruption of those in power, attacks capitalism and sees something intrinsically wrong with human nature through the human archetypes that the animals represent. The exaggerated characteristics of the animals compare to Hicks' exaggeration of Southern types in that both are looking at the wider characteristics of humans and their flaws and what these say about our society.

Orwell attacks the hypocrisy of those in the power as the pigs preach against drinking alcohol and engaging in trade with humans, yet they themselves do both of these things. It is similar to the televangelists Hicks raged against, those like Jim Bakker and Jimmy Swaggart who were involved in that which they preached against. In the novel, we have Moses, the raven, Orwell's satire on religion. Moses gives the downtrodden animals stories of Sugarcandy Mountain, a paradise they will go to when they die. He becomes a useful tool for those in power, giving the workers a belief that if they work hard and endure their miserable lives they will be rewarded. It is in keeping with Hicks' attacks on religious leaders who espouse a duty from God, wanting money in God's name, blinding the masses with the idea that whatever happens it is God's will. This is merely a means to keep the masses unquestioning.

In satirising American culture, Hicks' concern was to expose the credulity of the masses, a theme central to *Animal Farm* with Orwell showing those in power actively seeking to keep the masses stupid and therefore influenceable. The pig, Napoleon, opposes Snowball's plan to educate the animals. Instead, he wants to keep them dumb, leading to a situation in the novel where "Several of them would have protested if they could have found the right arguments." This dumbing-down is carried on through the pigs removing access to education; whilst for Hicks it is created by the omnipresence of inane television shows. Just as the sheep in *Animal Farm* represent the unquestioning masses, so the sheep's bleating often drowns out an opposing voice. We can see this idea with Hicks' reference to sheep in many of his shows, employing the baying sound to suggest the American public mindlessly obeying the spin they are given.

Similarly, the animals in *Animal Farm* have empty ceremonies, which celebrate battles and involve saluting their flag of a hoof and horn. Orwell is attacking the appropriation of patriotism by those in power, using it to give them the appearance of respectability whilst also fostering the idea that any questioning of those in power is unpatriotic and must therefore play into the hands of enemies. Hicks' material on flag burning exemplifies this with the way that partaking in it is presented as anti-American. Moreover, frequent Hicks targets such as Reagan and the televangelists always wrapped themselves in the American flag, using it as a means to persuade the country to get behind them because it was the American way. Hicks saw that "You can get away with anything if you just have a flag behind you" (45). It's a patriotism employed to get people in line and alienate those who question its integrity, what Noam Chomsky referred to as "the stranglehold of ideology and tradition of conformism that makes a mockery of the values we pretend to hold" (45a).

Hicks often cited those in power as "fear-mongering," those whose ideology was to unite people through fear of an enemy. Reagan had employed this with the fictitious threat from the Soviet Union and Draconian drugs policies that played to the fears of white middle class Americans. It can be seen with the pigs in *Animal Farm* and their frequent references to the farm's one-time owner, Mr Jones: "surely there is no one among you who wants to see Jones come back?" Orwell, like Hicks, is well aware that fear can trap people into accepting what they know to be wrong. Thus we have Hicks' America swamped by fundamentalism, its ideology based on a threat of retribution in hell.

We have too, in *Animal Farm*, the manipulation of the masses through language. Squealer is the propaganda machine delivering the pigs' spin on events: "they had nothing to go upon except Squealer's list of figures, which invariably demonstrated that everything was getting better and better." This correlates to Hicks' philosophy on television, in that it has become the sole means of information for an apathetic public too lazy to think for themselves. News is made palatable, easily digestible, with complex issues simplified, progressively dumbing down the culture and its people, so that just like the animals in *Animal Farm*, they haven't the intellectual tools to question their leaders. Added to this, the simplification of the animals' Seven Commandments to the axiomatic "Four legs good, two legs bad" is a device to stifle any kind of thought or discussion, much as Hicks sees the media's presentation of drugs and other issues as one-dimensional and part of an attempt to suppress debate and alternative viewpoints.

In Orwell's essay *Politics and the English Language* he complained about words being used "to dress up simple statement(s)." This decoration of language is seen in Hicks' routine on porno stars being described as "models" with Hicks cutting through the pretensions and manipulation with "how is gissum being worn this year?" and "Here's Dallas with a penis ensemble" as he mocked these stars before adding "yeah, I'm an amusement engineer." Despite being more frivolous, Hicks sees such linguistic ornamentation as another fraudulent way to misshape opinion, thus making it a political issue.

In the essay Orwell writes of political language "designed to make lies sound truthful and murder respectable." He complains about the labelling of bombings as "pacification" and the displacement of people being called "transfer of population" or "rectification of frontiers." It's seen in *Animal Farm* with Squealer referring to reductions of food as a "readjustment." It was something seen in the Gulf War where saturation bombing became "laying down a carpet" and civilian casualties became "collateral damage," words designed to make the obscene realities of conflict more palatable to the American public. Moreover, because the military was in full control of Gulf War reporting, it set the language agenda so that such dishonest phrases became common currency. Indeed, a CIA memorandum in November 1991 said the media "have helped us turn some intelligence failure stories into intelligence success stories" (46). For Hicks, this abuse of language is apparent when weapons being sold to Iraq are described as "machine tools" in the U.K. and "farming equipment" in the U.S. It is also evident when Hicks mocks news reports that refer to "The *Elite* Republican Guard," language designed to scare the American public. As Hicks noted, "Well, after two months of continuous carpet bombing and not one reaction at all from them, they became simply The Republican Guard, not nearly as elite as we may have led you to believe. And after another month of bombing, they went from The Elite Republican Guard, to The Republican Guard, to the Republicans made this shit up about there being a guard out there." Hicks sees that government is using language as a political tool, using "Elite" to infer a need for the military to take action, whilst at the same time the inevitable military success appears more heroic with such an apparently mighty force being overcome.

For both Orwell and Hicks, language is an apparatus used by governments to present untruths to the masses. It is most obviously seen in

Nineteen Eighty-Four, Orwell's novel focusing on a totalitarian government of the future, the kind who for Hicks "partition information." It uses language, or "Doublethink" to persuade the masses to accept two contradictory ideas, so we have "joycamp" referring to a forced labour camp, "Ministry Of Peace" referring to the department in charge of war and "Ministry Of Love" concerned with torture. It is a world where "the Party would announce that two and two made five, and you would have to believe it. "Doublethink" is apparent in Hicks' routines, where we have a population ignoring the contradictions of the Kennedy assassination, and just as *Nineteen Eighty-Four*'s government want to erase and control history with its "who controls the past controls the future: who controls the present controls the past", so we have people telling Hicks to "quit talking about Kennedy" and his routine on the Rodney King trial which sees the police officers re-writing history by reinterpreting the beating video: "It's all on how you look at...If you play it backwards you see us help King up and send him on his way."

Television is complicit in this deception with the bipartisan politics of Hicks' America mirrored by the generally unquestioning television networks. In *Nineteen Eighty-Four*, the government uses the media in the shape of Big Brother with telescreens everywhere delivering constant propaganda for Oceania's government. "Hate Week" (alluded to by Hicks with his "The People Who Hate People Party") involves news stories that follow Oceania's victories in the war, leaving the public ecstatic with patriotic happiness. Hicks sees the same jingoistic joy, the "bloodlust" that makes people feel better about themselves during the Gulf War. And like Oceania ignoring the bad news of bombs falling on London, so there was a careful avoidance of civilian casualties by the American media during the Gulf War.

The government controls the media's language through "Newspeak", giving only a limited or biased view of events. This control limits the masses understanding and keeps them passive. The telescreens are ubiquitous and there is no alternative so that gradually the masses accept it, exemplified with the novel's hero Winston Smith unable "to fix his mind on any one subject for more than a few moments at a time." It's the constant repetition of manipulated news that sees the masses accept untruths, echoed in Hicks' booming TV voice administering "You are free to do as we tell you! You are free to do as we tell you!" For the animals in *Animal Farm*, the masses in *Nineteen Eighty-Four* and the people of Hicks' America, freedom is an illusion they are made to believe through television.

Television's part in the conspiracy that Hicks had seemingly been piecing together all his career is evident in the way the mainstream shied away from him, and is best seen when Hicks was dropped from the Letterman Show in 1993, which Hicks described as "a series of Orwellian cuts and edits" (47). Hicks' views were unpopular because they challenged the status quo. Because of this, they were a threat that the mainstream didn't want to allow. Orwell wrote of this in *The Freedom of the Press* with "Anyone who challenges prevailing orthodoxy finds himself silenced with surprising effectiveness. A genuinely unfashionable opinion is almost never given a fair hearing, either in the popular press or in the highbrow periodicals."

As 1992 drew to a close Hicks was adeptly uncovering a conspiracy equal to Orwell's Big Brother. The impending ousting of Republicanism by Bill Clinton and the Democrats didn't impress Hicks, seeing the change of government as little more than a charade. For him politics in America was "'I think the puppet on the right shares my beliefs.' 'I think the puppet on the left is more to my liking.' Hey, wait a minute, there's one guy holding up both puppets!'" Again, it echoes the illusions created by those in power in *Animal Farm* and *Nineteen Eighty-Four*, a point emphasized by Hicks' opinion of the political debates in the run up to the 1992 presidential elections, observing that "It's like watching the live-action version of *Animal Farm*" (48), continuing this theme when Clinton came into power with "we're just entering a new level of deceit. It's gilded. We're now entering the *Animal Farm* era of political correctness" (40). Hicks saw through Clinton's front of liberalism and political correctness as merely another means to control what is said, like George Carlin's view that "one person's correctness is another person's incorrectness" (41). Indeed, vice president Al Gore's wife, Tipper, had been behind the P.M.R.C.'s imposing of warning stickers on albums. It's the use of political correctness as a way to ignore problems like racism and poverty, its aim seeming to be to avoid offending the liberal middle classes, who in turn could be absolved of guilt merely by paying lip service to such issues.

Clinton wasn't really offering anything new, which is why he got elected and prospective Democratic candidate Jerry Brown got marginalized. Brown had sought the Democratic nomination with a liberal, almost socialist agenda, refusing to take campaign contributions larger than $100. Hicks hated the way Brown was portrayed in the media as "Governor Moonbeam" because he injected an element of spirituality into his campaign. Brown's angry rants were certainly in tune with Hicks and the

172

way the media smothered his voice mirrored Hicks' own marginalisation by the entertainment industry.

Clinton's defeat of Bush in the presidential elections came on the back of a mere 55 per cent turn out, of which only 43 per cent voted for Clinton. Nonetheless it led many liberal commentators to believe this was the dawning of a new era. Indeed, Hicks was also in celebratory mood, rejoicing about "That rampaging Republican beast brought to its knees." He saw this beast as the Republican elephant, which he and fellow comics had been trying to bring down for over a decade, an allusion to Orwell's *Shooting an Elephant* with its reference to the end of the British Empire. However, he was enough aware of politics ("all governments are lying cocksuckers") to know that Clinton wasn't going to change much, referring to him as "a poor man's Kennedy" (17), whose election, in effect, manufactured more complacency by convincing people that social issues and inequality were going to be addressed. And those lying cocksuckers were at it again when just before Bush left office he pardoned six members of the Reagan administration for the Iran-Contra affair, much like Ford had pardoned Nixon over Watergate.

When he'd given up alcohol and drugs in 1988, Hicks' comedy had moved towards more political material. After quitting smoking it was as if he were pushing all vices aside, all distractions that might hinder his journey in search of the truth. Now firmly established in the U.K. and with plans to subvert television through *The Counts Of The Netherworld*, he achieved another nomination by the American Comedy Awards for Best Male Stand-Up in January 1993. He was up against Richard Jeni, Ritch Snyder, Will Durst and George Wallace, Jeni being the eventual winner. But Hicks' new found optimism wasn't diminished; particularly happy that he'd finally found a management team he'd always needed with Colleen McGarr and Duncan Strauss, a partnership in tune to his talents and the possibilities for progress.

He was also putting together his next comedy album, *Arizona Bay*, though Invasion Records didn't think it ready for release. It included his musical score mixed with the routines, what Hicks described as his "comedic *Dark Side Of The Moon*", in reference to Pink Floyd's concept album. *Arizona Bay* was to be an all-encompassing view of America as a microcosm of the world, music being used because for Hicks, it "heals the comedy" (3). And some comedy it was too, the best of his career thus far as he attacked television lies, government lies and a society distorted by consumerism. Perceptive, involving, successfully hitting so many targets and given a mesmerising quality by the musical score, *Arizona Bay* showed the depth of Hicks' knowledge of the world, uncovering truths as he moved closer to the centre of a conspiracy amongst those who ruled the planet.

14
Conspiracies

...And then came the Waco siege at Mount Carmel. Deep in the Texas Bible belt, Mount Carmel was populated by Seventh Day Adventists led by David Koresh amid an atmosphere of teaching and ideas with something of a sixties commune vibe to it. The religion itself dates back to the early nineteenth century when its members were intellectuals, amongst them John Harvey Kellogg, a Seventh Day Adventist pioneer and the inventor of cornflakes. They believed in the evolution of humanity with God giving mankind minor revelations as it progressed. A breakaway division of the Seventh Day Adventists was formed at Mount Carmel in 1934. Vernon Howell (as Koresh was known until he changed his name in 1989) was first at Mount Carmel in 1981. A guitar player, his preaching style was casual, more concerned with teaching, though his reading and teaching of the Seven Seals of Revelation saw him as another Christ.

In March 1992, FBI cameras were set up to spy on Mount Carmel whilst at the same time a group of eight officers tried to infiltrate the group, suspecting them of stockpiling illegal weapons. Though the Davidians had many weapons, they were for selling legally at gun fairs, most of them boxed ready for sale. Not wanting a confrontation, Koresh even offered to allow agents from the Bureau of Alcohol, Tobacco and Firearms (ATF) to inspect Mount Carmel for illegal weapons, but his offer wasn't taken up.

On February 28th the following year, the ATF blocked roads, donned full combat gear and prepared to raid Mount Carmel. The press had been tipped off about the raid as the ATF thought that the successful operation they envisioned might be good publicity for them for two reasons. Firstly, the ATF faced congressional budget hearings in March. That they were filming the raid themselves suggests they wanted footage to show congress to support their request for further funding. Another reason for seeking publicity was to divert attention from a public relations disaster that had occurred the previous year.

The ATF and FBI had only recently been involved in a similar situation back on August 21st 1992 when three U.S. Marshalls were watching the cabin Randy Weaver shared with his wife Vicki and children Rachel, Sara and Sammy in the mountains of Idaho. Also there that day was family friend Kevin Harris. The Marshalls were hoping to arrest Weaver with possession of a shotgun sawn off below the legal limit. Randy Weaver was something of a survivalists, eschewing the consumer society for a plywood cabin amid the beautiful natural surroundings of the Selkirk Mountains. The Weavers attended gatherings put on by the Aryan Nation, and though they did not agree with the Nation's racist views, they had similar feelings about governments having too much control over people's lives. It was at one of these gatherings that Randy was approached and asked to saw off a shotgun at below the legal limit. Assured of the man's decency, Weaver agreed to do it, but the man asking was an undercover ATF agent seeking to set Weaver up and force him to either become an informant on the Aryan Nation or go to prison. Randy refused and subsequently didn't attend court for the charges.

On the 21st the U.S. Marshalls first shot the Weaver dog, then their son Sammy in the back, killing him. When Kevin Harris opened fire the Marshalls returned fire and in the ensuing chaos one Marshall was killed. So began a siege with 400 army troops called up to surround the cabin, along with tanks, armoured personnel carriers and FBI snipers, their sights set on the Weaver home, coldly killing Vicki Weaver in front of her children with a bullet in her head, whilst also shooting and injuring Randy and Kevin Harris.

The FBI branded Randy a "white supremacist", deliberately employing language with racist connotations so as not to provoke sympathy for the Weavers from American liberals. The media dutifully followed suit as the siege continued. Indeed, there was little information being fed to the media apart from propaganda to make the Weavers seem evil. Even comedian Bill Maher, on his show *Politically Incorrect*, bought into the spin when he said, "If you're bringing your kids up in Aryan Nations you are causing danger because you're spawning hate in America."

The siege lasted ten days before the Weavers surrendered, both Randy and Kevin Harris concerned about gangrene in their wounds, leaving the cabin in which Vicki Weaver's body still lay.

As Randy Weaver approached a trial, which looked likely to be a disaster for the government, ATF and FBI, so the Waco siege provided a timely distraction, beginning to dominate the news on television and in papers.

The media were eager to present Koresh as the ATF wanted with reports branding him a child molester, a gun nut, and using manipulative language like "Sinful messiah" and "cult leader." Hicks poked fun at the media presentation, with his take on Koresh as a "frustrated rock musician with a messianic complex, armed to the teeth and trying to fuck everything that moves. I don't know how to tell you this, sounds like every one of my friends in Austin…I've been compared to Koresh before. People said I was like Koresh, except without the guns and pussy."

The raid of February 28th was ostensibly to arrest Koresh and get him off the property, yet at no point during the preceding days was any effort made to arrest him as he left the property, which he did regularly before the ATF created a siege situation.

The raid saw helicopters circling Mount Carmel and ATF agents charging in by the truckload, throwing in flash bang grenades and provoking a gun battle. As the shooting began, from inside Mount Carmel, Douglas Wayne Martin made a 911 call. Martin (an educated lawyer who didn't fit the media stereotype of occupants brainwashed and held under duress) pleaded for help and for the raid to end, but there was no cessation until after several hours when the ATF, having run out of ammunition, retreated. Two Davidians had been killed and four ATF agents. The ATF claimed the Davidians opened fire first, yet holes in the doors to Mount Carmel showed the bullets were mainly incoming. In later congressional hearings this door went missing after being requested as evidence (as did a videotape of the raid). ATF agent, Jim Cavanaugh, testified that the helicopters hadn't opened fire, yet film showed a helicopter shooting one Davidian, standing at the top of a tower, dead. The same misinformation that Hicks had mocked in his routines on the Kennedy assassination was to be a feature of the siege and its aftermath.

The FBI then took over, surrounding Mount Carmel with soldiers, tanks and snipers, moving the burgeoning media presence back some two miles away from Mount Carmel, to a place that became known as Satellite City. Of the negotiations that then began, the FBI only relayed to the media the information it wanted them to know. It continued to paint Koresh as a religious maniac, peddling the child abuse line and referring to Mount Carmel in hostile, militaristic terms like "compound" and "bunker" which the media dutifully adopted in its reporting. There was little questioning of the idea that Koresh wasn't brainwashing Mount Carmel's inhabitants, even when some parents and children voluntarily left the compound after the February raid (to be immediately arrested and separated from their children). When questioned about the placing of the media two miles away the FBI argued it was for safety reasons, despite ATF records showing the rifles at Mount Carmel only had a range of one mile.

Thus, the media didn't see FBI tanks crushing vehicles around Mount Carmel as they cleared the way for an assault. Pictures were only shown, edited, several days later. Meanwhile, the FBI showed its caring side by sending in first aid on March 4th (with bugging devices concealed inside).

The developing story naturally piqued Hicks' interest. To him it was "the most fascinating story of the year, bar none." Hicks liked left-field news items, ones that pointed out the weirdness of life and were so compelling that in a sense they united a nation, to such a degree that they were ripe for misrepresentation. For someone willing and eager to question the media's presentation, this was a news story he had to see first hand. On its seventh day, Hicks and Kevin Booth travelled to Waco to film.

Driving to the siege, Hicks got his first listen to Denis Leary's *No Cure For Cancer* album (recorded in October 1992 and released in 1993). Leary had been employing material suspiciously similar to Hicks' as far back as 1991, but at the time Hicks had laughed it off, even making jokes about it in interviews. A comedian taking ideas and bits of material from others was nothing new, but with Leary's debut album it went beyond what was acceptable, nothing short of outright stealing. It angered Hicks not least because Leary had released the album through the major backing of A&M Records, garnishing a reputation, gaining publicity and making big money as the album sold well.

The *No Cure For Cancer* show is filled with the same themes as concerned Hicks. Hicks had being doing material on the warnings on cigarette packets for some time, poking fun at how the supposedly shocking language has little effect on smokers. Leary took this idea, although he did have a slightly different angle with his routine about the packets' warnings having no impact on smokers, musing that even if they were called 'Tumours' people would still buy them. His railing against non-smokers also takes Hicks' reference to non-smoking on aeroplanes whilst Leary's sucking deep on his cigarette and exhaling (on the album's stage show) has the same delighted and defiant wheeze as Hicks.

Leary seems to be stuck in some kind of time warp with his drugs material, egotistically celebrating his excesses and doing cocaine jokes that Robin Williams had been doing in the mid-1980s. Hicks had been doing a bit about cocaine making you put up with people you wouldn't normally put up, talking about doing it with killers, at Comix Annex shows in the mid-1980s. Leary adopts this premise in imagining doing cocaine with Hitler, then like Hicks, uses Keith Richards' drug excesses as a template with

"Keith, we can't do any more drugs because you already fuckin' did them all…we have to wait until you die and smoke your ashes."

Leary employs Hicks' phrases with such lines as "whining fuckin' maggots", "two words", with referring to his beliefs as "personal", and with "nobody wants to hear it." In this there seems to be some assimilation of style as well as content, the aforementioned phrases succinctly conveying exasperation at and isolation from mainstream culture (the kind of confident isolation that suggests strength of conviction).

There is also the contrast between Jimi Hendrix dying from drugs and Motley Crue still living, evoking a similar idea as Hicks' comparison of Hendrix to Debbie Gibson. Leary even does a Vegas Elvis impersonation when imagining Jesus living an Elvis-like existence had he gotten old. It is with his routines on rock music that he steals most heavily from Hicks, adding to his hatred of The Bee Gees with the line "bring me the head of Barry Manilow." Like Hicks he employs John Lennon as the benchmark for good music with "We live in a country where John Lennon takes six bullets in the chest. Yoko Ono was standing right next to him, not one fuckin' bullet…Explain that to me! Explain it to me God!" The plea to God goes back to Hicks' disbelief that Reagan was elected, a riff in which he desperately demands explanation from the Lord. Like Hicks, Leary says "I just don't get it" when talking of the appeal of other rock stars (for Hicks it's MC Hammer, for Leary it's Bon Jovi), almost word for word copying when he continues with "I missed the fuckin' point some place. The boat left and I wasn't on it." Similarly, with JFK, he says "That's what's wrong with this country, we always shoot the wrong guys," as he talks about Ted Kennedy being the one who should have been shot.

Leary moves onto the Judas Priest case where the band have supposedly inspired two people to commit suicide, almost word for word taking Hicks' riff with his "Heavy metal fans are buying heavy metal records, taking the records home, listening to the records and then blowing their heads off with shotguns? Where's the problem? That's an unemployment solution right there folks." Even the pacing of the riff takes from Hicks, but Leary doesn't have the imagination to use the subtle detail of Hicks' "two less gas station attendants," and is content not to develop the routine, unlike Hicks, who uses the whole Judas Priest case to mock ignorance and stupidity.

Hicks' smoking routines arguably got him noticed in the 1980s with clever lines like "I go through two lighters a day." One trick pony Leary returns to smoking on the album with "I love to smoke. I smoke seven thousand packs a day." He then takes Hicks' routine on a tracheotomy and voice box and does the microphone to the neck routine, although instead of an individual, Leary imagines a whole family with voice boxes. Though Leary does have an inspired moment where he pictures a man with a voice box talking to the similarly voiced serving machine at McDonald's, it's merely a side order before more Hicks pilfering. Whereas Hicks used Yul Brynner for a celebration of smoking, Leary takes baseball star Babe Ruth, but there is the same rhythmic listing of enjoyed vices with Ruth saying "I smoked twenty five goddam black Cuban cigars a day, I have meat for breakfast, lunch and dinner, I fucked eighteen prostitutes a night. Course, I'm dead now." Not only does this compare to Hicks' "Yul Brynner: smoking, drinking, girls are sitting on his cue-ball noggin' every night of his life," but Leary's final line is again, word for word, a take from Hicks' Yul Brynner saying "I'm dead now."

When we hear the whining arguments of non-smokers, Leary adopts the same pious, smug voice as Hicks (though he can't carry it off fully as, at times, it descends into the whine of a spoilt child), and the same incessant, rhythmic reeling off of reasons why smoking is bad. And then, in response to the non-smokers' arguments, Leary invokes Jim Fixx: "Remember Jim Fixx, the big famous jogging guy? Jogged fifteen miles a day, did a jogging book, did a jogging video and dropped dead of a massive heart attack when? When he was fuckin' jogging that's when." It goes beyond taking a brief riff, Leary shamelessly plundering a whole routine from Hicks.

Leary wants people to see him as an outsider, as someone separate from the crass mainstream, as someone with artistic integrity. For him the smoking is what sets him apart from conservative, politically correct America. But it's all he's got. Unlike Hicks' connecting of ideas and opening material out to social and political issues, Leary is stagnant, more in tune with America than he would have you think. Though he makes fun of Americans' cultural deficit in the way the word "croissant" has been turned into "croissandwich", he turns it into a celebration of his countrymen doing whatever they choose and fuck the rest of the world if they don't like it. He is the meat eating, smoking, gun-toting American male who makes no allusions to his personal freedom not impinging on anyone else's. His sneering and snarling delivery has none of the humanity of Hicks' performances and he doesn't have the courage to venture out into social or political material. The fact that he mocks the socially conscious lyrics of R.E.M. says everything about his ideology.

At the end of the *No Cure For Cancer* concert, he seems to be showing some originality when he talks about men having to be macho and not being able to cry. Yet this leads into sentimentality and mawkishness as he talks about his own child and his desire to do right so that his son can have a better future. It has none of the poignant optimism with which Hicks ended his shows. Instead Leary hopes his son "can live in a world without war, in a country without colour, with clean air to breath and clean water to drink, so that maybe twenty-five years from now he can turn to me and say 'you know something dad, I really like this place.' And I can say, 'Well son, I did my best.'" Beyond the puke-inducing false sincerity, quite where this sentiment fits in with all that has gone before is mystifying. Leary obviously wants to reach into the optimism of Hicks, but it's a self-satisfied optimism that seems little more than a tag to unify and give credibility to the narrative that has gone before. He even concludes the show like Hicks by dropping down dead.

At the end of the day his ideology rings somewhat hollow when it becomes clear he is a comedian prepared to hawk products like Holstein Pills beer in adverts which play on his angry man persona, selling the idea of being edgy and dangerous. After the success of *No Cure For Cancer* he happily jumped into a series of lame Hollywood movies including *National Lampoon's Loaded Weapon 1* (1993) and *Demolition Man* (1993) with Sylvester Stallone, only producing a second comedy album, *Lock 'N Load*, in 1997 when his film career bottomed out.

Hicks and Booth drove to Waco on the seventh day of the siege, Booth filming and Hicks as a kind of guerrilla reporter. They didn't get any closer than the other news media, so they set up filming on the outskirts. Hicks' reporting is somewhat subdued, often repeating points and making general observations about the weather and the siege being "a slumber party that just really got out of hand." His dispatches seem to reflect the atmosphere of the area after the initial raid, the sense of a cooling down period. More than that, it reflects the lack of access to information about the situation.

In his reporting Hicks recites a passage from the Bible, Deuteronomy 13, verse 4: "Ye shall walk after the Lord, your God, and fear him, and keep his commandments and obey his voice and ye shall serve him and cleave unto him," observing that Koresh was " a man heavily armed and heavily cleaving to his Lord." Hicks makes some humorous comments on the situation, referring to Koresh's seventeen wives not allowing him out as they are still shouting at him, joking that the cows around Mount Carmel "are actually FBI agents dressed as cows," and musing on those inside the building possibly playing Scrabble, Monopoly and Risk. To Koresh's reading of Genesis, Hicks notes that after Genesis "God created the sub-machine gun…Man named all the animals and then began shooting them one by one"; something of a re-working of his routine on Jesus returning to Earth with an Uzi machine-gun. Generally, in his reportage, Hicks is casual, disappointed, struggling to get a hold on the situation. Nonetheless, the subsequent video release from Sacred Cow is an interesting document, suggestive of where Hicks' television career might have headed, mixing comedy and current affairs in a way not dissimilar to the subsequent work of Michael Moore.

During Hicks' tour of Australia in April 1993, another exhausting schedule of sixteen shows in three weeks during which he began to feel ill beyond just the regular touring fatigue, he was bringing in Waco material, supremely interested in the developing news story and how it would play out.

As the siege went on, the FBI continued its underhand tactics. When Koresh struck a deal to send out children and in return get milk for the babies inside Mount Carmel, the FBI did not honour it straight away, telling the media Koresh had turned down the offer. When they did finally send the milk in, they put listening devices inside the plastic bottles.

On March 8th and 9th Mount Carmel sent out videotapes in which the residents spoke of why they were there and their belief in what they were doing. In no sense did it appear that they were being held against their will. The FBI didn't release the tapes to the media as it continued a campaign of demonising Koresh (a third tape sent on March 26th was also not released to the media). You didn't have to be a conspiracy nut to see an insidious connection in the collusion between the government and media, all the more so when on March 15th the ATF issued a gagging order preventing its agents from talking about the bungled operation of February 28th. Those who did speak out condemned the disorganisation and miscalculations of the raid.

The FBI stepped up the pressure by cutting off electricity supplies and communication lines. They introduced psychological tactics by playing loud music day and night, songs like Nancy Sinatra's *These Boots Are Made For Walking* or blaring the distressing cacophonous noises of screeching, crying babies and animals being slaughtered, shining lights into Mount Carmel at night, seemingly trying to rack up the tension as if wanting to provoke a conflict. Equally, the FBI troops were in "hog-heaven" as they mooned and gave middle finger gestures to the building. The media continued to tow the party line, having little choice as they were kept so far back. Amazingly, two people managed to get through and join those at Mount Carmel.

On April 19th 1993, the 51st day of the siege, the FBI began their assault on the compound. When it was over, seventy-six Davidians were dead, and as the building burned to the ground, the ATF proudly raised its colours on a flagpole. Then the lies really began. Despite the FBI's initial concern being about firearms, the new spin was playing more on the child molestation angle being the reason for going in. And yet, a local sheriff had visited Mount Carmel many times to check on the children and found nothing untoward. Meanwhile, the FBI, back-tracking to save its credibility, said that Koresh had promised five times to come out and hadn't. However, a study of the negotiation tapes and transcripts shows that to be a lie, recording only one occasion when Koresh agreed to come out and then changed his mind.

The FBI's actions in attacking Mount Carmel were brutal and excessive. At 6.02am Bradley tanks began destroying the buildings and firing in CS gas canisters. A few minutes later - claiming to being fired upon - the Bradley tanks began to shoot many ferret rounds into the building, which included the highly poisonous and flammable methylene chloride. Dick Rogers, the FBI Hostage Rescue Team Commander, told the subsequent hearings "The FBI never fired one shot at the Davidians," yet there is infrared footage, which shows rounds being fired off from the tanks that are battering the building. As the assault proceeded the FBI used a loudspeaker to boom out "This is not an assault. This is not an assault." After a while, their "hog-heaven" sensibilities come out with a mocking ad-libbing of "David, you have had your fifteen minutes of fame."

CS gas was pumped into the building (hundreds of canisters in the first two hours) despite the fact that the FBI knew gas masks wouldn't fit the babies in there. Tanks rammed and tore down the buildings, blocking escape routes and ripping bodies apart. Women and children inside retreated from the gases into the kitchen storage room, only for the room to then be rammed by tanks and filled with CS gas, a gas that works like cyanide when in a confined spaces. Evidence found in the aftermath showed the effects, with bodies snapped back on themselves, as was the case with one eight year old girl. As highly flammable CS gases filled the air inside the building, holes in its walls, created by the tanks, allowed air to come through so that when the fire started at midday it spread very quickly.

When he returned to America, Hicks was concerned with analysing the Waco situation, particularly through footage screened on public access television, aiming to uncover truths about the FBI and ATF's murderous role. To the claim "Oh, we had to bust the compound down 'cos we heard child molestation was going on," Hicks replied, "Yeh, if that's true, how come we don't see Bradley tanks knocking down Catholic churches?" Hicks was aware of the medical reports from doctors examining children who'd left Mount Carmel which stated there were no signs of sexual abuse. He didn't buy into the party line and once again saw how the media was complicit in the conspiracy with its misinformation.

Hicks had seen "footage which was not shown on any mainstream media source of the Bradley tanks shooting *fire* into the compound," thus suggesting that television channels were in effect ignoring the evidence being screened on public access. "So the major news said that the Branch Davidians started the fire...and all they (the FBI) did was shoot tear gas, and yet I've seen with my own eyes – and my squeegeed third eye – footage of a Bradley tank shooting fire into the compound...Isn't that odd that no major news source has picked up on that? You'd think that's newsworthy." Though the media seemed happy to follow the FBI's spin, it wasn't helped by the way the FBI kept journalists back from the story. In its end of year report in 1993 the Society of Professional Journalists noted, "In the case of Waco, journalists were kept so far away from the front lines that they were not able to properly scrutinize the actions of the law enforcement agencies and negotiators," whilst in the aftermath, "Court appearances were held secretly. Hearings were closed to the press. Key documents ranging from motions to government responses to arrest and search warrants were sealed."

For Hicks it was a conspiracy controlled by the FBI not wanting the mainstream media to broadcast the footage he had seen on public access because "it went against the party line story which was that they shot tear gas in order to 'help' the mothers and the children to get out," to present to the public that "while they're destroying the compound they are getting the mamas and children out." Hicks referred to it as the FBI's "soft sell," which was pretty much accepted by the masses in the aftermath of the fire. Most people saw the whole siege in terms of a crazy religious nut thinking he was God, brainwashing people and getting them to commit suicide. And though Hicks' view was out of tune with popular opinion in America, subsequent investigations into the Waco affair revealed him to be in tune with the reality of the situation.

Waco was perhaps the most powerful indication since the Warren report that the government in America could cover up anything. Hicks wasn't afraid to point the finger, believing that what happened showed "that the government, from the FBI, the ATF, up to Janet Reno and including Clinton are liars and murderers." At the hearings FBI spokesman Bob Ricks said "We did not introduce fire to this compound" and that "non-pyrotechnic delivery systems were utilised." Yet military pyrotechnic devices were found in the aftermath whilst public access TV showed footage of fire coming from Bradley tanks. It was Attorney General Reno who gave her approval in April for an assault using CS gas targeted at various parts of the building, to be carried out over forty-eight hours with the intention of making the inhabitants of Mount Carmel leave when the building became uninhabitable. There was a clause in this plan that allowed the FBI to begin sending CS gas into the whole building if they were fired upon. Claiming to be fired upon after only a few minutes, the FBI then bombarded the building, precipitating the disaster that was to follow. Either Reno hadn't read the report properly or she was a liar. And if she hadn't read the reports and hadn't understood the dangers of CS canisters then she should have resigned, or for Hicks "committed hare kari." When Reno gave evidence to the hearings she told them that the tanks were unarmed, crassly likening them to " a good rent-a-car." Again, she is either a liar or so misinformed as to be a liability in her position as Attorney General.

Concerning the fire, Reno also told the hearings "I have absolutely no doubt at all that cult members set it", a view supported by President Clinton, who refused to accept Reno's resignation the day after the carnage, callously asserting that it wasn't going to happen "just because some religious fanatics murdered themselves." It is unlikely that Reno and Clinton were getting such poor information that they didn't know the truth, and equally as unlikely that after seeing the footage of the tanks starting the fire they could be so stupid as to accept some FBI lie. Therefore, she and Clinton were liars and Hicks was, once again, one of the few who were prepared to point this out (although, into *The Simpsons* episode *Bart's Girlfriend* from June 1994 was slipped a sign on the church marquee "Evil Women in History: From Jezebel to Janet Reno").

The congressional hearings also concluded that the Davidians had killed themselves. In the media world with its quick newsbites, ignoring of the details and appetite for new news stories, this conclusion was pretty much accepted by the masses.

For Hicks "the whole thing was an absolute disaster and debacle," not only because of the lives lost but also because it showed the total and uncaring control of those in power and how they were allowed to get away with it. He saw how the government used the media because "They don't want the voice of reason spoken fully, because otherwise we'd be free, otherwise we wouldn't believe their fuckin' horseshit lies, nor the fuckin' propaganda machine – the mainstream media."

In many ways the Waco disaster crystallised Hicks' thinking, uniting many of his themes and encapsulating all that he saw wrong with his country. We have the truth being marginalized (to public access television) seemingly at the behest of those in power, the "lying cocksuckers". Meanwhile, information presented to the public is simplified or sensationalised so that "bovine America" can make quick judgements between good and evil and subsequently get on with the task of enjoying the unfolding story as entertainment. Hicks saw the Waco cover-up in the same way as that surrounding the Kennedy assassination, in that it showed the total control of those in power over the unquestioning, "docile masses." For those who did question, who did pursue the truth, there appeared to be a conspiracy every bit as insidious.

When the trial of the surviving members of the siege began in January 1994 the conspiracy was obvious with a Republican, Judge Smith, presiding over another cover up, putting a gagging order on the defence team so they couldn't make their cases to the press. Although the jury only wanted to find the defendants guilty of firearms offences, the judge linked this to manslaughter and gave five defendants forty-year sentences, whilst one other received a twenty-year sentence and another got five years. In his summing up, Judge Smith towed the party line too, concluding that "the first shots were fired from inside the front door of the compound" and "by a combination of suicide and murder inflicted by Davidian upon Davidian, all but a handful of the Davidians were killed."

Despite the fact that the news story was still very "alive" as 1994 progressed, for the most part the media neglected any debate on the after effects of the siege or the implications of the government's actions. As a news story it was superseded by the more flashy and exciting Hollywood tale of O.J Simpson's arrest for double murder. Here was a more easily digestible news story, as superficial and unedifying as the world from which it came: "Go back to bed America."

Since Bush's New World Order speech, many in America had come to subscribe to a theory that this meant an elite of the super rich governing the planet for their own ends. These people called themselves Constitutionalists, believing that the Constitution gave them the rights that government (and the New World Order) was trying to erode. The media portrayed them as crank conspiracy theorists or dangerous neo-Nazis, yet made no attempt to uncover any truth or analyse why they might feel so disenchanted by conventional society and politics. Throughout the 1990s many militias were forming in the South, believing that the U.S. government was part of this new world order and that they had to be armed, in preparation for a day when they might have to battle for their freedom. It created some strange bedfellows, the theory attracting those eager to oppose gun control and neo-Nazi groups as well as those living in communes whose philosophy was very much in tune with the hippies of the 1960s. Hicks' conspiracy theories may even have found a home there. Indeed, Kevin Booth's Sacred Cow company has been behind the promotion of Alex Jones, a radio and talk show host who organised the rebuilding of the Branch Davidian church at Mount Carmel. Jones is at the forefront of those who believe in a new world order made up of bankers, a shadowy elite known as The Bilderberg Group.

The conspiracy theories angle had been a mainstay of Hicks' acts from his early days. He would tell one heckler "Please don't debate me, it's my one true talent. I have twenty-three hours a day to develop these fuckin' webs of conspiracy." Through Hicks seeing the connection of things, he was able to see the conspiracies behind events, making him an excellent debater, to such an extent that he would often end his shows by seeking questions from the audience. Indeed, his early fascination with Elvis (and all the conspiracies and contemporary "sightings" wrapped up in that myth), then later and more pertinently with JFK, is due to his awareness of many different viewpoints and ideas on issues and his delight in being able to select appropriate arguments whatever the debate. His continued interest in the Kennedy assassination was because he believed it showed "how the totalitarian government that rules this planet partitions out information." It linked to the way pop culture and the entertainment industry sought to steer people away from the truth, away from questioning those in power, wanting Bill to "quit talking about Kennedy." His feelings were clear in his routine about the assassination museum in Dallas and The Sniper's Nest from which Oswald was supposed to have fired at Kennedy. Hicks ironically acknowledges the accuracy of the scene, "because Oswald's not in it" but also sees the conspiracy in the way that tourists cannot get close to The Sniper's Nest. Again this was a government/CIA cover-up because it didn't want "thousands of American tourists" getting too close and realising "Oh my God, they're lying!" Hicks cleverly updates the routine with a potential conspiracy when he tells of a CIA plot to assassinate Saddam Hussein and the only problem being "convincing Hussein to fly to Dallas."

Once more there is a sixties influence to Hicks' angle on conspiracy theories. The counterculture referred to a power behind the machinations of government and big business as "The Man", believing as Hicks did that it was out to crush individuals and impose conformity. It is a view seen in Dr Timothy Leary's *The Declaration Of Evolution*, Leary pointing out that the establishment "have in every way attempted to impose a robot uniformity and to crush variety, individuality, and independence of thought." With Hicks, it was television that crushed his voice, prevalent inanity smothering a voice of reason. In addition, Hicks' growing awareness of the world through his studying of comedy in the 1970s came at a time when the Watergate scandal exposed the secret scheming of those in power, all the way up to President Nixon. The shows Hicks was watching on his portable television satirised the conspiracy and the gullibility of the public, whilst a general mood of paranoia and mistrust filtered into American society and its culture with the growth in all forms of surveillance (as can be seen in such films as *The Parallax View* (1974) and in the dystopian society of Woody Allen's film, *Sleeper*).

As in literature and films where we are presented with archetypal images of conspiracy filled worlds ruled by dictatorial governments, so there correlates the figure of a shadowy revolutionary working on the margins of society to overthrow the establishment. With Hicks' lack of mass success in America, he is certainly a figure working on the peripherals, conveying his "revolution of ideas" to small and loyal fans in the dark and dingy clubs of Austin, Chicago and San Francisco, hoping to one day generate a movement that would rise up against those in power and reject their values. He is the man going unnoticed to different secret locations, leading a "meeting at the docks" or founding his own compound as he seeks to spread the truth, saying during his appearance on Jonathon Ross's show in 1992 that "I hope to overthrow the American government and replace it with a freely elected democracy." And after the election and Bush's defeat, it's a different conspiracy angle with, "It must have been a secret service plot to keep me out of the country the night Bush lost."

All the threads of Hicks' philosophy – drugs, rock stars, TV, the news, government – subscribed to a view of some shadowy figures controlling everything through careful management of the entertainment industry and the information the media is allowed to present. Even little nuggets from seemingly innocuous routines alluded to the conspiracy: "did I miss a meeting?" implying Machiavellian plotting going on behind Hicks' back, and "It's a CIA plot to make you think malls are good" offered as an explanation for the music of Rick Astley and Debbie Gibson. Perhaps as a result of his wide reading of issues, particularly Noam Chomsky's illuminating texts uncovering America's complicity in terrorism and genocide around the world, Hicks is always looking for what is going on beneath the surface, what machinations are at work engineering a story or issue before it is presented to the public. This enables some witheringly accurate political material, but also gives depth to more innocent routines, such as that on Scotland's Loch Ness Monster, the whole myth uncovered by Hicks as a means to get "thousands of American tourists to bring their fat fucking families and their fat dollar bills" to boost the country's economy.

In Hicks' world these shadowy figures echo Big Brother in Orwell's *Nineteen Eighty Four*, though Hicks attaches to them a more contemporary urge to control for financial reasons, seeing that governments are responsible to corporate interests, that "Our elections are a charade...and tomorrow they're selling your life from out under you." Democracy is therefore an illusion (which one cannot argue with when analysing election results that see presidents voted in by a minority of those eligible to vote). People don't decide who becomes president, as Hicks says on *Sane Man*, it's "Who does Shell want in there?"

Hicks' creates a vivid picture, playing to archetypal conspiracy images, as he describes a scene where "Whenever a new American president is elected they are brought into a small dark room in which the twelve biggest industrial, corporate, military, economic heads are sitting. One of them pulls down a film screen and shows the new president a video of the JFK assassination from an angle they've never seen before. They then turn to the president and say, 'Any questions?'" Though he taps into pre-conceived notions with his conspiracy imagery, contemporary referencing of the issue of a few powerful owners of corporations running the country links the scene to reality and a viewpoint which gained prominence with the anti-globalisation movement of the late 1990s. Way ahead of the zeitgeist, Hicks' material at the beginning of the decade alluded to the corporate take over of the world with a view that commercial interests are what drives governments, concluding that the Reagan/Bush interventions in Central America were "so Pepsi can put a plant down there."

When Hicks talks of the "Twelve guys who run the fuckin' world," it's a theory in tune with those groups who thought the Randy Weaver incident and the Waco siege were examples of what Bush's "New World Order" speech really meant. This is a world order controlled by bankers and corporate bosses, one eager to crush individuals they cannot control and silence the voices of those who do not buy into a consumer lifestyle. Moreover, this world order seeks to maintain control by keeping and increasing the power held by the few. It's a view backed up by events of the early 1990s in the U.S., a period when there were massive corporate takeovers, such as Disney taking over the American Broadcasting Company and the merger of Time-Warner and CNN, whilst Rupert Murdoch was gradually becoming holder of the most TV stations in America. What these mergers meant was more of a party line being towed in the media, an agenda based on fundamentalism and conformity. And for Hicks' "twelve guys who run the fuckin' world" one needs to look no further than details of how vast corporations are growing ever larger, swallowing up the competition, to such an extent that General Motors is now wealthier than Denmark.

The new demons emerging also seemed part of the right-wing conspiracy and were well aware of the power of television. In the 1970s and early 1980s the ABC TV network had been critical of the Reagan administration, even broadcasting the nuclear war disaster movie *The Day After* (1983). In 1985 ABC was taken over by the conservative organisation Capital Cities, which had connections with the C.I.A. and aligned itself with Republicanism.

ABC gave Rush Limbaugh his career break in 1988 with his radio talk show, which went national and gradually reached an audience of over twenty million listeners. Limbaugh, a fat, opinionated, right wing fear-mongerer spouted the messages coming from Republican Party headquarters. In 1988 he published his *35 Undeniable Truths*, which consisted of anti-feminist, anti-homosexual and anti-Soviet sentiments and a belief that progress came through economic growth. These "truths" included "Peace cannot be achieved by developing an 'understanding' with the Russian people" and "Evolution cannot explain Creation" an ideology completely at odds with Hicks'. More worrying, he had a racist streak. As a broadcaster in the 1970s he'd once told a black caller "Take that bone out of your nose and call me back," whilst in the 1990s he said, "Have you ever noticed how all composite pictures of wanted criminals resemble Jesse Jackson?" (49).

Limbaugh was a man full of hot air who peddled right wing rhetoric as fact, preaching only to supportive audiences because he was unable to defend his untruths if debated. His TV show, *The Rush Limbaugh Show* began in 1992 and by 1993 his ultraconservative rants had gained him a large enough audience for him to become a powerful media and political figure. With 1994's updated *Undeniable Truths* including the statement, "Ronald Reagan was the greatest president of the twentieth century," it's almost like Orwell's *Nineteen Eighty-Four* and its notion of re-writing history.

An even more frightening abomination was senator Jesse Helms, a political figure with deeper fascistic tendencies than Limbaugh. In the 1970s and 1980s he'd supported the murderous regime of Chile's General Pinochet whilst also being a central figure in the ultraconservative ideology of 1980s Republicanism. Naturally, he supported a ban on flag burning, which led to some common ground with Hicks, who said he wouldn't support flag burning, "unless it's knotted, soaked in kerosene and stuck up Jesse Helms' rear." The vile Helms also called homosexuals "disgusting", made patronising remarks to and about women, and was opposed to gun control, abortion and government support for the arts. His bigotry was also compounded by his outright racism. In 1990 the TV commercial for his election campaign showed white hands crumpling a job rejection letter with the voiceover saying, "You needed that job and you were the best qualified. But they had to give it to a minority because of a racial quota."

He was everything Hicks detested, seeking to sway opinion through fear and hatred and not through compassion and reason. In addition, Helms was a vile representation of Southern stereotypes, the kind Hicks had been so mercilessly mocking throughout his career. And yet, Helms had power and a willing audience. His place in the conspiracy was obvious from his support of the tobacco industry. For Hicks, Helms was a "tobacco pushing motherfucker. You are the worst fuckin' drug dealer in the fuckin' world. You scrawny, right wing, fear mongering sucker of Satan's cock." The pushing of tobacco correlates to the drugs conspiracy; government misinformation on the effects of drugs due to the powers that be fearing people with open minds, whilst allowing the humdrum and corrosive, but highly profitable profusion of tobacco: "Drugs that open your eyes to make you realise how you're being fucked every day of your life: Those drugs are against the law. Coincidence? I don't know." Cigarettes are fine for their effects are so limited that there is no danger of enlightenment for users. For Hicks, it becomes as much a conspiracy as that surrounding Kennedy, one that outlaws the evolution of thought (such evolution being feared by a government set on maintaining secrets such as the truth behind the assassination).

Hicks imagined Limbaugh's dark secret of being a man "who likes to lay in a tub while other men pee on him" whilst Helms would be found out when he died and there is discovered "the skins of young children drying in his attic." These are not Hicks' best observations, but the anger comes through and conveys his sense of frustration that his satire has had little effect as Limbaugh and Helms have risen to power, their bigoted opinions finding widespread support in "bovine America."

By the end of April, *Rolling Stone* magazine voted Hicks as Hot Comic of 1993, such approval mirroring the good vibe evident in his mood and sense of where he was heading. He seemed to be hitting the right groove and producing some of his best material. Moreover, there was an increasingly appreciative audience, especially in the UK, where the broadcast of *Revelations* on May 27th garnered more positive attention, whilst in America there seemed to be a widening of critical acclaim, if not particularly popular interest. Nonetheless, he still played to enthusiastic audiences at places like the Laff Stop, where on June 7th he recorded some material for the proposed *Rant In E Minor* album at the same time. His keen interest in *The Counts Of The Netherworld* remained, saying about the show "Carl Jung had the theory that there is a collective unconscious that mankind shares, and I agree with that. The only difference is I don't think it's supposed to be unconscious. As the Agents of Evolution, the job of the Counts of the Netherworld is to shine the light into mankind's unconscious mind and try to wake up the world." His ideology, connected to spirituality, had given him a clear vision of where he was heading and how he could use the medium of television to prompt others to join his "revolution of ideas."

Then, in mid-June 1993, he was diagnosed with pancreatic cancer. Dr William T. Donovan of The Good Samaritan Cancer Institution had nothing but admiration for the way Hicks handled news of the disease: At first, "...it was as if somebody had shot him, because he was a bright person and he knew what cancer of the pancreas meant," but there was never any anger about his condition, Hicks' immediately focusing on how he could beat the disease. "He was just a very gentle person," concluded Donovan (44). From initial devastation, Hicks quickly decided to embrace a positive outlook and not let the illness sway him from his targets, particularly when he saw his country swept up in the superficial optimism of the Clinton government.

Bill Clinton's vision of America seemed little more than a chance for rose-tinted spectacles to once again become fashionable. His centre politics were an illusion as the centre was now occupied by right wing ideology. Clinton maintained the selling of arms to oppressive regimes, such as Turkey, who used the U.S. weaponry to suppress and kill thousands of Kurds. In addition, this new Democratic president had also instigated the biggest war and arms budget in history whilst also continuing the bullying and bombing of weaker nations. When George Bush visited Kuwait in April 1993, the country's authorities arrested seventeen people for an alleged plot to assassinate the former president with a car bomb. For Hicks, Clinton "became one of the boys", as reactionary as his Republican predecessors, when he used this as an excuse for ordering twenty-two cruise missile strikes on June 26th 1993 (at a cost of $3 million a missile), killing six people. Hicks took up the assassination idea, cleverly reversing the conspiracy angle with, "You know what we should have done, we should have embarrassed the Iraqis...*We* should have assassinated Bush, and said 'that's how you do it towel-head, don't fuck with us.' And see, if Bush had been the one who died there would have been no loss of innocent life."

Soon after the diagnosis, he played The Funny Firm in Chicago, but there was still no big audience breakthrough in America. For all his playful paranoia, Hicks saw the conspiracy to keep his voice out of mainstream entertainment, and with the diagnosis he was more determined than ever to uncover the conspiracy. His work rate did not diminish as more material was recorded for *Rant In E-Minor* and he continued to tour. According to Kevin Booth, "He was going at 1,000 miles an hour and couldn't bear to be in any mundane situation that distracted him from writing" (50). When faced with attempts to censor, the satirist becomes stronger, censorship being fuel to the satirist's fire, giving credence to his views.

As he underwent chemotherapy he returned to smoking with a passion and in the summer of 1993 did mushrooms at Kevin Booth's parents' ranch in the Fredericksburg countryside, taking "what Terence Mckenna called 'an heroic dose'."

Things continued to go well in critical terms with favourable reviews like that in the *San Francisco Chronicle* (August 8th 1993), which asked 'Is Bill Hicks the Voice of 1990s Comedy?' It's review of the show was excellent: "Hicks may be the freshest - surely most daring - voice in stand-up in years...Midway through his act, I realised just how banal and predictable comedy has grown." It also puts Hicks in with the innovators of comedy in America: "You have to go back to Mort Sahl, Lenny Bruce, George Carlin and Richard Pryor to recall such an individual, piercing, idiosyncratic mind." The illness contributed to the irony of being "Voice of 1990s Comedy", but Hicks was now more determined than ever to tell the truth and in the autumn and winter of 1993 he would deliver his most apocalyptic and angry work to date. Although it is fair to say his illness contributed to it, the catalyst was his twelfth and final Letterman show appearance on October 1st 1993.

David Letterman hadn't cut it when he'd briefly tried stand-up in Los Angeles in 1975, choosing instead to pursue a career in television and the fame and fortune it brought. In November 1978 he made the first of his twenty-two appearances on the national institution that was *The Tonight Show* with Johnny Carson, which he would go on to guest host fifty times. In 1980 his morning show began and was such a success that in February 1982 *Late Night With David Letterman* started on NBC.

When the show was first broadcast, despite Letterman employing Carson's self-satisfied and easy manner, it was seen as something fresh and original. Letterman brought new comic talent to television, though it was always on his and the network's terms, which basically meant don't upstage the host and don't be too controversial. With the show's success, Letterman thought he was the man in waiting for the prestigious Johnny Carson spot, but instead in 1993 NBC decided to give it to Jay Leno (who had been regularly guest hosting since 1987).

Letterman left NBC, taking his show to CBS, somewhat bitter about his rejection and eager to prove he could gain a bigger audience than Leno. This necessitated the further dilution of the show and its content, in order to garner more mainstream appeal when it began on 30th August 1993. Letterman acquiesced and the show became a big hit.

With Bill Hicks and the Letterman show, the two perspectives had previously managed to co-exist, albeit uneasily, Hicks' material at some distance from that which Letterman's controllers found acceptable. It required some compromise, what Hicks called being "de-clawed" (51), yet it served both of them with Hicks getting exposure and Letterman building an audience on being hip and edgy. But now, the two had moved further apart. 1993 had been a momentous year for Hicks; the wider recognition and quality of his material had emboldened him, then Waco had angered him, not to mention not being able to get *Arizona Bay* released. There was the continuation of terrible TV and proliferation of talentless stars, and Clinton showing his true colours by bombing Iraq. Furthermore, his illness had brought his priorities into focus, setting him on a mission to enlighten without compromise.

But the Letterman show had also changed, its original audience having grown up, probably sold out after making some money in the eighties. Letterman himself was more popular, his smoothness, offbeat material and deadpan delivery giving him the veneer of someone with individuality and daring. But there was a careful scripting and structuring of the show and Letterman had peddled his persona for so long that it seemed smug.

The show was now a big hit in the ratings, beating Jay Leno's show and attracting more lucrative advertisers after being moved an hour earlier. Hicks had been called in as a replacement for a former mafia cook from the Gambino clan, who had been going on to promote his *The Mafia Cookbook*. Hicks' set had already been pre-approved and when he filmed his segment at 5.30pm there seemed to be no problems. The audience liked it and according to Hicks "Dave gave me an Havana cigar during the break." He felt happy because it was "the closest to me I've been on the show" (51). It wasn't until some hours later when Hicks - then back at his hotel - was telephoned by the show's executive producer Robert Morton, who informed him that his performance was being cut. Morton laid the blame at CBS Standards and Practices, but when CBS denied this Morton admitted responsibility.

It seemed Hicks' segment had been cut because it was felt the material might not go down too well with the show's sponsors. The Letterman producers pinpointed what they called "hot points" which included Hicks' attack on pro-lifers: "If you're so pro-life, do me a favour. Don't lock arms and block medical clinics. If you're so pro-life, lock arms and block cemeteries." He had also wondered about how the Easter Bunny and chocolate eggs came to be linked to Jesus, before finishing with his old routine on Christians wearing crosses: "Do you think when Jesus comes back he's gonna want to see a fuckin' cross?" His pro-life material was particularly relevant in 1993 with Helms and Limbaugh continuing their anti-abortion rhetoric of the Reagan years and an increase in violence against doctors at abortion clinics. In March 1993, Michael Griffin had shot and killed Dr David Gunn in Florida, whilst in August, Rachelle Shannon had shot an injured Dr George Tiller. This was just the tip of an iceberg that saw blockades, hate mail and arson attacks, all justified once again by invoking a vague idea of doing it for "the children", or in the name of God. Such claims were lambasted by Hicks' abortion material, most adroitly with his pointing out the irony of "pro-lifers killing people."

He became the first comedy act to be censored at CBS's Ed Sullivan Theatre, following on from the banning on Elvis Presley's hips in 1956. Hicks was incensed, as was his mother, Mary Reese Hicks, for whom he'd done the routine prior to filming, her reaction being that she "hooted and fell out of her rocker" (51). Logically, if Mary's more conservative sensibilities had not found the routine objectionable, then why would the supposedly younger, hipper and more liberal Letterman audience? He couldn't understand who he was supposed to be offending, what kind of audience Morton had in mind, mystified that he might be offending an audience when he was part of that audience when not doing a show. He wrote a 39-page letter to *The New Yorker* magazine's John Lahr, which he later developed into a piece titled *Bill Hicks* on *Television...Sometimes*, in it setting out a lucid argument against such censorship and a stinging attack on what he saw as a corporate conspiracy.

Apparently Letterman was both saddened and angry about how events transpired, yet he himself didn't like jokes about Jesus on his show. It all became clear that financial concerns lay behind the censorship when, three nights later, a pro-life commercial appeared during a break in Letterman's show. It proved to Hicks that "Freedom of expression is guaranteed, if you've got the money" (2), and further to that, "If television considers themselves the moral arbiters of our society, I think that goes a long way towards explaining the trouble and the chaos that exists" (2).

Television was complicit in the conspiracy, be it by peddling government propaganda or denying audiences intellectual engagement. Even *Saturday Night Live* had a guest appearance by George Bush in 1993, sending himself up, causing Hicks to comment that it was "now like the old *Carol Burnett Show*" (40). Throughout his career Hicks had been effectively marginalized by television, little short of censorship of his voice. This is what separates him from the likes of Kinison and Pryor. For all Kinison's danger and bad language, he played to an all American macho image, the white Anglo-Saxon, beer drinking ordinary dumb America who likes his alcohol and pussy and thinks being liberal means not being racist in public, but being allowed to fear and hate homosexuals and by extension love the all American Christian way of things. And this got him television appearances, albums on Warner Brothers, parts in films and huge arena shows.

Pryor never sold out in terms of material, but he certainly had sufficient exposure with his many films. His material, whilst edgy and sophisticated was less cerebral, less challenging than Hicks'. By the time he made it big with concert films he wasn't threatening to those in power. It was more his pioneering of his art, his personal life and the aura that came with them that created the myth of Pryor as a threat. The entertainment industry (and therefore the establishment) did not feel the need to suppress him as they had with Hicks. Diagnosed with multiple sclerosis in 1986, going public in September 1991, doing his last stand-up in 1995, Pryor is now seen in the same light as Mohammed Ali; as an iconic and warmly respected figure, no longer perceived as a threat by white middle class America now able to afford admiration.

Hicks' anger at the Letterman censoring was quickly manifested in his explosive shows afterwards, his October 10th show at Comedy Corner beginning with "This is my last ever show" before indulging in fantasies about killing Billy Ray Cyrus, Marky Mark and Michael Bolton. He did the banned set, certainly not offending this (probably Letterman watching) audience with his take on pro-lifers and Easter. Once again it's comedy as a catharsis with Hicks releasing his anger and bitterness, raging against "bovine America" and the suffocation of voices of reason. The show is a shocking tour de force, a Grand Guignol of graphic images and honest, naked emotion, yet it still manages to remain very funny with Hicks maintaining his comic instinct to entertain.

His disappointment with the Letterman show conversely sees him keener to attack Jay Leno. Leno had started in the stand-up circuit in the mid seventies before his first appearance on *The Tonight Show* in 1977. By 1987 he had become the exclusive guest host, his easygoing style and inoffensive jokes allowing people to feel good about themselves, even doing the old Bob Hope thing of performing for troops when he did shows for those stationed in the Gulf in 1991. He didn't take risks, his affable personality perfectly in tune with *The Tonight Show*'s more conservative audience, so that he was chosen to succeed Johnny Carson instead of the seemingly more off-the-wall David Letterman.

Hicks had admired Leno when supporting him in the mid-1980s, but had grown to detest everything he stood for by 1993. It wasn't just Leno's appeal to conservative Middle America, but also the way he had lost his sense of humour with his elevation to *The Tonight Show*, apparently content that he was now interviewing such people as Joey Lawrence from the show *Blossom*, turning the show into a "cultural train wreck" of b-list celebrities fawned over by Leno. Hicks' adept impersonation of Leno has the talk show host reaching something of an epiphany with, "Good God, what have I done with my life?" before unloading a 9mm gun into his mouth. Another conspiracy is subtly implied in the aftermath of Leno's suicide: "his brains spew out, forming an NBC peacock on the wall behind, because he's a company man to the bitter fuckin' end." It prompts an idea that, behind Leno's façade of affability, there is something more sinister at work, perhaps even a mission to lower standards through his television show. What most raised Hicks' ire was Leno's association with commercials, selling Doritos "not even when he needed the money," peddling "snacks to bovine America" in order to add to his already vast wealth. Perhaps the cruellest line (at least for a comedian) from Hicks' impersonation is Leno's final, desperate cry of "Anyone remember when I was funny?"

Hicks continued to get his message across when he appeared on Austin Public Access show *Capzeyez* on 23<rd> October. Hicks is relaxed, wearing jeans, t-shirt and leather jacket as he takes questions from host and callers, at times contemplative, at times jabbing his finger, lifting himself from his chair to address the camera directly. His central theme is that of television's part in the conspiracy, "I believe that there's this agenda in mainstream media...to keep people stupid, docile and apathetic, and therefore the elite who own these corporations...their agenda is to keep us stupid and apathetic." He seems somewhat worn down, resignation in his voice when he says, "I'm kind of at peace with myself as well. I don't really care anymore." However, he becomes more positive when talking about going to England to work on *The Counts Of The Netherworld* and not being back in America until 1995.

After recording further material for *Rant In E-Minor* at The Laff Stop, Hicks took part in Sacred Cow's *Halloween Special*, smoking again as he sits behind two pumpkins and responds to phone calls, his tone of voice less angry as he talks for the most part to his type of people (his mother even calling at one point). Supposedly speaking from Hell, Hicks jokes about seeing Tony Danza, Bruce Willis and all those connected with the TV show *Full House* down there. It is a frivolous and somewhat subdued Hicks, a weary resignation in his voice when he laments that "we live in a world where a plea for sanity sounds like sour grapes...in a society which worships only two things, fame and money, and if you're not famous and rich then you're not anything really is what we're told by the media." Again it is the voice of the downtrodden, the proletarian comedian who could never be in a sit-com, never seek the empty thrills of stardom. When one caller asks "Is it true you're doing your last performance in Austin?" Hicks replies "Yes," checks himself, then says, "No, it's the second to last performance," perhaps a hint that he knew what the future held.

He was getting support for his stand against the Letterman show censors as he increasingly used radio shows such as "shock-jock" Howard Stern's to give his version of events. Newspapers were also sympathetic, particularly when John Lahr's article, *The Goatboy Rises* appeared in *The New Yorker* on November 1<st>. The lengthy piece from theatre critic Lahr combined a career perspective with an in-depth analysis of the machinations behind the Letterman banning. Not only did it view Hicks in theatrical terms, as a pioneer of his art, but also as a social commentator espousing his views on television and its cultural effects. In addition, we can see in it and Hicks' 1993 performances the development of his philosophy, from his early career mocking TV celebrities to a deeper insight into how the medium seems part of a wider conspiracy to dehumanise through intellectual regression.

The article's favourable reception generated publicity for Hicks' cause and drew a good crowd for what would be his last gig at Igby's on 17th November 1993. Coming on to Hendrix's *Fire*, Hicks is dressed in autumnal colours "reflective of my bright and cheerful mood" (6), the glasses and beard presenting him fully as the sophisticate. Hicks begins with announcing it as his "final live performance" saddened at his "total anonymity in the country I love." As one of his final live shows, it is a somewhat poignant document of a comedian at the end of his tether. There is resignation when he plays with an image of himself as a cynic, likening his outlook to a camel filling its hump with hate and God stirring the ingredients of cynicism when "making a William." It's a theme seen in his ideas of forming "The People Who Hate People Party" and mockery of American audiences' desire to hear "dick jokes." Hicks' confession of being addicted to the TV show *COPS* and acknowledgment that trash TV is like some irresistible atrocity exhibition seem to suggest a comedian feeling his message has not gotten through, that he will be remembered as a dirty mouthed cynic. Thus we have the dark imagery of a dying Marky Mark laid in the snow, blood oozing out as his body sinks, plus the TV show with a "woman giving birth in a dumpster to an armless flipper child" and the base humour of a graphically illustrated orgy involving Rush Limbaugh, Ronald Reagan and Nancy Reagan. There is too the frustration at the success of fellow comedians like Carrot Top and Gallagher. Gallagher's routine of smashing fruit is mocked as Hicks imagines Africa's starving wanting to see his show merely to get some of the food when it is smashed to pieces.

Yet in contrast to this misanthropy there is the spiritual yearning of wanting to "rid the world of these fevered egos that are tainting our collective unconscious and making us pay a higher psychic price than we can fuckin' imagine." Frequent evocations that it is time to evolve reveal that Hicks is not defeated, that within his spirituality and sense of enlightenment there is hope. Though he pronounces, "We have mis-created this world" he sees "the body is an illusion" and looks to a heaven where smoking is permitted and "Hendrix is on harp tonight." He closes the show to Rage Against The Machine's *Killing In The Name* and the repetition of the lyrics "Fuck you I won't do what you tell me." He places a melon on the stool, as if he has become so frustrated that he is going to sell out and become like Gallagher, gesturing motions to hit the melon with the microphone stand before striking the stool and leaving the melon in tact. This is the defiant Hicks who will never conform, scowling as he raises two middle fingers in true punk style and lip-synchs "Motherfucker!"

He went over to England at the end of November to get the go-ahead for *The Counts Of The Netherworld*, finding strength of purpose from a belief that he could get the show made, continuing the following year when he was still making plans, writing and believing in a recovery. But his condition was clearly worsening, his weight loss more evident. On January 6th 1994, at Caroline's in New York, selflessly agreeing to fulfil a commitment, he went on stage for the last time, did about forty minutes, and then had to walk off.

15
<u>Enlightenment</u>

It was time for Hicks' retreat into another world, to his parents' home in Little Rock, to prepare himself for the next level, some fine-tuning of his soul and spirit, some last feeding on knowledge. He listened to music like Miles Davis and Elvis Presley and found solace in Van Morrison's *Astral Weeks*, an album of raw melancholic beauty permeated by mystical lyrics and the mesmerising feel of two or three chord structures. Stand out track, *Sweet Thing*, evokes the beauty of nature with its languid rhythms and poetic lyrics vividly conveying a thriving landscape of possibilities. It is an impressionistic album, ethereal images floating through songs combined with a pervading sense of mystery. Morrison's album works as a song cycle, its connected narrative beginning dream like before moving towards darker images, its contradicting moods and atmospheres mirroring Hicks' own feelings.

A believer in fate and destiny, Hicks saw life as a circle becoming complete as he returned to the heroes of his formative years by watching documentaries on Jimi Hendrix and The Beatles, re-reading *The Adventures Of Huckleberry Finn* and studying *The Tibetan Book Living And Dying*. "There's still a lot of work to do" was a common refrain from Hicks at this time. He worked on a book, titled *New Happiness*, in addition to other writings he had been occupied with since his diagnosis, including a screenplay called *The King's Last Tour* about Elvis faking his own death. There was a sense of optimism, engendered by Bill's belief in a one-consciousness universe where even death has a meaning. According to Colleen McGarr, "He was getting a lot more light-hearted, because he felt really good" (44). He was at peace with himself and the world, able to face death because he knew there was a God, not tied to any religion, just some creative being out there, whose workings were based on love, not fear. He knew life was too goddam weird for there not to be anyone out there, perhaps even a "prankster God". He looked forward with hope and readied himself for the next life, saying "I've never been more happy or at peace about it. It's been a long enough road, but what is length in the context of eternity?" (52).

That friend Kevin Booth said of him, "Bill was the first person I ever met whose goal it was to become enlightened," (6) is testament to a man always searching for meaning, restless in his need to know the answers to profound questions; a man seeking to connect with the bigger picture and the intangibles of the universe that suggest there must be something spiritual about existence. Keenly in touch with the world around him, towards the end of his life an awareness of his place in the open scheme of things helped him cope with the illness. This awareness had manifested itself as a youngster when he loved the outdoors and sought to discover the world, appreciating creation and seeking knowledge from the world around him. He believed that people took for granted the beauty of life on Earth, that they should be able to "name all of the animals" before they could fully evolve.

In his teens, Hicks had absorbed Transcendental Meditation; a process of relaxing the body through meditation in order to achieve spiritual awareness, an enlightened state that transcended consciousness. The founder of TM, Maharishi Mahesh Yogi had taken elements of Hinduism and simplified them, announcing in 1972 a world plan to share TM through centres around the world. Hicks' heroes The Beatles had visited Yogi in 1967, generating worldwide interest and prompting a growth in practitioners, which reached a peak in the mid 1970s. TM allowed Hicks (much like drugs did) to tap into his creativity, giving him a feeling of there being some greater force. Drug trips, invariably taken in natural surroundings, only cemented his belief in creation as he saw the beauty of the world and had his mind opened up to many possibilities.

Though he attacked organised religion for the constraints it imposed, Hicks did have faith that there was some omnipotent creator at work and that beyond life there was another realm of existence, one of spirit. He believed "Our bodies are an illusion," and that the mind was humanity's most powerful component, that its openness was what guided experiences after death. It is why, in Hicks' comedy, God, the mind, spirituality and the soul are inextricably linked, and why deities are often humanised by mundane activities and recognisable dialogue. Hicks wants to suggest that connections with spirituality are possible, not through organised religion but through imaginative leaps of a shared consciousness. He may have made quips about "channelling Elvis," but taken out of the hands of charlatans not so far removed from shallow televangelists, Hicks had a serious interest in the feasibility of contacting the dead. After being diagnosed with cancer, Hicks returned to the book *A Course In Miracles* by Helen Schulman. A book he had read before, he now studied in detail Schulman's notes made from humanist messages she had received. The dominant religious outlook of the U.S. may even have labelled such activities as the work of Satan, because there's was a faith based on unshifting dogmatism. For the perennially open minded Hicks, ideas taken from religion were always those that emphasized compassion and enlightenment.

From Hinduism, Hicks identified with Shiva (also known as Siva), the third of three forms of God (after Creator, Preserver, Shiva was The Destroyer). Also known as King of Dancers and giver of joy, Shiva's mission is to set humanity free from ignorance. Undoubtedly this was how Hicks saw himself and his comedy with routines that opened up an audience's view of the world and mocked the trivial things that drag us down. Just as Shiva spends much of his life alone in meditation in the Himalayas, so Hicks was often a solitary figure when in Los Angeles, spending time reading and filtering the television world into his material. More than that he saw himself as a lone voice of reason, particularly in his unresponsive home country. Shiva is often depicted with a third eye in the middle of the forehead, echoing Hicks' "squeegeed third eye," inferring that this gave him the ability to see further into the soul of humanity and identify truths that those in power don't want widely known.

There is constant reference to the soul in Hicks' routines, be it rock music with soul or politicians who have none and choose greed instead. Misconstrued as cynical, Hicks was merely identifying the cynicism of those with power. He could make fun of his own dark soul, claiming he smoked because "I need the tar to fill the pot holes in my soul," but in fact his soul was rich, filled with love and a desire to instil in others compassion, to evolve further and hopefully help others evolve in the process. Part of his anger came from a frustration that people weren't evolving, were in fact regressing: "We have at our fingertips the greatest minds of all time, the greatest knowledge and the history of the greatest thinkers of all fuckin' time, but no, let's have little white girls singing" (of the popularity of Tiffany and Debbie Gibson). The human race wasn't developing, was too self-satisfied with what it had, with all the material goods: "I'm tired of this back-slapping aren't humanity neat bullshit. We're a virus with shoes, that's all we are."

Evolution is a central theme of Hicks' comedy and philosophy, his words a means of "planting seeds" of ideas, which he hopes will help people's minds to grow. He sees a world where people seem to have ceased to grow, content to consume and feed off creation without reciprocation. This is the "bovine America" he so detests, the America which appears to have come as far as it can intellectually, Hicks employing the caricature of Southern types to mock people whose lives revolve around TV, whose lives are governed by fear. These are the people not shouting "Revolution" but instead are impotently crying for "Evolution!"

Hicks saw that "Evolution didn't end with us growing opposable thumbs," that it meant a continuing seeking of knowledge to unlock the meaning of life. Though he joked about the next evolutionary step being losing a vertebrae so men could have the ability to suck their own cocks, more pertinently, humanity's next evolutionary step would see it "putting your guns aside," casting away lies and hatred and embracing a world of love.

Such enlightenment coincides with Hicks' belief in life beyond planet Earth; the sense that we are not alone in the universe and that if we evolved we could "explore space, both inner and outer, for all eternity." Running throughout his material is disgust at the narrow-mindedness of society, a theme also apparent in his belief in alien species; that humanity's place in infinite space meant there must be life beyond Earth, but humanity was too tied up in the mundane, in things that held back our evolution, to ever explore such possibilities. For Hicks, "Outer space awaits our presence, we are better and more unique than this and all eternity is our playground." Within this line there is the desperate yearning for mankind to use its knowledge and spirituality to gain a deeper understanding of its place in the universe. "Playground" not only suggests the experience could be more fun than the day-to-day slog the human race has locked itself into, but also connects back to the feeling of innocence lost when John F. Kennedy was killed.

Whilst tripping with Kevin Booth and David Johndrow in 1987, Hicks had a UFO experience, and though all three were separate at the time, they shared the same vision. In Hicks' recollection, "We had this shared vision of being visited by a ship and these seven balls of light which (inside) you could see these little skeleton figures inside, moving in this light, and they led us onto their ship and we were asking them, all telepathically, 'Why are you doing this?' and they said, 'Because you wanted to know.' And we said, 'Why us?' and they said. 'Because you'll see it for what we are.' And we said, 'How do you do what you do?' and they said 'we're gonna show you.' And they opened up their ship and we all saw this bright light" (3).

Hicks liked adventure and fantasy computer games, sought to have his imagination stretched and all possibilities explored objectively. His fascination with UFOs is an extension of this (as well as being part of his interest in conspiracy theories). He once said "With a five-minute UFO experience I got a taste of holiness I never got in twenty years of religion." In this he sees that organised religion is blinkered, that if indeed there is a God of all creation then surely there must be something more than just Earth.

Hicks had long been a fan of science fiction and writers like Tom Robbins, Ray Bradbury and Kurt Vonnegut, whilst – as already noted in Chapter Seven – he ascribed to Terence McKenna's view that aliens had left drugs on the planet to help facilitate mankind's evolution. Hicks' taste in the genre was for those works that maintained a contemporary relevance by employing recognisable characters, their narratives offering metaphors for modern society, eschewing the somewhat boring flights of fantasy of the more elaborate genre offerings. And what this often produced was a distinct and confident narrative voice, one that could articulate disparate stories and ideas in much the same way as the stand-up. Hicks enjoyed Tom Robbins' *Another Roadside Attraction* not just because of the originality of a plot concerning a roadside diner run my mystical hippy-types who acquire the body of Jesus Christ, but also because of Robbins' vibrant writing style, allowing him to philosophise when employing monologues and flashbacks, digressing and going off at tangents in a manner the comedian favoured.

The left-wing leanings and anti-capitalist sentiment of genre novels like Bradbury's *Fahrenheit 451*, where a totalitarian government burns books, are apparent in much of Hicks' comedy. Hicks' rednecks may merely not understand the appeal of reading, but his fundamentalists are the kind who *would* destroy literature they found offensive, although this may not be necessary as in Hicks' world the drug of television has become a more subtle government tool to suppress thought. Hicks even suggests the fascistic practice himself when making a connection between drugs and good music: "Drugs have done good things for us. If you don't believe they have, do me a favour – take all your albums, tapes and CDs and burn them, 'cause you know what, the musicians who made that great music that has enhanced your lives throughout the years? Rrrrreal fuckin' high." It's a reasoning that cleverly targets middle class hypocrisy; all comfortable with music that history has subsequently deemed as classic, yet at the same time buying into a state sponsored message that drugs are inarguably bad.

One of his favourite science-fiction books was Robert A. Heinlein's *Stranger In A Strange Land*. It is the story of a man raised by Martians who returns to Earth as a messiah figure, founding his own church. He preaches love, teaching humanity to evolve, untouched by the selfishness of humans. It's a plot that can be seen in Hicks' riff about aliens dropping Jimi Hendrix on Earth saying, "We'll pick you up in twenty-eight years. Jimi, show 'em how it's done."

The appeal of the science-fiction genre is in its specific trait of taking contemporary society and looking towards how it would develop if it progressed along the path it was currently taking. In many ways, Hicks could be labelled a science-fiction comedian, seeing how the world was shaping up and projecting it into his own picture of a dystopian future. It is seen in his projection of himself as a dead smoker making anti-smoking commercials like Yul Brynner's, but it also has a panoramic view of society with characteristics exaggerated to suggest what the future might become. This is apparent in his future vision of a mall culture where people spend their days shopping, never seeing daylight, and in a world where people are too scared to leave their living rooms in case they are attacked by "some crack-addicted, A.I.D.S. infected pit bull," locking themselves indoors, in front of the television; Orwell's *Nineteen Eighty-Four* for the consumer generation. It is similar to John Carpenter's science-fiction film, *They Live* (1988), a film Hicks had enjoyed with its portrayals of corporate bodies as aliens, using subliminal advertising to brainwash people. Again it's part of Hicks' conspiracy angle, the way that those in power are so separate from the essential ideals of humanity yet still seem to have the power to maintain control.

In 1991 and 1992 in Fyfe, Alabama, there were many UFO sightings and reports of inexplicably dead and mutilated cattle. The mutilations were often accompanied by sightings of helicopters, leaving some to believe the military were testing weapons on the cattle. Unlike rednecks who brought guns to UFO sightings, Hicks was enlightened enough to see the positive, praying for an alien culture to arrive which would take him away from Earth and all its detestable traits. He aspired to have the kind of knowledge that alien races must possess, his greatest fear being that such species would be as backward as the people of Earth, that they would be redneck aliens who would not choose to land in New York, but instead jovially announce, "We're going to enter out mother ship in the tractor pull."

Such belief in alien races and spiritual enlightenment saw Hicks seeking out the intangible for answers, going beyond materialism to enrich his soul. Once more, it is a view informed by the idealism of the 1960s, Hicks seeing life in much the same way as Dr Timothy Leary: "old white rulers...have glorified material values and degraded the spiritual" (*The Declaration Of*

206

Evolution). Hicks' spirituality was without constraints, freed from the need to accumulate products (interviews with friends and family noting his frequent tendency to give things away). Such freedom imbues his material with that sense of a ride, free flowing like some hallucinogenic experience where he sees Jesus riding a unicorn whilst in heaven he parties with Yul Brynner. An ability to see the connection between things allows Hicks to see creation as a structured thing and therefore everything that happens has a reason and is linked to fate. It follows then that death is merely part of a process, which will eventually see people evolve into spiritual beings floating through the cosmos.

It is a spirituality that comes from individual discovery, the individual then having the responsibility to convey this to others. It is what Hicks spent his career doing, until the end when he cut himself off, saying goodbye to his friends before ceasing to speak on February 14th.

At 11.20pm on Saturday 26th February 1994 Hicks died in Little Rock. His fans were completely shocked by the apparent suddenness of the news. Tributes from the UK were fittingly passionate, and though in America the mainstream obituaries seemed more muted, Jeff Rusnak did perfectly summarise the loss with, "an artist who had the power to enlighten has been cut off mid-sentence...Hicks was a courageous and necessary voice. He will be missed" (53). Lewis Grizzard's death the following month garnered more attention and widespread lamentations. A newspaper columnist, writer and performer, Grizzard's humour had been likened to Twain's with humour based around stories of small town life in the Southern U.S., particularly the town of Moreland, Georgia. Some of his work did contain a satirical perspective, but it was a cosy type that didn't seem too dangerous, as much a celebration of Southern stereotypes as a mockery of them. Though Grizzard, like Hicks, employed the language of the South, it often created a somewhat sentimental picture. In short, his humour was a more palatable kind than Hicks', who was again nominated by The American Comedy Awards for Best Male Stand-Up in 1994 (along with Will Durst, George Wallace, Dom Irrera and Carrot Top). This time the judges rather insultingly concluded that Carrot Top was the year's best.

Obituaries in the British press showed the feeling of a country losing one of its own. William Cook in *The Scotsman* wrote that his death "has robbed stand-up of the most exciting young comic on either side of the Atlantic," whilst Rupert Edwards in *The Independent* lamented, "His death...has robbed comedy of a uniquely passionate talent." Such eloquent and precise summaries were a feature of the British press's response, fittingly conveying the country's admiration for what Hicks had achieved.

Bill Hicks was buried in the family plot in Leakesville, Mississippi. At the memorial service Hicks' brother, Steve, read out a piece Bill had written and requested be read: "I left in love, in laughter, and in truth, and wherever truth, love and laughter abide, I am there in spirit." A more touching epitaph one cannot imagine, conveying as it does the humanism and selflessness that was Hicks' life and work. His spirit then floated up into the cosmic one consciousness where he continues to enjoy the ride throughout eternity and infinity.

16
A Spiffy Eternity

Bill Hicks can rightly be defined as a social commentator whose work chronicles his times. Just taking a snapshot of the 1980s and early 1990s one can see how much his comedy linked to the era. Reference books for those years and the important events that transpired will record a history chronicled in Hicks' comedy. He had the tabloid headlines (From Ted Bundy and Pee-Wee Herman to Madonna) together with the important issues (Reaganomics, the L.A. Riots, The Gulf War). His philosophy hasn't dated. Indeed, since his death interest in him has grown and his ideas are as relevant as ever.

Fourteen months after Hicks' death, American was shocked when a bomb blew up the Alfred P. Murrah Building in Oklahoma City killing 168 people. Initial theories linked the attack to Middle East terrorists, until it transpired that an American, Gulf War veteran Timothy McVeigh, had carried out the attack. McVeigh aligned himself to right-wing militias fighting against government control and justified the bombing as a response to the government's actions in Waco (the bomb exploding on April 19th, two years to the day after Waco's catastrophic climax). It caused America to look at itself in a way Hicks often sought, though eventually it became a rather tenuous self-examination as McVeigh became the lone nut figure, whilst the conspiracy theories Hicks so loved became common currency in the wake of the bombing, growing throughout the 1990s as Earth approached the millennium. Moreover, as with the debate over Waco, the implications of the Oklahoma bombing were sidelined by saturation news coverage of the trial of O.J. Simpson. When the dead bodies of Simpson's ex-wife, Nicole Brown Simpson, and her friend, Ronald Goldman, were discovered on June 12th 1994, former American football hero turned actor O.J. Simpson became a prime suspect. His attempt to escape the law on June 17th saw news broadcasts becoming more like a Hollywood movie with a car chase involving Simpson and the police beamed live across the networks, providing enough fun for viewers in need of another *Smokey And The Bandit* sequel. The trial that played out between July 1994 and October 1995 held the nation's attention with its sensational mix of celebrity, sex and death: news as entertainment, in the same generic cess-pit as the *COPS* show. Indeed, in June 1995, CNN estimated they made $45 million in additional advertising revenue from coverage of the O.J. Simpson trial.

Interest in Hicks has flourished since his death, much more so than with Kinison (though both have had movies about their lives mooted). He is perhaps more popular now than he ever was in his life, increasingly looked back on with the same reverence as Lennon and Hendrix. A steady stream of articles, including Mike Sager's excellent *The Gospel According to Hicks* from GQ magazine (1994) and a chapter in Will Kaufman's book *The Comedian As Confidence Man* (1997) proclaiming Hicks "a true heir of Jonathan Swift", have kept his memory alive, along with more unusual referencing like issue 31 (November 1997) of the comic *Preacher* by Garth Innis and Steve Dillon. In the adventure, The Preacher sees Hicks in a nightclub, the comedian's speech bubbles using material from his albums. Meanwhile, British film *Human Traffic* (1999), a celebration of drug culture, had the main character living life by Hicks' philosophy and used a clip from Hicks' show.

Though there existed much 'new' material unreleased, it wasn't until February 1997 that the Rykodisc label released Hicks' final two albums, *Arizona Bay* and *Rant In E Minor* (along with re-releases of *Dangerous* and *Relentless*), reminding people of Hicks' great talent and inventiveness. *Rant* in particular was an apocalyptic masterpiece, for many fans a first chance to hear material from Hicks' last gigs.

Cynthia True's biography, *American Scream*, appeared in 2002 and was lapped up by fans eager for the first look at Hicks' personal life and background. Though well-researched and interesting, True's book offers little insight from those closest to Hicks. More tantalising is the promise of a future book by Kevin Booth in collaboration with Austin journalist Ken Lieck.

Rykodisc seem to have finally realised the interest in Hicks by releasing albums of previous unavailable material in November 2002. *Love Laughter And Truth* is a somewhat perfunctory collection of cobbled together bits of shows whilst *Flying Saucer Tour Volume 1* is a full show (in front of a difficult audience) and promises to be the first in a series of releases. It would be nice to think that some videos could be released of the many bootlegs floating in cyberspace, for an appreciation of Hicks' shows really comes from seeing his use of physical comedy when delivering material.

Bill Clinton returned to office in 1996. The sex scandals surrounding the president and Monica Lewinsky had the media going into another false frenzy, the kind so often cited by Hicks. Thus the debate becomes not about presidential perjury, but the more titillating analysis of whether oral sex can be considered adultery. As a distraction, Clinton ordered the 1998 bombing of the Al-Shifa pharmaceutical plant in Sudan, claiming it was used for chemical weapons, yet subsequent examination of the facts has revealed the plant was "the only source of 90 per cent of the basic medicines of one of the poorest countries" (43).

Television news continues to become more like entertainment with sound and graphics borrowed from MTV and its coverage of sensational news stories that have little bearing on people's lives. In 1997 the average length of TV news soundbites in America had gone from 42.3 seconds in 1968 to 9.9 seconds in 1997 (54). This is news unwilling to tackle issues in any depth, eager to keep the viewer interested by presented news as fast food. In essence, it is there as an arm of government, not to ignite debate but to reassure by ignoring complex and challenging issues: "Go back to bed America" reverberates long after Hicks' death.

It would be fair to say that with the emergence of HBO, American television is producing some of its best programming in decades with shows such as *The Sopranos*, *Six Feet Under*, *Oz*, *The West Wing* and *The Shield*. Nonetheless, the trend for the voyeuristic pornography that is reality TV has not abated. One can only delight in the possibilities of Hicks' take on *The Anna Nicole Smith Show* and the recent travesty of *Star Dates*. In the latter we have ordinary people dating D-list celebrities (with Gary Coleman amongst them), as if to suggest that Joe Public's ultimate aspiration is to be a part of the celebrity world.

Pre-September 11th, there seemed to be more hope for cinema with recent years seeing a growth in low budget "indie" films that treat audiences like adults. Though the aftermath of the terrorist attacks provoked murmurings of a need to tone down the vacuous spectacle of blockbuster action movies, it remains to be seen whether proposals for a fourth *Rambo* film (and its rumoured plot concerned with killing Osama bin Laden) are the beginnings of a renewed pursuit of patriotic posturing.

Music, on the other hand, has certainly maintained its descent into irrelevance. Hicks' harking back to an era when music had soul is as pertinent now as it was for the eighties, the nineties and the new millennium (as celebrated to great success by the likes of Will Smith, Robbie Williams and Cliff Richard). Against Hicks' rock heroes, only Nirvana came close in terms of world appeal and artistic integrity, and of course a rock star dying young; lead singer Kurt Cobain's suicide due in no small part to a conflict with rock traditions and the role he felt uneasy with, the kind of pigeonholing detested by Hicks. But Nirvana were a joyless band who didn't touch the peaks of reckless abandon achieved by The Rolling Stones, Jimi Hendrix and The Beatles, whilst the "grunge" movement Nirvana pioneered soon became assimilated into the mainstream, the genre tag now a term applied to corporate whores such as Nickleback. There have been great bands and great music - The Smiths, The Pixies, the pioneers in the UK's Madchester scene as well as Seattle's grunge scene - but for the most part, the charts and entertainment industry have rewarded the usual talentless, forgettable and uninspired 'stars'. This is a world where Mariah Carey can sell millions and Robbie Williams is considered the wild man of rock and roll. The trend for teenage pop stars has not abated and the successors to Tiffany and Debbie Gibson are multitudinous, with Britney Spears at the forefront peddling a clean-cut image and selling Pepsi Cola.

Commercials continue to dominate lives, selling sex more explicitly than ever whilst respected stars like Ed Harris and Samuel L. Jackson sell out to hawk products, forever tarnishing any 'cool' image their movies may have generated, with plugs for Vauxhall and Barclay's Bank respectively. This is perhaps what Hicks so detested about adverts, that with their main objective of selling they lose all integrity, and thus anyone or anything associated with them is tainted. As a man who loved rock music and all it represented, its exploitation by marketing and advertising was abhorrent not because he had any love for those who sold out, but because their actions in the realms of one consciousness somehow dishonoured an ethos. In a world where Dennis Hopper involves himself with a commercial that exploits the hippy philosophy of his film *Easy Rider*, little seems sacred. In this world maybe even Hicks' quip that one day it'll be "It's Jesus for Miller" doesn't seem so fanciful.

On Friday February 26th 1999 at 11.20pm, five years to the minute after Hicks' death, friend Fallon Woodland posted an e-mail on the Sacred Cow website: "...the ONLY thing that is gone at all is Bill's physical body...bill was and is bigger than life and he is certainly bigger than death and that is why this day does not toll heavily in my heart..." It says everything about the optimism Hicks' worldview engendered, that for friends and fans his philosophy lives on.

The best comedians are social commentators, tapping into trends and current affairs, opening up a new perception of events, and questioning the validity of the media's presentation and the general public's acceptance of the information they are presented with. This often leaves their comedy becoming dated, like that of Lenny Bruce. Hicks' material, although based on current events during his lifetime, looks at bigger and more general truths that retain their relevance. Issues such as personal freedom, the need to question governments and media manipulation will always be relevant (unless the world evolves into some kind of Utopia). Therefore, since his death, Hicks' philosophy is more relevant than ever. We need his voice and ideas when events such as the April 20th 1999 shooting at Columbine High only provoke a lip-service response for gun controls and remind us of Hicks' classic line about only "a fool and a communist" seeing the link between the prevalence of guns in America and the number of deaths. Moreover, analysis of why two boys at Columbine had decided to kill their peers found a convenient enemy in rock and roll, in particular the music of Marilyn Manson. The hysterical demonising of Manson and voracious dissemination of his lyrics to find a reason for the killings is in stark contrast to the indifferent shrug afforded to Smith & Wesson's 1999 gun catalogue which showed a child with a handgun, nostalgically beside his father, and a caption which read "Those sure were the good times – just you, dad and his Smith & Wesson." How prescient too were Hicks' inflammatory remarks, in the aftermath of the Waco debacle, about Catholic churches being at the centre of child abuse? Investigations in 2003 have uncovered evidence of at least 1,200 priests involved in the abuse of more than 4,000 children.

We needed Hicks' voice too when American politics, in such a shoddy state, allowed George Bush Junior (amongst whose supporters was one Chuck Norris) to become president in 2000 after weeks of arguments over the counting of votes in Florida. With Dick Cheney as his vice-president (a man with a record of voting against the release of Nelson Mandela, against abortion even in cases of rape or incest and voting against a holiday to commemorate Martin Luther King) George W. Bush became leader of the most powerful country in the world in the least convincing fashion. Investigations have since found much evidence that Bush never actually beat Al Gore, and that a lot of the voting in Florida was rigged. For example, in the summer of 1999, Katherine Harris, Bush's presidential campaign co-chairwoman and the Florida secretary of state in charge of elections, paid $4 million to Database Technologies to remove anyone "suspected" of being a former felon (55). This targeted mainly black men, preventing 31% of them from voting. The black vote is traditionally for the Democrats, some even taken off the register having already served their time and being made eligible to vote again. In addition, there were anomalies with overseas votes (mostly military and Republican votes) being counted when they shouldn't have been allowed. One can almost hear Hicks' doubtful pondering of "Coincidence?" when one analyses these facts. Moreover, Hicks' assertion of "Twelve guys who run the fuckin' world" is borne out with analysis of the donations given to Bush's 2000 election campaign. The tobacco industry donated $7 million and coincidentally Bush stopped federal lawsuits against cigarette manufacturers. The oil and gas industry donated $25.4 million, and coincidentally Bush abandoned the restrictions on CO_2 emissions whilst also ignoring the Kyoto agreement on global warming. The legion of insidious measures Bush has undertaken would have provided Hicks with enough material for a triple album, but in his place there is a valuable source in Michael Moore's book, *Stupid White Men*.

Moore is undoubtedly one of Hicks' successors, and although he is more of a journalist and filmmaker than a comedian, he uses humour to expose hypocrisy and deceit amongst the rich and powerful, whilst also mocking the bigots and fundamentalists that were often targeted by Hicks. Through his work in television, particularly his series *The Awful Truth*, we get a sense of Moore's disbelief at what often goes unnoticed in American society: from statistics revealing the number of black citizens being shot and killed by the New York Police Department, to an inspired feature on pro-lifers killing doctors, with Moore joking that the rubble from bombed clinics would be recycled to build orphanages, subtly making the same point as Hicks when noting that those who condemn abortion will not take the responsibility for looking after those that are subsequently unwanted. On Moore's show there is evident a bemusement and exasperation common to Hicks' routines about the behaviour of his fellow citizens, and like Hicks, Moore is unafraid to fly in the face of popular opinion as he criticises America's gun culture in his film *Bowling For Columbine* and appears on talk shows mocking Bush and his aggression against the Middle East. In comparison to Hicks as a revolutionary using satire to challenge ideas, Moore is the revolutionary seeking to prompt active involvement through face-to-face confrontations with those perpetrating injustices; his stunts ranging from the sublime to the ridiculous, yet more often than not dominated by a sense of irony Hicks would have been proud of.

In terms of stand-up comedy, few contemporaries have emerged to challenge Hicks' legacy. Dennis Miller has something of the style and material and some of Hicks' ideas, to the point of using the word "rant" in his books and albums. He'd progressed from presenting *Saturday Night Live*'s 'Weekend Update' to hosting his own chat show in 1991. His stand-up routines include many of Hicks' themes as he attacks TV and popular culture and analyses the subjectivity of language, but Miller's material is weaker and he has nothing of Hicks' opening up the experience, moving out of immediate space and taking the audience with him. His ideas don't have that universal feeling and as well as some of his material being distinctly pedestrian, it is also underpinned by the same right-wing ideology apparent in some of Sam Kinison's material, with its belief that need is a weakness and its celebration of the American way of survival of the fittest. Moreover, Miller's routines about law and order and advocating of the death penalty reveal an ideology crossing over into Rush Limbaugh territory.

Chris Rock really comes close to Hicks in terms of stand-up. He is not particularly dangerous to the establishment, but he has got some funny and perceptive things to say. A voracious reader of newspapers, Rock is a political comedian, even more so than Richard Pryor. Like Hicks, Rock challenges the anti-intellectualism of his background, particularly in a routine Niggers Vs. Black People where he advocates putting money inside books as a means to avoid it being robbed by "niggers" who seem to fear learning and its means to self-empowerment. His routines are rooted though in a black perspective, mainly because Rock feels the need to refer to it in his material. He doesn't need to. He is a perceptive, sophisticated and brilliant stand-up comic. His routines on "black" relationships are universal, and his analysis of language shows how sophisticated his comedy material is. One only hopes he does not waste his talents on Hollywood movies.

Two comedians, Doug Stanhope and Joe Rogan, have been compared to Hicks over the last few years, not least because they have both worked with Kevin Booth. Joe Rogan, himself an admirer of Hicks, has some similarities in terms of material. Like Hicks, there is the controversial subject matter, his graphic sexual imagery and routines on masturbation owing as much to Kinison as to Hicks. Rogan too seeks some kind of evolution of thought and attitude, adeptly and incisively mocking white trash America and cutting into society's false morality. Rogan is very funny, but at this stage of his career shares with many other American comics a rather insular perspective.

Doug Stanhope has some concerns similar to Hicks, his love of smoking, pornography and drugs directly correlating to his frustration at society's hypocrisy concerning those vices. Thus we have Stanhope indulging in what might be termed "Hicksian" rants against Middle America, all manner of killjoys and religious moralists, characters often – as with Hicks – denoted by an idiotic Southern drawl when reason is missing. Stanhope shares Hicks' frustration with society's inexplicable behaviour and is a clever observer of the strange and peculiar in everyday life, to such an extent that it allows him to expose false morality. But there is a divergence between the two. For Hicks, celebrating drug taking, smoking and pornography were intrinsically linked to freedom of choice, to intelligent humans being allowed to make their own choices (so long as they didn't harm another human being). Though Stanhope freely admits "I'm a huge fan of pornography" and delights in presenting his three packs a day nicotine addiction and copious consumption of cocaine, the tone and unforgiving imagery create a nihilistic mood where altruism is merely implicit, something happily coincidental with Stanhope's hedonism. On the other hand, Stanhope is caught up in the inconsistencies of political correctness, indulging in carelessness misogyny with women generally presented as whores or strippers whilst at the same time showing a willingness to mock not only his own masculinity, but also a priapic culture in general. Indeed, sharing the same Malthusian outlook as Hicks, Stanhope is decidedly PC when suggesting the way to prevent an overcrowding of the planet is to encourage homosexuality with pro-sodomy billboards.

Similar to Hicks seeing political correctness as another form of censorship, Stanhope can be forgiven for allowing a desire to break down barriers result in sometimes-unpalatable moments. When the risks pay dividends, the dark imagery is original and perceptive, as with a routine where the consigning of smokers to sections on trains calls up images of Jews on their way to Auschwitz. Hicks, self-titled "dark poet" had such a capacity for storytelling, for creating a vivid picture through his use of language and imagery that one almost forgot the obscene and shocking pictures he was conjuring up. Stanhope, though less humanitarian, is similarly adept at building up images smoothly and fluently, becoming increasingly dark as he leads the audience into his disturbing world, his frustration with truck drivers building to a crescendo as he talks of masturbating to footage of the L.A. riots and trying to time his ejaculation to coincide with Reginald Denny's beating. Despite Stanhope lacking Hicks' warmth and sensitivity (for Hicks the "no sympathy" angle was more of a mood swing than a philosophy, for Stanhope it often seems like an ideology), his lack of pretension and willingness not to conform ("I'm not pro-choice, I'm pro-abortion") suggest his career development will be worth watching. Moreover, his most recent material has shown a growth of sophistication with material about society's lack of differentiation between drug users and drug addicts, as well as more political material, most of it aimed at George W. Bush.

David Cross has emerged as one of the few comedians willing to go out on a limb and puncture the empty patriotism of Bush's post-9/11 America, and by doing so show an objective view of his country, one that like Hicks has a world perspective. From referring to Los Angeles as a "non-stop parade of delusion" to his labelling of post-9/11 flag-waving as an "empty gesture", Cross is comparable to Hicks when conveying a sense of himself as a voice of reason, one seeking to question those in power, pointing out the flaws in accepted arguments and mocking the arrogance of white America. He perceptively develops the flag-waving routine to mock the selling of patriotism through television commercials, an obsession with flags that sees Cross presenting a mock advert, one concluded with "all flags made by Chinese prison labour" just as Hicks had U.S. flags which were "made in Korea."

Cross adeptly satirises the false morality and sensitivity of post-9/11 America and the entertainers consumed by the moral dilemma of whether they should perform after the terrorists attacks. And punching through the fog of jingoism, Cross succinctly evaluates Bush's War On Terrorism in much the same way as Hicks did with the War On Drugs. For Cross, "You cannot win a war on terrorism. It's like having a war on jealousy."

Born in Atlanta, as a fellow Southerner, Cross, like Hicks, paints a vivid and grotesque picture of the region's dominant stereotypes: "morbidly obese people...sitting on their fuckin' couch...watching their satellite dish, all day and all night, and watching their fifteen year old kids, and their fifteen year old's three year old, and they're all running around...and they've poor dental work, and fuckin', y'know, they're junkies and speed freaks and alcoholics, and they're sitting there with their, y'know, running sores." Cross is concerned with escaping narrow-mindedness, is cynical about religion ("tribal, superstitious nonsense") and also like Hicks, but in contrast to Stanhope or Rogan, is proud to be an intellectual, happy that he is separate from bovine America. His delivery is as assured as Hicks' and one hopes that as his career develops he continues to make sharp and fearless observations.

In contemporary stand-up, the comedian most like Hicks is Will Durst, not only because he remains a peripheral figure in the American comedy scene (with even more unsuccessful nominations for the American Comedy Awards than Hicks), but also in terms of his insightful material.

As a political comedian, Durst's material thrives on an appetite for current affairs in much the same way as Hicks, both seeking to view events from a different perspective as they uncover the absurdity and ironies of everyday life. Back in 1991 Durst was doing a routine similar to Hicks about the U.S. selling arms to Iraq, although unlike Denis Leary's stealing from Hicks, Durst has an original way of presenting it. In the routine Durst uses the example of America selling weapons to both Iran and Iraq during the war between the two countries. He moves stage right, gesturing handing over a gun to one side, then moves stage left to whisper to the other, "he's got a gun" before moving back to the person he has first armed with "he knows about the gun." It echoes the America represented by Hicks' Jack Palance, one eagerly stirring up trouble.

Durst too is not afraid to criticise America, even in the wake of the September 11th attacks, mocking the retaliatory bombing of Afghanistan with "all we're doing is rearranging rocks," pointing out the absurdity of using burrowing bombs that only create more caves and the contradiction of dropping food at the same time as bombs. Similar to Hicks, this leads on to the media's presentation of the war with Durst ridiculing the lack of illumination in the coverage of U.S actions in Afghanistan, calling the TV news "rumours with sponsors." And just as Hicks raged against the apathy of "bovine America", so there is Durst, bewildered that nobody was prepared to riot after the obvious corruption in the 2000 elections, reasoning that it was because the American public "have the attention span of high speed lint." Durst's America is plagued by the same ignorance as Hicks', with people who "love the home shopping network because it's commercial free" and are baffled by suicide terrorists because "how do they get paid?" Though he eschews sexual material, rarely swears and doesn't delve into the dark, violent imagery of Hicks' routines, Durst's sense of disbelief at events is comparable to Hicks, as in the way he perceptively unlocks the ironies inherent in accepted views.

In the United Kingdom, two comedians have emerged in the 1990s that are willing to push boundaries and uncover truths. The first, Mark Thomas, despite television shows on Channel 4, maintains a position on the margins as he looks into issues neglected by the media and confronts those perpetrating wrongs. Similar to Michael Moore in actively challenging those in power and seeking to make them accountable, Thomas is nonetheless an accomplished stand-up, one as in touch with contemporary issues as Hicks undoubtedly was. Indeed, as a passionate campaigner for workers' rights (both at home and abroad) and a fierce and knowledgeable critic of globalisation, he is perhaps more of a political comedian than Hicks. As a result, despite a fine sense of irony when raging at political hypocrisy, his material can be more engaging for the insight he offers rather than its comic pay-offs. Nonetheless, Hicks would have been proud to note Thomas' routine on the benefits of cannabis echoing his own, with Thomas' assertion that Paul Macartney had been inspired to write *Helter Skelter* whilst stoned, yet in sobriety had managed the inane "Frog Chorus."

The second U.K. comedian to emerge, Chris Morris, perhaps picking up from the surrealism and willingness to be controversial of Peter Cook, has also left his mark. His TV show *Brass Eye* tackled issues such as drugs, sex and crime, exposing the false sincerity of celebrities willing to speak on behalf of causes they knew nothing about. One special episode on paedophiles provoked outrage from the tabloid and conservative press, who seemed blind to the sophisticated way it mocked the hysterical coverage of paedophiles. If that wasn't enough, a mock feature in *The Observer* newspaper, written by Morris and Armando Iannucci and concerned with September 11th and its aftermath, was as controversial as anything Hicks has done. *Six Months That Changed A Year* (17th March 2002) brilliantly satirised how the tragedy was exploited by politicians and sensationalised by the media, so that we have "Tony Blair publicly drains every drop of blood from his wife to help the injured of New York" and "Sources say that the Pentagon attack, already notorious as 'a TV dud', is now badly in need of a relaunch." One particular mock quote, attributed to Noam Chomsky, takes something from Hicks' routine about the police officers in the Rodney King trial explaining that the beating videotape looks different when played backwards. In the Morris/Iannucci piece, the joke is on Chomsky for his ability to take opposing viewpoints to the consensus: "If you run the twin towers footage backwards, the towers stand up again – we need to ask why has the footage only ever been run forwards?" The essence of the piece is a theme seen in much of Hicks' material, that of how the public don't seem to question the news they are presented with, thus allowing a potent mix of forced sensitivity, distorted patriotism and sensational simplification to create a climate in which the truth is ill defined. Quite clearly, Morris and Iannucci are as intent as Hicks was to puncture myths and say what people were afraid to say.

The attacks on the World Trade Centre on September 11th 2001 have left an indelible mark on the American consciousness and sense of itself. On the one hand it created introspection amongst Americans and a questioning of the country's interventions in foreign affairs. More dominant though (or at least more vocal) has been the patriotic fervour and desire for America to flex its muscle further. Hicks would have certainly felt angry at the lack of reason in the U.S. responses to September 11[th,] creating what Hicks would identify as a climate of fear and hate. Typical of this is the USA Patriot Act, giving police increased power to tap telephones and look at internet correspondence, allowing secret government searches without warrants, and permitting the CIA to detain non-US citizens indefinitely without trial. But breeding fear is profitable with the military industrial complex enjoying a boom in arms sales since the twin towers attacks.

With the bombing of Afghanistan as President Bush's response to the terrorist attacks, we have a situation echoing Hicks' "bullies of the world" routine all over again. At first Osama bin Laden was the new demon and, just as Hicks had the American bully arming those it wished to crush, so bin Laden had once been armed and trained by the American government when the C.I.A. was organising al-Qa'ida to fight the Russians in the 1980s. Relevant too is the closing line from the *Sane Man* show where Hicks contemplates the expense of building weapons and how that money could be used to alleviate much of the human suffering around the world. One cold fact mirrors such a sentiment; that at least 3767 civilians were killed by U.S. bombs between October 7th and December 10th in Afghanistan, a country whose annual budget of $83 million is one tenth of the cost of a B-52 bomber (56). Moreover, the number of deaths attributed to the twin towers attacks engendered a feeling not only of immense loss, but also a determination that something would be done about it. Yet, there isn't the same determination to do something about preventable deaths around the world, such as the 6,000 children who die every day from diarrhoea because they have no clean water (57). It is this kind of disparity and "irony on a base level" that Hicks was so adept at making comic gold out of.

America's need for an enemy, once the Soviet Union, then the war on drugs, has now become the war on terrorism. Though it's a war that cannot be won, Republican spin forces the country to get behind it. And anyway, the war on drugs needed to take something of a "ceasefire." After spending $75 billion on the drugs war in the last five years, there was something of an admittance of failure when in October 2002 the U.S. military began cutting back its budget, ostensibly to fund the war on terrorism. At the same time, President Bush's niece, Noelle, was jailed for ten days for drug offences. Coincidence? Meanwhile, in 2002 Attorney General John Ashcroft launched *Operation Pipe Dreams*, an incomprehensibly idiotic attempt to prevent marijuana usage by targeting shops that sell bongs. Unreasonable and petty, it says everything about an administration that has run out of ideas, but at least Ashcroft has chosen an apt title.

September 11th has become something of an American obsession. On the one hand, there are the poignant pictures of those lost and unaccounted for, pinned up on walls in New York's Grand Central Station. At the other extreme, there is something of a Billy Ray Cyrus feel about having hunky fireman on calendars whilst souvenir shops sell t-shirts, postcards and all manner of tacky memorabilia. Cyrus' heir apparent has emerged in the shape of country singer Toby Keith, whose album *Unleashed* went to the top of the charts. Songs on it include *Courtesy of the Red, White and Blue (The Angry American)* with its celebration of the bombing of Afghanistan and lyrics "We'll put a boot in your ass. It's the American way." Keith represents "bovine America" and its superficial looking at issues and knee-jerk responses. That this attitude is dominant could be seen when Bill Maher criticised the U.S. in the aftermath of September 11th on his show *Politically Incorrect*, resulting in Sears and Federal Express withdrawing their ads and some television stations refusing to broadcast the show. The conspiracy to silence voices of dissent is still prevalent in television, still seen in Bush's for us or against us posturing.

Following the World Trade Centre attacks, October 2001 saw anthrax being sent through the post, creating a panic that Middle East terrorists were again at work. The scare produced thousands of hoaxers, amongst them Clay Waagner sending 700 letters containing fake anthrax to abortion clinics. The pro-lifers that Hicks so detested still managed to justify Waagner's actions as he had succeeded in preventing many abortions. Indeed, the prevalence of right-wingers in positions of power after Bush's election has allowed all manner of Draconian measures, such as Texas passing the Women's Right To Know Act on May 21st 2003. A breathtakingly illiberal law, it forces women to look at photographs of a foetus at various developmental stages and makes doctors warn about abortions increasing the risk of breast cancer (without evidence) before women can go through with the procedure. In addition, following moves to prevent the U.S. Agency for International Development from giving money to groups providing not only abortions, but also merely information about abortions, Bush has recently banned foreign aid to family planning organisations that might use that funding for abortion counselling.

In Bush's America, traditional American values of democracy and justice are distorted, whilst moral codes become based on fear and hate, pushing views that are imposed when rational argument is bludgeoned by a mantra of "for us or against us." This is an America that now seems to echo with Hicks' "You are free to do as we tell you" because the War On Terror has created a climate where authoritarian measures can be defended with a quick nod to 9/11. Similarly, 2001 saw The Parents Television Council attack American TV for its adult themes, which it thought children were seeing. It's a return to Hicks' anger that protecting "the children" is often used to justify dictatorial actions. The PTC did have some praise though for a show called *Doc* about a country doctor going to New York, calling it "uplifting and inspirational". The show's star was none other than Billy Ray Cyrus. Hicks would have appreciated the irony and the connectedness of it.

There's positivity around Hicks' legacy. For all the misanthropy, he was essentially an idealist having to face reality and the calculated cynicism of others. Though the names may have changed, the same fevered egos and lying cocksuckers are prevalent in society, so that returning to Hicks' material one can see and hear how they still resonate with relevance, and are still searingly funny. Thankfully, the body of work he has left behind is considerable. Now he's jamming with Jimi Hendrix and partying with Yul Brynner as the Earth continues to make the same fuck ups as before. But hey, it's just a ride. "Have a spiffy eternity."

17
ANOTHER PERSIAN GULF DISTRACTION

The ostensible aim of the Afghanistan bombing campaign was to find Osama bin Laden, identified by the Pentagon as the mastermind behind the 9/11 attacks. However, once it became clear American forces couldn't locate or capture him, Saddam Hussein returned to centre stage, the Bush government trying to intimate that Iraq had links to al-Qa'ida, despite several official reports having stated that no connection existed, and that furthermore, there were significant ideological differences between the two. However, just as Hicks mocked the deceitfully emotive drive towards war when imagining a government argument that "Saddam Hussein likes to fuck dogs in the ass and then take their spine out and use it as a toothpick," so there was the constant linking of Hussein to worldwide terrorism. Deliberately evoking memories of September 11th and creating a sense that a chemical weapons attack was imminent, both Bush and his U.K. lapdog Tony Blair ignored a substantial anti-war movement, culminating in a conflict between the world's most powerful country (and the allies it managed to coerce) and a country in Iraq that might just have trouble defending itself against the Hare Krishnas.

Towards the end of 2002, when events were pointing towards some action against Iraq, various musicians contributed to an album, *The Fire This Time*, a venture that aimed to tell the true story of the first Gulf War through mixing spoken word and music. Suitably, Hicks was sampled for two tracks on the album: Pan Sonic's *Whore Of Babylon* sampling the "bullies of the world" routine and Barbed's *We're Doing Well Now* sampling the "Elite Republican Guard" routine. Meanwhile, *Totally Bill Hicks* was released on DVD in the U.K., with many reviews commenting on the timelessness of Hicks' Gulf War material. In routines dominated by subtle and ironic connections, it is appropriate that Hicks' comedy could be so effortlessly connected to the events of the 2003 conflict.

Hicks called the first war "The Persian Gulf Distraction" because he saw it as President Bush's means to focus the nation's attention away from his failing domestic policies whilst also generating enough patriotism to elevate his flagging popularity. Much the same accusation can be levelled at George W. Bush, using the second Gulf War to distract attention from a domestic recession and his administration's failure to get to grips with the Enron scandal, plus of course the embarrassing inability to find Osama bin Laden. Although it may seem somewhat fanciful, perhaps even a part of the conspiracy angles Hicks so loved, the facts support the idea of a "distraction." For example, Jack Leslie, sometime advisor to the Bush administration and chairman of PR firm, Weber Shandwick Worldwide, said of the Iraq war: "Better this than a lot of domestic issues that could be at the forefront" (58). Thus, as with his father, Bush exploited the situation (and particularly the "fear" Hicks saw as dominating right-wing ideology) to boost his popularity: Prior to September 11th, George W. Bush's popularity rating was 50%, whilst afterwards it rose to 82%. It subsequently slipped back, falling to 53% by March 13th/14th 2003, before "The Persian Gulf Distraction" began on March 18[th,] when war was declared on Iraq and his rating rose to 68% (58). Meanwhile, in the U.K. it proved equally convenient for Tony Blair when the Labour Party sneaked out the news that the British tax payer would have to rescue MPs pension funds.

Within the war's first four days, 300 cruise missiles had been launched against Baghdad, each costing $1 million. One can't help thinking of Hicks when one ponders such figures and despairs at the obscenity of it all, a voice somewhere in the wilderness raging against such a waste of resources when it could be used "feeding and clothing the poor of the world – and it would pay for it many times over, not *one* human being excluded." With such devastation caused by the initial bombing campaign – complete with Hollywood moniker, "Shock And Awe" – we also get a sense of Hicks' point that "There never was a war. A war is when *two* armies are fighting," adeptly pointing up a disparity in military strength that applied to the first war and was even more apparent during the second.

Central to Hicks' comedy in general and his Gulf War material in particular was his analysis of how language is used by governments to manipulate the masses. So, when weapons sold to Iraq in the 1980s are described as "machine tools" or "farming equipment" by way of excuse, Hicks is intent that the bamboozling of the American public should be shown up, his routine creating an absurd scenario where this "farming equipment" miraculously becomes a tank to combat the dangers of farming. Hicks saw how language can be used to soften up that which is unpalatable, as in his routine about the Waco siege when he mocked the "soft sell" of the FBI claiming their operation was to help mothers and children. Such tactics were evident in the 1991 war when civilian deaths were referred to as "collateral damage" as if they were an acceptable and minor detail, the language softer still with the second war when they were labelled "unintended consequences."

In a similar way, calling what was actually an invasion a "war" is meant to instil patriotism, make the cause seem nobler and generate public support. Further to this, the government and military easily managed to promote (in the U.S. media at least) the tag of "Operation Iraqi freedom," as if this were some selfless act of benevolence. It fits in with the Bush administration suggesting a "coalition" of world forces, when really the invading armies were predominantly U.S. and U.K. troops and a few Australian and Polish forces. The term had been employed in the first conflict, Hicks sarcastically referring to "that huge coalition, that *giant* coalition" of 1991, pointing out it consisted of merely U.S. and British troops and some French.

As a counterbalance to the soft sell, but for comparable aims, we have the presentation of a war that may not run smoothly, thus presenting a worst case scenario so that when this doesn't transpire the public can be led to believe that allied troops are having great success. This is apparent in frequent references to an "air war," giving the impression that two air forces are engaging in active fighting when in reality there was no such air combat. With this, it is natural that every air force mission will be presented as a success.

Donald Rumsfeld's briefings, during the war's early stages, frequently pointed out that the war might last several months, continually emphasising the threat Saddam Hussein's forces posed. This is the essence of Hicks' "Elite Republican Guard" routine in which said Iraqi forces are presented as "the ultimate desert warriors" throughout the campaign, until their lack of presence eventually leads to them quietly disappearing from military briefings. Hilariously, the recent conflict saw the Republican Guard once again referenced, this time more often as the "Special Republican Guard," equally as threatening as their "Elite" predecessors. However, once again there was no reaction, and when the war was over Lieutenant-Colonel Terry Ferrell simply dismissed the mystery with "They didn't show up."

Hicks had made a connection between what the government wanted to show of war and what subsequently turned up in the media. His attention mostly directed at television, he saw how the relaying of video footage of amazing technology and the sense that soldiers were enjoying the adventure, made the war seem almost like a Hollywood film, and just like Hollywood films, the enemy's evil and threat is often exaggerated, hence the "Elite Republican Guard" are presented "like these guys were the bogeymen…twelve feet tall desert warriors." Hicks often cited CNN as the main culprit, but during 2003 it was undoubtedly the Fox News Channel that took bias to a new level, extensively using "Operation Iraqi Freedom" as a banner, referring to U.S. troops as "we" and "us" and imbuing their reports with a patriotism that was insulting to viewers.

Also in this cathode ray smokescreen, there was an emphasis on the heroism of "our boys and girls," something most obviously seen with the rescue of Private Jessica Lynch (prompting headlines alluding to the film *Saving Private Ryan*). She had been recuperating in an Iraqi hospital after her unit had been ambushed, then U.S. forces entered to retrieve her, the filmed mission immediately becoming a major news story. Despite being presented as a daring initiative, there were no Iraqi soldiers at the hospital to prevent the rescue. Indeed, there had been an attempt by the Iraqis to return Lynch, but the ambulance in which she was being transported had come under allied fire. The Pentagon, keen to boost domestic morale, released only a five minute edited version of the rescue video and gave little exposure to the same mission retrieving the dead bodies of Lynch's comrades. Moreover, after the rescue the Pentagon said she had received stab and bullet wounds. Some time afterwards the truth was revealed that she had been neither shot nor stabbed and had in fact received her injuries when her vehicle crashed.

This kind of selective presentation is targeted in Hicks' material on drugs, the Waco siege and the first Gulf War, where the news media loses any sense of objectivity and becomes little more than a tool of government. By keeping the television media under control, government can convince the public that they have freedom and are being presented with unbiased viewpoints from which they can reach their own conclusions. But Hicks sees through this façade with "You are free – to do as we tell you!" And with the idealised images of war presented to the U.S. public, there is a sense of television visuals as an anaesthetic, images of war which mesmerise in their efficiency and cleanliness, the subliminal message being "Go back to bed America."

The much-criticised 1991 "pool system" for journalists found a natural successor with the "embedding" of journalists in 2003. A term that suggested a getting deep into the situation, it is really just attaching reporters (after military approval) to military units, and therefore being under the restrictions imposed by those units. Over 600 journalists and around 100 cameras were embedded, with journalists 'free' to report what the military allowed, as with the interviewing of soldiers, who were specially selected and briefed on what to say before being interviewed. Indeed, the military went further, compiling footage themselves which showed them in a good light, such as Iraqis surrendering or pictures of the military being friendly with civilians.

For television in the U.S., Jerry Bruckheimer (co-producer of piece-of-shit movie, *Flashdance*) and Bertram Van Munster created *Profiles From The Front Line*, a kind of reality TV programme about the U.S. soldiers on the front line. It was approved by Donald Rumsfeld and served as a means to stir patriotism and sympathy by humanising the conflict, not by conveying the reality of war and all its human carnage, but by showing the sanitised day-to-day existence of U.S. soldiers. It broadcast no footage of U.S. soldiers mistreating civilians, as in one case where a unit was physically abusing a civilian on a roadside and being secretly filmed a la Rodney King. When they spotted the camera pointing at them, the soldiers opened fire.

Television seems complicit in another conspiracy, wilfully presenting an inaccurate picture of the conflict, for despite the control of the military, there was every opportunity for the British and American media to use pictures from Arabic television station Al-Jazeera, which was showing unflinching images of civilian casualties. Though horrific, they at least displayed a reality missing from much mainstream television, emphasizing that beneath the spectacle of "shock and awe" with its exploding buildings, there is a human consequence; one that should be evident if the news is supposed to be objective. The fact that Al-Jazeera determinedly put across images not concurrent with the U.S. portrayal of war might explain why American aircraft bombed the Baghdad bureau of Al-Jazeera, killing a reporter, despite the television station having given its co-ordinates to the Pentagon to prevent accidental bombing. It offers another one of those incidences where Hicks, ironic articulator of connections, might have pondered "coincidence?" doubtfully.

Western television's acquiescence to government is evident in the way events, which were favourable to the U.S. and U.K. forces, were reported without corroboration. When the rumour of an uprising in Basra circulated, it took hold, repeated and embellished until it was reported as fact. There never was an uprising, but for allied forces seeking to convince the Iraqi public that there was a groundswell of support for Hussein's overthrow (as well as showing domestic audiences that Iraqis were embracing their "liberation"), the non-existent uprising served as useful propaganda. It was also seen with the search for weapons of mass destruction, the military inciting a media frenzy with each find of respirators, all manner of barrels and tanks, and various bottles that hinted at chemicals. Lead stories were then dominated by the possibility that this was part of the evidence of chemical weapons, only for the subsequently negative test results to go unreported.

This was a war characterised by rumour, effectively playing into the hands of Bush and Blair, for within the confusion, where claims and counterclaims dominated, where versions of events were changing by the day, the general public could barely get a handle on developments before a new story or angle came to prominence. Thus, when fifty-five Iraqi civilians were killed after a missile hit a marketplace, the allied military announced they would "investigate", blurring the story, delaying a definitive account in the hope that some future distraction would push the incident further to the margins of the general public's consciousness. Moreover, as well as not admitting responsibility for the marketplace bombing, allied military suggested instead that it might have been caused by an Iraqi missile. Yet Iraq had few missiles, whilst hundreds of allied cruise missiles were dropping on Baghdad every day. Indeed, U.S. missile pieces were found amid the wreckage of the marketplace bombing.

Because much of Hicks' material is concerned with using irony to expose deceit and misrepresentation, his material seems particularly prescient when looking at the careful media management of the second Gulf War. This control is all about keeping the masses from questioning the actions of government, presenting a good clean war where the objectives are simplified to a battle between good and evil. It becomes an emotive atmosphere where the voice of reason is not heard, so that just as Hicks throws in "here's a foetus and he's a Hitler" we have the Bush administration making spurious links between Saddam Hussein and the tragedy of 9/11 in order to justify a war.

After the first conflict, Hicks was one of the few American comedians prepared to mock his country's involvement, because in a land where patriotism is engendered by the values of democracy and freedom of speech, it is a peculiarity that the same country can be so highly sensitive to the exercising of that freedom of speech when it is putting across an anti-war argument, labelling it, without irony, as unpatriotic. For Hicks, this dichotomy is crystallised in his routine about flag burning with its certainty that if freedom means anything then there must be "the freedom to burn the fuckin' flag." Always prepared to go against the prevailing mood, Hicks saw how it is not only apathy that can drive "the docile masses" towards

228

acquiescence, but also fear. It is a fear of alienation and condemnation, one particularly apparent in 2003 with George W. Bush's ethos being that those who did not support the war against Iraq were in essence supporters of terrorism, and by implication, supporters of those that carried out the September 11th attacks.

The attempts to silence voices of dissent links back to Hicks' Letterman banning and the conspiracy angles where a cabal of powerful men controlled all forms of entertainment. When Natalie Maines, lead singer of Texan singing trio the Dixie Chicks, announced at a London gig, "Just so you know, we're ashamed that the president of the United States is from Texas," she could not have imagined the irrational response back home. With something of a mob mentality, there were public CD burnings organised by the Cumulus Media radio chain, whilst America's largest radio station owner, Clear Channel, banned Dixie Chicks records (Clear Channel regularly donated money to the Republican Party). Similarly, actor Tim Robbins had been invited to the National Baseball Hall of Fame, but subsequently found his invite cancelled after his anti-war comments. It seems no coincidence that the Hall's president had once been part of the Reagan administration. One can't escape the sense that Hicks' shadowy elite is at work, but more than that, in a climate where a man was even arrested for wearing an anti-war t-shirt in a New York mall, fear and hate have clouded clarity, Hicks' "voice of reason" smothered by what he would have dubbed "phoney hysteria." A recent piece by Norman Mailer quite chillingly pinpoints this combination of control and patriotism as leading to "a pre-fascist atmosphere in America already."

Once again, television is actively involved in the conspiracy, all the major networks denying peace groups, who tried to pay for airtime, the right to exercise their freedom of speech through anti-war commercials. Most tellingly, an internal NBC report (successfully) recommended cancelling Phil Donahue's somewhat liberal leaning news show on cable TV news network MSNBC, because "He seems to delight in presenting guests who are anti-war, anti-Bush and sceptical of the administration's motives" (58). Post-conflict, such totalitarian behaviour has even extended its reach to Arabic television channel, Al-Jazeera, its reporters subjected to detentions and arrests as well as the threat of closure by Paul Bremer, the U.S. proconsul in Iraq.

Linked to this marginalizing of dissenters is an inexplicable sensitivity towards the soldiers, who are invariable presented as ordinary, heroic and fighting not because as Hicks might have it, they are "hired killers," but because they are seeking to right injustices. From this we get an argument intended to nullify the war's critics, one heard frequently during the 1991 conflict, but mostly confined to the U.K. in 2003. It saw Tony Blair and his cronies at their most sanctimonious, arguing that in a democracy it is fine to debate the rights and wrongs of going to war, but once war starts it is everybody's duty to support the troops, suggesting that such criticism damages their morale. Such emotional blackmail is not only abhorrent but also completely ridiculous, its logic being that once a war begins all debate must end and everyone should either agree it is a right war or just shut up. Hicks saw through the absurdity of the argument with his 1991 quip that he "was in the unenviable position of being for the war, but against the troops."

It is in his material about soldiers being "in hog heaven out there" that Hicks so fearlessly swims against the tide of popular opinion, his caricatures of soldiers in the Gulf not presenting them as selfless heroes, but as something of a cross between dumb surfer dudes and good time college jocks. They have little concern for humanity, treating war as a game when carelessly launching the missiles they have excitedly selected from a weapons catalogue. To see how this perspective applied to the 2003 conflict one need only look at U.S. Vice Admiral Timothy Keating's speech to his troops at the beginning of the conflict: "When the president says 'Go', look out – it's hammer time," a statement followed immediately by the MC Hammer song, *Hammer Time*. It is an attitude that filters down, a U.S. staff sergeant who'd painted his face for the attack on Iraq viewing the war in terms of a Hollywood movie: "This is not the face of a peacekeeper. I'm doin' the whole Last of the Mohicans kinda thing" (59). One can almost here Hicks' dumb Southern drawl with the dim-witted statement from one U.S. soldier: "We bomb 'em. Y'know, it's cool to me 'coz I like explosions" (60).

Hicks' intent was to cut through the false image of soldiers often presented in the news, one that serves government by being a useful emotive tool for countering opposing views. He was well aware that a quarter of U.S. soldiers killed in 1991 were as a result of friendly fire, as if those in charge of weapons were so enjoying the experience of war that they were out of control. Twelve years later, friendly fire was again a frighteningly regular occurrence, whilst there were also many occasions when trigger happy – or nervous – U.S. soldiers fired on unarmed civilians, or stray allied missiles killed civilians, such as the one that killed five Syrians attempting to leave Iraq by bus. This could effectively be described as "hog heaven" – a situation where there appears to be little accountability amid a free reign to cause riotous carnage.

Once again, in 2003, we got a sense of what Hicks referred to as "the bullies of the world" with U.S. technology imposing its will on an impoverished country, dropping cluster bombs (banned by over 100 countries), weapons designed to scatter around 200 smaller bombs on impact, sending out shards of steel, often not all exploding so that they would be left around like land mines. For Hicks, this kind of weaponry, as with the use of highly advanced stealth bombers in 1991, is an obscenity, prompting him to ask, "couldn't we feasibly use that same technology to shoot food at hungry people?" But people don't seem to be a priority in these conflicts, U.S. war spending for the three weeks of its duration put at $55 billion whilst only $275 million was allocated for humanitarian aid to Iraq (61). In addition, we have the "disparity in casualties" that Hicks noted, over 3000 Iraqi soldiers killed against under 200 allied dead. Even more shocking were figures provided by Iraq Body Count (IBC), an independent U.S. and British research group, which estimated that between at least 5,000 and 7,000 civilians had been killed during the war, with a possibility that the figure might be as high as 10,000.

These are what journalist John Pilger refers to as the "unpeople," those whose lives and struggles are not significant enough to grab the attention of the mainstream media. Certainly Bush and Blair did not show the same superficial grief for a loss of innocent life exceeding that of the September 11th attacks. This is the kind of hypocrisy Hicks so raged against, from his early career mocking corrupt televangelists to the religious conviction of Reagan and Bush Senior somewhat contradicting their involvement in terrorism and genocide in Central America. So, in 2003 we had the Bush administration talking of international law when U.S. soldiers were paraded on Iraqi television, and though such actions did go against article 13 of the Geneva Convention, the U.S. military had done exactly the same thing previously. Indeed, far worse was to follow some weeks after the war had been declared over, when the Pentagon insisted – against military advice – that the dead bodies of Uday Hussein and Qusay Hussein be photographed for distribution to the world's press. Shockingly, and with a level of paranoia characteristic of those engaged in deceit, the Pentagon felt that perhaps the Iraqi people might not be convinced by the photographs, ordering that the faces be shaved and made up before being filmed.

The call for compliance with the Geneva Convention seems most hypocritical when compared to conditions at Camp Delta, the U.S. naval base at Guantanamo Bay in Cuba, where hundreds of "prisoners" have been confined, initially after the Afghanistan conflict, but gradually added to as the War On Terror casts a global net. At Camp Delta, conventions are regularly flouted, such as allowing the demeaning spectacle of men kneeling on the ground, wearing blacked out goggles and earphones to be filmed. These "prisoners" aren't allowed canteens, religious premises, means of exercise, access to lawyers or the freedom to communicate with their families.

These alleged terrorists are interrogated with "stress and duress" methods that are little short of torture; involving solitary confinement, sleep deprivation and psychological intimidation. And, if this doesn't work, then prisoners can be sent to countries such as Egypt where, in U.S. military parlance they are "rendered" for inquisition – electric shocks and beatings – with questions drawn up by U.S. intelligence.

As Hicks would have it, those in government are "lying cocksuckers," which seems a fair assertion after the second Gulf War with the level of hypocrisy and distortion of truth. The maltreatment of prisoners by the Iraqi army made front page headlines in the predominantly right-wing U.K. newspapers, whilst television broadcasts refused to show such images exactly because they didn't want to break the Geneva Convention. Compare this to the lack of analysis of the much more significant breaking of protocol 11 of the Geneva Convention by the allies. Protocol 11 prohibits attacks on infrastructure that is deemed necessary for maintaining public health. Yet U.S. missiles targeted electricity lines upon which water treatment plants depended, leading to outbreaks of dysentery and cholera.

Such actions contradict the messages of both U.S. and U.K. governments that the attack on Iraq was not against the ordinary people of the country, but only against Saddam Hussein and his evil cohorts. Though the Iraqi leader was undoubtedly an unpleasant human being and guilty of abhorrent crimes, there existed in the allied portrayal of him a level of hypocrisy that would have aroused Hicks' ire. Moreover, the shifts of emphasis when using Hussein as a reason for going to war once more linked to Hicks' throwing up of different emotive arguments, or "whatever it takes" to get the public to support a war. So, war is necessary because Hussein's rule is undemocratic (in contrast to the shining monument to democracy that was Bush's 2000 election victory). Or, we have both Tony Blair and George W. Bush claiming war as a moral duty, because Hussein's regime is repressive and involves the brutal treatment of his own people. That neither leader feels the same moral urge to intervene against other dictatorships around the world is one thing, but there is also America's forty years of support for the repressive, brutal and illegal Israeli occupation of Palestine. What's more, to see how Republicans really feel about brutal dictators, one need look no further than the State of Florida, governed by the president's brother Jeb Bush, and home to Jose Guillermo Garcia since the 1990s. A former head of El Salvador's military, Jose Guillermo Garcia oversaw the death squads that murdered thousands of civilians, but he is just one of many former dictators and murderers living freely in Bush's America.

For Hicks, those in power employ a selectivity of facts that can be regarded at best as hypocrisy, but is really little more than a form of lying. He saw it with the war on drugs and government presenting all drugs as bad, except the ones that are taxed and are therefore useful to government. Similarly, in the lead up to war, much was made of the dangers from chemical and biological weapons with frequent citing of the 1998 atrocity when Hussein ordered the gassing of 5,000 Kurds in Halabja. In fact, those politicians in search of a convenient soundbite could have gone much further, noting that Halabja was one of over 50 attacks on villages in Northern Iraq that were part of a systematic massacre of 120,000 Kurds. However, perhaps those pious politicians were only too aware that such detail would only further accentuate their own passivity at the time, for back in those Halcyon days the U.K. Conservative government was still happily doing business with Hussein. Even after the first war, back in 1994, botulism developed in Maryland was transferred to Iraq, after approval by the State Department (62). Was this, one wonders, merely "farming equipment," the kind innocently used to fend off wasps?

Weapons of mass destruction eventually found its way to being the central reason for attacking Iraq (after previous arguments failed to capture the public's imagination), and within this the "lying cocksuckers" were at their most obvious. The "lying cocksuckers" of the British government, on 24th September 2002, produced "evidence" that Iraq had purchased uranium for nuclear weapons from Niger. A few weeks later, this persuaded U.S. Congress to permit Bush's war preparations. It subsequently transpired that this evidence was false, the consequences of which are still unravelling for Tony Blair.

Initially, claims were made that Iraq was obstructing weapons inspections, something certainly plausible when considering Saddam Hussein, but something that in this instance was a lie, for chief U.N. weapons inspector Hans Blix noted that the United Nations had undertaken over 400 inspections of more than 300 sites and concluded "that access to sites has so far been without problems" (63). In fact, for lies about weapons of mass destruction, one need look no further than the Pentagon who responded to a report in the Sydney Morning Herald on 22nd March, that U.S. aircraft had used napalm bombs during the attack on Baghdad, with a denial: "We completed destruction of our last batch of napalm on 4 April, 2001." But confirmation that they did – or should that be admittance of lying - came over three months after war ended.

Subsequent to the end of the war, the search for biological or chemical weapons has shown up the lying cocksuckers for what they are, Maureen Dowd of the *New York Times* likening Donald Rumsfeld's attempts to find weapons of mass destruction to O.J. Simpson "vowing to find the real killers" of his wife. One can hear the descending cadence of Hicks' routine about presentation going from "the Elite Republican Guard, to the Republican Guard, to the Republicans made this shit up" when one listens to the U.S. and U.K. governments' reasons for not finding the weapons that so necessitated a war: They have been hidden in secret bunkers. The country is so large that more time is needed to find them. They've been moved to Syria. Without any trace of irony, one U.K. politician suggested that Hussein wasn't using said weapons during the war because he feared the negative reaction of other countries!

Eventually, with weeks passing and still no discovery, the argument shifted again, with British Foreign Secretary Jack Straw, when asked on 14th May 2003 about finding weapons of mass destruction, simply saying, "It's not crucially important." Two weeks later, when Donald Rumsfeld was pressed on the subject, he reached an even more bewildering conclusion: "It is also possible that they decided they would destroy them prior to conflict" (which kind of suggests compliance with U.N. resolutions).

The fruitless hunt for these weapons is perhaps symbolic of the whole war and its aftermath; the subsequent attempts to control and police Iraq suggesting little forward planning from the Bush administration. Whilst looters filled the streets of Baghdad and elsewhere in Iraq, American companies were being awarded lucrative contracts to rebuild Iraq, or – more honestly put – loot the country's oil supplies.

Just as Hicks proposed that those in marketing and advertising could find a money-making angle in everything, so the second Gulf conflict attracted all manner of corporate vultures, amongst them plans for a Playstation game called *Shock and Awe*, a board game based on the war called *Axis of Evil* and even *Shock and Awe* trainers. And just as Hicks' routine had those in marketing and advertising seeking a commercial angle from his stand-up –

"Oh, you know what Bill's doing, he's going for that anti-marketing dollar" – so we had Invasion releasing an album of his 1992 Oxford Playhouse gig as *Shock And Awe*. Despite this, the album itself is one of Hicks' best, the comedian coming across as relaxed, confident and in tune with his British audience.

Perhaps the most unbelievably crass exploitation of the conflict came from the Pentagon, which had planned, starting in August 2003, to set up an online futures market allowing people to speculate on the possibility of terror attacks. It was abandoned after objections, but the Pentagon claimed it was an attempt to find the "broadest possible set of ways to prevent terrorist attacks... Research indicates that markets are extremely efficient, effective and timely aggregators of dispersed and even hidden information" (64). This sounds suspiciously like Hicks' marketing man seeking to defend poisonous baby food: "Oh, we made, ah, we made arsenic a childhood food now...Yeah, we just said, you know, is your baby really too loud? You know, the mums will love it."

Not only does Hicks' 1991 war material feel as fresh and relevant as it ever did, but his take on governments and his general ironic perspective can be applied to the 2003 conflict with little contrivance. His philosophy and the connections therein are held together by recurring themes and a compelling ideology so that when one is confronted with the obvious ironies of the 2003 conflict, one is immediately drawn to Hicks' sense of the absurdity of things. For a war meant to free Iraq from terror and make the world a safer place, it has fallen way short of its objectives in creating a country beset by car bombs, internal terrorism, snipers and civil strife, and a world situation where more people hate America and wish to do it considerable harm. Indeed, the war has ensured the world is a more dangerous place, making nations such as Syria, Iran and North Korea fearful of American power and therefore giving them a reason to further arm themselves.

We now live in a world where fear and hatred have consumed not only Western cultures, but also Eastern cultures; a world where paranoia and mistrust seem to govern the actions of governments, who in turn can be little trusted by those they are supposed to represent (think of the 28 pages extracted from the congressional report into the September 11th attacks, details that have been classified, and we have the beginnings of a conspiracy every bit as complex as that involving Kennedy). In this atmosphere the satirist thrives, although it usually takes one that has left a significant and lasting impression to remain relevant after death. This perhaps explains why interest in Hicks continues to grow, the release of the *Shock And Awe* album (Hicks' sixth posthumous release if one includes 2001's best of) followed by a new U.S. documentary, *Outlaw Comic – The Censoring Of Bill Hicks*, from the Trio network.

What he was, and still is, for U.S. audiences, is a fearless, iconoclastic voice articulating the views of many Americans whose opinions are either ignored or countered by sensationalism. He frequently referred to America as "the country I love" and made it his duty to mock the selfish, gung-ho stereotypes that were so prevalent throughout the Republican 1980s and 1990s. But in 2003, George W. Bush has created more anti-American feeling and seemingly emphasised the stereotype. In the end, Hicks' comedy is relevant now as it offers that voice of reason so lacking in the current administration. In seeking to answer the question about why anyone would fly two planes into the World Trade Centre, President Bush has undertaken measures that curb personal freedom and impinge on human rights whilst also coming up with a conclusion that bombing two impoverished countries might be the answer. The tragedy is that such actions distort real American values, using retaliation as a placebo, and in effect never allowing the public to comprehend why there are individuals so virulently opposed to their values. It would be more educative to take one of Hicks' quips as a symbol, one that seems throwaway, but on closer inspection captures the essence of why there is anti-American feeling. It is his response to the inexplicably popular comedian, Gallagher: "Only America could produce a comic who ends his show by destroying good food with a sledgehammer. Gee, I wonder why we're hated the world over."

Sources

Bill Hicks albums:
Dangerous (1990, Rykodisc)
Relentless (1992, Rykodisc)
Arizona Bay (1997, Rykodisc)
Rant In E-Minor (1997, Rykodisc)
Love Laughter And Truth (2002, Rykodisc)
Flying Saucer Tour Vol. 1 (2002, Rykodisc)
Shock And Awe (2003, Invasion Group)

Bill Hicks videos:
Sane Man (Sacred Cow Productions 1989)
One Night Stand (HBO Independent Productions Inc 1991)
Relentless (Tiger Television Limited 1992)
Totally Bill Hicks (including *Revelations* and *It's Just A Ride*. A Tiger Aspect Production for Channel Four Television 1994)
On The Seventh Day: Bill Hicks At The Cult Compound (Sacred Cow Productions 1994)
Bill Hicks On Austin Public Access (aka *The United States Of Advertising*) (Sacred Cow Productions 1993)

Other:
American Scream -The Bill Hicks Story by Cynthia True (Sidgwick & Jackson, 2002)

http://www.sacredcowproductions.com

http://www.darktimes.org

Specific sources

Chapter 3: *What's New, Pussycat?* : References taken from album *Woody Allen Stand up Comic* (Rhino Entertainment Company 1999) and *The Lenny Bruce Originals Volume 1* (1991 Fantasy Inc).

Chapter 4: *Wild And Crazy Guys*: references taken from *Steve Martin Live* (Vestra Video International 1984).

Chapter 5: *Breaking The Rules*: references taken from Sam Kinison albums *Have You See Me Lately?* (Warner Brothers 1988) *Leader Of The Banned* (Warner Brothers 1990) and *Live From Hell* (Priority Records 1993) and the documentary film *Sam Kinison: Why Did We Laugh?* (Sundog Productions 1997).

Chapter 6: *Richard Pryor & Physical Comedy*: references taken from the films *Richard Pryor: Live In Concert* (Special Event Entertainment Inc. 1979) and *Richard Pryor Live On The Sunset Strip* (Rastar Films 1982) and album *Craps (After Hours)* (Island Records 1994).

Chapter 9: *Republicanism On The Rampage*: reference to the video *Nothing Goes Right* (Orion 1987).

Chapter 13: *Go Back To Bed America*: Orwell quotes taken from *Orwell and Politics* (Penguin, 2001).

Chapter 14: *Conspiracies*: source material: *Waco-The Rules Of Engagement* (BBC documentary directed by William Gazecki) and *The Ashes Of Waco: An Investigation* by Dick J. Reavis (Syracuse University Press, 1995).

No Cure For Cancer by Denis Leary album (A&M Records 1993) and DVD (BMG Entertainment 2002).

Chapter 16: *A Spiffy Eternity*: references taken from album *You Can't Make Stuff Up Like This* by Will Durst (2002, worst of durst comedy ltd.). Sources for Doug Stanhope material are the CD albums *The Great White Stanhope* (1998 Uproar Entertainment), *Something To Take The Edge Off* (2001 Stand Up!-ismist Recordings), *Die Laughing* (2002 Stand Up!-ismist Recordings).

David Cross quotes taken from *Shut Up, You Fucking Baby!* (2002, Sub Pop Records).

References

1. *The Dark Side Of Bill Hicks* (The Public News, January 8th 1988).
2. *Capzeyez*, on Austin Public Access (23rd October 1993, Sacred Cow Productions).
3. Len Belzer Radio Show interviews with Bill Hicks between 1989 and 1993.
4. *The New York World* (20th November 1884).
5. *Bill Hicks: High Plains Jester* by Jack Boulware *(The Nose,* issue 11, 1992).
5a. *George Carlin: Personal Favorites* (DVD, MPI Home Video 1996)
6.*The Goat Boy Rises* by John Lahr (from *Light Fantastic Adventures In Theatre*, Bloomsbury Publishing 1996).
7. *Hicks Adds Cud-ly Character To His Routine* by Ernest Tucker (The Chicago Sun-Times, June 25th 1993).
8. *Woody Allen-A Biography* by John Baxter (page 290, HarperCollins 1998).
9. *Woody Allen On Comedy* (Laugh.com CD 2001).
10. Hicks interviewed by Duncan Strauss (1993).
11. *Andy Kaufman: Performance Artist or Stand-Up Comic?* By Peter Firman (2001).
12. *Dada and Surrealism* by Christopher Bigsby (Methuen 1972).
13. *Easy Riders, Raging Bulls* by Peter Biskind (1998, Bloomsbury Publishing plc).
14 *Comic Kinison Still Far From Being Family Fair* by Greg Doggell (The Los Angeles Times, Friday December 28th 1990).
15. *Hate-Mongers Are a Sad Chapter in the History Of Comedy* by Randy Lewis (The Los Angeles Times, Sunday April 22nd 1990).
16. *Halloween Special* (1993 Sacred Cow Productions).
17.*Touch Me, I'm Hicks!* by Stephen Dalton (N.M.E. 14TH November 1992).
18. *The Gospel According To Hicks* by Mike Sager (GQ magazine, September 1994).
18a. Quoted in *Stir Crazy* by Brian Case (Uncut magazine, February 2003).
19. *A Dangerous Comic On The Cutting Edge* by Jonathan B. Fox (Just For Laughs, 1992).
20. *It's Just A Ride* (Channel 4 documentary).

21. *Kavort!* (An entertainment and listings magazine from Southampton, U.K., November 1992).

22. *The Archaic Revival* by Terence McKenna.

23. *The Food Of The Gods* by Terence McKenna (1992, Bantam).

24. *Austin Tribute Concert*.

25. *A People's History Of The United States From 1492 to the present*, chapter *Carter-Reagan-Bush: The Bipartisan Consensus* (Howard Zinn, Longman, 1996).

26. *The Public News* (January 6th 1988).

27. *Nicaragua: The Threat Of A Good Example* by Dianna Melrose (Oxfam, Oxford 1985 pg 26), cited in (34).

28. *The Puppets of Pandemonium: Sleaze and Sloth in the Media Elite* by Howard Bloom (from *You Are Being Lied To* edited by Russ Kick, 2001 The Disinformation Company Ltd.).

29. *The Comedian as Confidence Man: Studies in Irony Fatigue* by Will Kaufman (Wayne State University Press).

30. *Bill Hicks Houston's king of comedy* (The Houston Post magazine, September 20th 1987).

31. *Bill Hicks: The Next Big Thing* by David Friedman (Newsday, September 26th 1990).

32. *British politics today* by Bill Jones and Dennis Kavanagh (page 15 Manchester University Press, 1994).

33. *Bloodless words bloody war* by Maggie O'Kane (The Guardian Weekend, December 16th 1995).

34. *Hidden Agendas* by John Pilger (Vintage 1998).

35. The Guardian, January 19TH 1991, from *Humanity-a moral history of the twentieth century* by Jonathan Glover (Pimlico 2001).

36. *Stand Up, Sit Down* (interviewed by Robert Klein, 1993).

37. Salon.com (March 13th 2002).

38. Carl Bernstein (The Guardian, June 3rd 1992)

39. *The Shrine Of Jeffrey Dahmer* by Brian Masters (Coronet Books 1993).

40. *After Kicking Butts And Booze, Bill Hicks Is Still Kicking Butt* by Bill Brownstein (The Montreal Gazette, January 15th 1993).

41. *George Carlin* by Stephen Thompson (*The Onion*, November 11th 1999, volume 35, issue 41).

42. *Black civil rights, white civil rights* by Samuel Francis (Washington Times, 22nd October (1993).

43. *The New Rulers Of The World* by John Pilger (Verson 2002).

44. *Enigmatic, admired, reviled, misunderstood* by Hap Erstein (The Montreal Gazette, March 28th 1994).

44a. *Manufacturing Consent – Noam Chomsky & The Media* (documentary film, 2002 Zeitgeist Films, Ltd.)

45. Interview with Zoë Taylor, Missouri D.J. (1992).

45a. *American Power and the New Mandarins* by Noam Chomsky (Pantheon, 1969)

46. From Memorandum to Director of C.I.A., from Task Force on Greater C.I.A. Openness, November 18th 1991, cited in (34).

47. Bill Hicks on Television…Sometimes (letter to John Lahr).

48. *Send in the clown: Bill Hicks offer referendum-day comedy relief* by Bill Brownstein (The Montreal Gazette, October 26th 1992).

49. *A Color Man Who Has A Problem With Color?* By Jeff Cohen and Steve Rendell (http://www.fair.org/ June 7th 2000).

50. *Icon: Bill Hicks* by Steve Hobbs (GQ).

51. Howard Stern radio interview (WXRK Radio, New York, October 7th 1993).

52. Quoted in (29).

53. *Bill Hicks Will Be Missed For Courageous Comic Voice* by Jeff Rusnak (The Fort Lauderdale Sun Sentinel March 4th 1994).

54. *Picture Perfect* by Kiki Adatta, cited in (34).

55. *Stupid White Men and Other Sorry Excuses for the State of the Nation* by Michael Moore (Regan Books 2001).

56. Marc Herold, University of New Hampshire, cited by Seamus Milne in The Guardian, December 20th 2001, referenced in (43).

57. U.N. Development Report, cited in The Guardian, October 22nd 2001, referenced in (43).

58. *Weapons Of Mass Deception* by Sheldon Rampton & John Stauber (Centre for Media and Democracy, 2003).

59. The Guardian, April 8th 2003.

60. BBC Correspondent – *War Spin* (2003).

61. The Guardian, April 12th 2003

62. US Senate report *US Chemical and Biological Warfare-Related Dual Use Exports to Iraq and Their possible Impact on the Health Consequences of the Persian Gulf War*, May 25th 1994.

63. Quoted in *20 Lies About The War* by Glen Rangwala & Raymond Whitaker (The Independent On Sunday, 13TH July 2003).

64. *Pentagon drops plan for terror betting site* by Andrew Buncombe (The Independent 30th July 2003).

241

Index

Leno, Jay: 67, 95, 161, 163, 194-195, 197-198
Letterman, David: 47, 49, 67, 85, 95-97, 111, 116, 123, 131, 132, 140, 154-155, 161, 172, 194-198, 229
Limbaugh, Rush: 190-192, 195, 199, 215
Love Connection (TV): 156
Lying cocksuckers: 14, 22, 23, 98, 114, 136, 137, 139, 173, 186, 222, 232, 233, 234
Madonna: 120, 122, 125, 152, 209
Marblehead Johnson: 116, 158
Marijuana: 50, 62, 69, 86, 89-90, 92, 104, 118, 220
Martin, Steve: 41-46, 49, 52, 54, 62, 71, 85, 135
Major, John: 138, 148
McKenna, Terence: 87-88, 164, 193, 205
Michael, George: 114, 120, 122
Miller, Dennis: 162, 214-215
Moore, Dudley: 133, 134
Moore, Michael: 182, 214, 218
Morris, Chris: 219
Murphy, Eddie: 52, 61, 85, 93, 111, 135
Mushrooms: 74, 86-90, 153, 193
Newhart, Bob: 30-31
New Kids On The Block: 60, 61, 121, 122, 153-154
Nicaragua: 100, 114
Ninja Bachelor Party (film): 36-37, 84, 116, 119, 140, 153
Nixon, Richard: 12, 17, 18, 21-23, 27, 31, 42, 43, 47, 50, 97, 118, 155, 173, 188
One consciousness: 9-11, 15, 25, 52, 91, 122, 126, 129, 136, 145, 208, 212
One Night Stand (film): 132
Orwell, George: 122, 166-173, 189, 191, 206
Pilger, John: 163, 231
Pineapple, Jimmy: 54
Pornography: 56, 152, 153, 154, 155, 157, 160, 165, 215, 216
Presley, Elvis: 12, 19-21, 25, 45, 47, 48, 114, 117, 124, 139, 167, 179, 187, 195, 201, 202
Pryor, Richard: 27-28, 42, 47, 52, 58, 67-85, 111, 113, 153, 193, 196, 215
Rage Against The Machine: 124, 199
Rant In E-Minor (album): 30, 116, 126, 192, 193, 198, 210
Reagan, Ronald: 31, 53-58, 68, 85-86, 89, 91-106, 109-110,113-115, 118, 121, 125, 136-137, 151, 163, 169, 173, 179, 189-191, 195, 199, 229, 231